Project Management Institute

ORGANIZATIONAL PROJECT MANAGEMENT MATURITY MODEL

(OPM3®) – Third Edition

Library of Congress Cataloging-in-Publication Data

Organizational project management maturity model (OPM3) / Project Management Institute. -- Third edition.
        pages cm
    Includes bibliographical references and index.
    ISBN-13: 978-1-935589-70-9 (alk. paper)
    ISBN-10: 1-935589-70-9 (alk. paper)
    1. Project management--Standards. 2. Project management. I. Project Management Institute.
    HD69.P750745 2013
    658.4'04--dc23
                        2013019656

ISBN: 978-1-935589-70-9

Published by: Project Management Institute, Inc.
                  14 Campus Boulevard
                  Newtown Square, Pennsylvania 19073-3299 USA
                  Phone: +610-356-4600
                  Fax: +610-356-4647
                  Email: customercare@pmi.org
                  Internet: www.PMI.org

PMI Publications welcomes corrections and comments on its books. Please feel free to send comments on typographical, formatting, or other errors. Simply make a copy of the relevant page of the book, mark the error, and send it to: Book Editor, PMI Publications, 14 Campus Boulevard, Newtown Square, PA 19073-3299 USA.

To inquire about discounts for resale or educational purposes, please contact the PMI Book Service Center.
        PMI Book Service Center
        P.O. Box 932683, Atlanta, GA 31193-2683 USA
        Phone: 1-866-276-4764 (within the U.S. or Canada) or +1-770-280-4129 (globally)
        Fax: +1-770-280-4113
        Email: info@bookorders.pmi.org

10 9 8 7 6 5 4 3 2 1

NOTICE

The Project Management Institute, Inc. (PMI) standards and guideline publications, of which the document contained herein is one, are developed through a voluntary consensus standards development process. This process brings together volunteers and/or seeks out the views of persons who have an interest in the topic covered by this publication. While PMI administers the process and establishes rules to promote fairness in the development of consensus, it does not write the document and it does not independently test, evaluate, or verify the accuracy or completeness of any information or the soundness of any judgments contained in its standards and guideline publications.

PMI disclaims liability for any personal injury, property or other damages of any nature whatsoever, whether special, indirect, consequential or compensatory, directly or indirectly resulting from the publication, use of application, or reliance on this document. PMI disclaims and makes no guaranty or warranty, expressed or implied, as to the accuracy or completeness of any information published herein, and disclaims and makes no warranty that the information in this document will fulfill any particular purpose or need. PMI does not undertake to guarantee the performance of any individual manufacturer or seller's products or services by virtue of this standard or guide.

In publishing and making this document available, PMI is not undertaking to render professional or other services for or on behalf of any person or entity, nor is PMI undertaking to perform any duty owed by any person or entity to someone else. Anyone using this document should rely on his or her own independent judgment or, as appropriate, seek the advice of a competent professional in determining the exercise of reasonable care in any given circumstances. Information and other standards on the topic covered by this publication may be available from other sources, which the user may wish to consult for additional views or information not covered by this publication.

PMI has no power, nor does it undertake to police or enforce compliance with the contents of this document. PMI does not certify, test, or inspect products, designs, or installations for safety or health purposes. Any certification or other statement of compliance with any health or safety-related information in this document shall not be attributable to PMI and is solely the responsibility of the certifier or maker of the statement.

TABLE OF CONTENTS

©2013 Project Management Institute. *The Standard for Program Management - Third Edition*

LIST OF TABLES AND FIGURES

1

OVERVIEW

1.1 Introduction

The Organizational Project Management Maturity Model (OPM3®) – Third Edition provides guidelines for improving organizational project management within organizations. It defines the *OPM3* model, which is comprised of the *OPM3* Construct and *OPM3* framework activities and processes. This edition of *OPM3* expands, reinforces, and clarifies many of the concepts presented in the previous editions. This standard leverages the Project Management Institute's (PMI®) foundational standards, including *A Guide to the Project Management Body of Knowledge (PMBOK® Guide)* – Fifth Edition [1],[1] *The Standard for Program Management* – Third Edition [2], *The Standard for Portfolio Management* – Third Edition [3], and *PMI's Lexicon of Project Management Terms* [4] as well as the *Project Manager Competency Development Framework (PMCDF)* – Second Edition [5].

OPM3 is organized into six sections:

Section 1 Overview—This section provides an overview of the foundational concepts of organizational project management (OPM) and *OPM3*. This section outlines the relationship between portfolio, program, and project management, the role of stakeholders, and a summary of the remaining sections.

Section 2 Foundational Concepts—This section sets the stage for applying *OPM3*. It takes an in-depth look at the *OPM3* model, domains, the organizational project management (portfolio, program, and project) processes, organizational life cycle and maturity, and continuous improvement.

Section 3 The Organizational Project Management Maturity Model *(OPM3)*—This section, considered the foundation of *OPM3,* describes two core components of the standard: the *OPM3* Construct and the *OPM3* framework. These are further elaborated in Sections 3.2 and 3.3.

Section 4 Acquire Knowledge—This section guides the discovery and preparation process prior to performing an assessment within a business environment. This section outlines the essential inputs, outputs, and tools and techniques.

Section 5 Perform Assessment—This section guides the plan and execution process before, during, and after performing an assessment. This section outlines the essential inputs, outputs, and tools and techniques.

Section 6 Manage Improvement—This section guides the evaluation, prioritization, and implementation processes after performing an assessment. This section outlines the essential inputs, outputs, and tools and techniques.

---

[1] The numbers in brackets refer to the list of references at the end of this standard.

Appendices—The appendices provide the history of the standard and present case studies on how *OPM3* has been successfully applied.

Glossary—This section includes the basic terminology used within this standard.

OPM3 is flexible and scalable, which benefits organizations of different types, sizes, complexity and geographic location. It supports most organizations most of the time, regardless of age, maturity, or other factors.

OPM3 incorporates the collective expertise of the organizational project management community from a wide spectrum of industries and geographic areas. This standard identifies and organizes generally accepted and proven organizational project management practices. The *OPM3* framework provides processes to assess an organization's practices against *OPM3* Best Practices. The assessment findings, without being prescriptive, guide an organization to undertake relevant improvements. The findings enable an organization to make informed decisions regarding potential initiatives for change. Appendix X1 provides a summary of revisions from the previous version of *OPM3*. PMI continues to receive feedback as organizations apply *OPM3* and uses the feedback to improve the standard.

For achieving a certain level of performance and effectiveness or continuously increasing an organization's competitiveness and profitability, *OPM3* helps to accomplish these goals.

Key benefits from applying *OPM3* include, but are not limited to:

- Greater market share,
- Improved competitive advantage,
- Improved customer satisfaction and retention,
- Improved time to market,
- Increased productivity,
- Operational effectiveness,
- Predictable delivery performance,
- Reduced cost and rework, and
- Stronger linkage between strategy and execution.

1.2 Purpose of *OPM3*

The increasing pace of change combined with the rising complexity of the economy and global competition requires executives to reexamine their strategy to fulfill stakeholder expectations and meet market needs. This refinement of strategy requires a new focus on product development, operational effectiveness improvements, and customer service enhancement. However, defining strategy by itself does not ensure success or meet market needs. Rather, executives need to focus on organizational agility and project management capability to ensure success. Organizations should seek ways to translate strategy into organizational success through a project-based approach. Successful organizations develop an environment for delivering individual projects and programs, while creating an organizational culture that treats temporary endeavors as projects. Such organizations manage projects and programs to support organizational goals. Their goal is to select the specific initiative needed to deliver organizational strategy, produce better performance, better results, and a sustainable competitive advantage. To accomplish this, an organization needs to know what specific organizational project management-related practices, knowledge, skills, tools, and techniques have proven consistently to be useful. In addition, a method to compare the organization's current state of organizational project management against industry practices, through the identification of capabilities requiring improvement and the establishment of a roadmap for achieving improvements specific to its needs.

The Organizational Project Management Maturity Model (*OPM3®*) – Third Edition establishes the foundation for and linkage between strategy and portfolio, program, and project management. *OPM3* describes the significant components of PMI's *Organizational Project Management Maturity Model* and provides an organizational view of portfolio, program, and project management to support achieving best practices. In addition, *OPM3* illustrates how the application of the best practices helps to realize organizational improvements. Best practices are the methods currently recognized in a given industry to achieve a stated goal or objective.

1.3 What is OPM?

Organizational project management (OPM) is a strategy execution framework that utilizes portfolio, program, and project management as well as organizational-enabling practices to consistently and predictably deliver organizational strategy to produce better performance, better results, and a sustainable competitive advantage.

OPM addresses integration of the following:

- Knowledge (of the portfolio, program, and project processes),
- Organizational strategy (mission, vision, objectives, and goals),
- People (having competent resources), and
- Processes (the application of the stages of process improvement).

The term "organization" does not necessarily refer to an entire company, agency, association, or society. It may refer to business units, functional groups, departments, or subagencies within the whole. While individual projects may be considered tactical, OPM is, by definition, strategic.

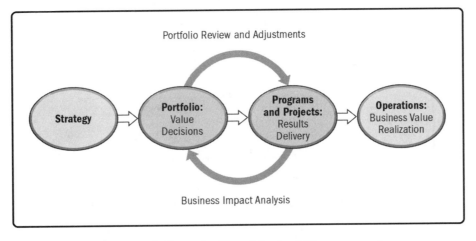

Figure 1-1. Organizational Project Management

Driven from strategy, OPM ensures that the portfolio aligns the set of programs and/or projects that yield the appropriate value decisions and benefits for the organization. Portfolio reviews occur on a regular basis, adjusted as market conditions or strategy change. An analysis of the business impacts on the portfolio guides the portfolio review and is adjusted as needed to deliver results or when other work makes it necessary to revise. These results directly link to business value realization. Feedback from value performance analysis influences the strategy of the organization.

1.3.1 Relationship of OPM and Organizational Strategy

Organizational strategy is a result of the strategic planning cycle, where the vision and mission are translated into a strategic plan. The strategic plan is then subdivided into a set of initiatives influenced by market dynamics, customer and partner requests, shareholders, government regulations, resource capacity, and competitor plans and actions. These initiatives establish strategic and operational portfolios for execution in the planned period.

The concept of OPM as depicted in Figure 1-2 correlates an organization's capabilities in portfolio, program, and project management and the organization's effectiveness in implementing strategy, vision, and mission. OPM purposefully links an organization's portfolio, program, and projects to its business strategy and supporting business objectives.

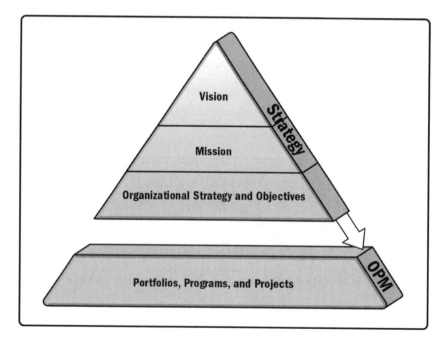

Figure 1-2. Relationship of OPM and Organizational Strategy

1.3.2 The Relationships Among Portfolios, Programs, and Projects

The relationship among portfolios, programs, and projects is such that a portfolio refers to a collection of projects, programs, subportfolios, and operations grouped together in order to facilitate the effective management of that work to meet strategic business objectives. Programs are grouped within a portfolio and are comprised of subprograms, projects, or operations that are managed in a coordinated fashion in support of the portfolio. Individual projects that are either within or outside of a program are still considered part of a portfolio. Although the projects or programs within the portfolio may not necessarily be interdependent or directly related, they link to the organization's strategic plan by means of the organization's portfolio.

As Figure 1-3 illustrates, organizational strategies and priorities are linked and have relationships between portfolios and programs, and between programs and individual projects. Organizational planning impacts projects by means of project prioritization based on risk, funding, and the organization's strategic plan. Organizational planning can direct the funding and support for the component projects on the basis of risk categories, specific lines of business, or general types of projects, such as infrastructure and process improvement.

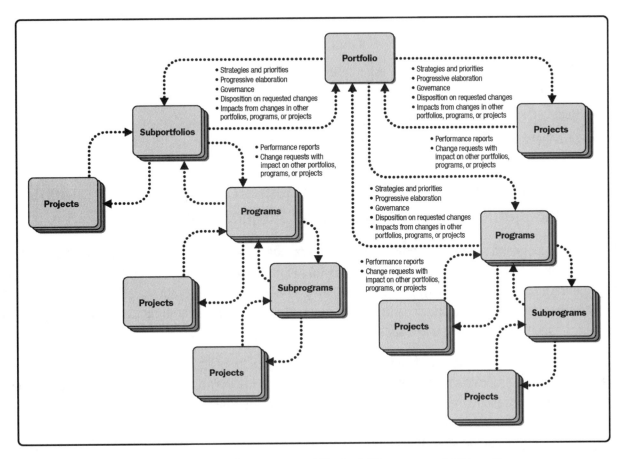

Figure 1-3. Portfolio, Program, and Project Management Interactions

1.4 What Is *OPM3?*

OPM3 provides a way to deliver strategy through clearly linked portfolios, programs, and projects. *OPM3* enhances effective use of human capital by developing portfolio, program, and project competencies (stakeholder engagement, estimating, scheduling, management, etc.). *OPM3* transforms the portfolio, program, and project domain processes into high-quality delivery processes that are well understood, stable, repeatable, and predictable. *OPM3* highlights opportunities for more flexible, adaptable, and improved management systems.

OPM3 is flexible, scalable, and supports organizations of different types, sizes, complexity, and geographic location regardless of age or maturity. *OPM3* benefits organizations, management, governance bodies, portfolio, program or project management offices (PMOs), OPM consultants, process improvement experts, change agents, department managers, and those engaged in project management activities. These benefits may include, but are not limited to:

- Greater market share,
- Improved competitive advantage,
- Improved customer satisfaction and retention,
- Improved time to market,
- Increased employee productivity,
- Operational effectiveness,
- Predictable delivery performance,
- Reduced cost and rework, and
- Stronger linkage between strategy and execution.

1.5 Relationships Among Portfolio Management, Program Management, Project Management, and Organizational Project Management

In order to understand portfolio, program, and project management, it is important to recognize the similarities and differences among these disciplines. It is also helpful to understand how they relate to organizational project management (OPM). OPM is a strategy execution framework utilizing portfolio, program, and project management as well as organization-enabling practices to consistently and predictably deliver organization strategy producing better performance, better results, and a sustainable advantage.

Portfolio, program, and project management are aligned with or driven by organizational strategies. Conversely, portfolio, program, and project management differ in the way each contributes to the achievement of strategic goals. Portfolio management aligns with organizational strategies by selecting the right programs or projects, prioritizing the work, and providing the needed resources, whereas program management harmonizes its project and program components and controls interdependencies in order to realize specified benefits. Project management develops and implements plans to achieve a specific scope that is driven by the objectives of the

©2013 Project Management Institute. *Organizational Project Management Maturity Model (OPM3®) – Third Edition*

program or portfolio it is subjected to and, ultimately, to organizational strategies. OPM advances organizational capability by linking portfolio, program, and project management principles and practices with organizational enablers (e.g., structural, cultural, technological, and human resource practices) to support strategic goals. An organization measures its capabilities, then plans and implements improvements towards the systematic achievement of best practices.

Table 1-1 shows the comparison of portfolio, program, and project views across several dimensions within the organization.

An organization that implements OPM can improve its processes by adopting recognized best practices to achieve consistent portfolio, program, and project success in support of strategic goals.

Table 1-1. Comparative Overview of Portfolio, Program, and Project Management

Organizational Project Management			
	Projects	**Programs**	**Portfolios**
Scope	Projects have defined objectives. Scope is progressively elaborated throughout the project life cycle.	Programs have a larger scope and provide more significant benefits.	Portfolios have an organizational scope that changes with the strategic objectives of the organization.
Change	Project managers expect change and implement processes to keep change managed and controlled.	Program managers expect change from both inside and outside the program and are prepared to manage it.	Portfolio managers continuously monitor changes in the broader internal and external environment.
Planning	Project managers progressively elaborate high-level information into detailed plans throughout the project life cycle.	Program managers develop the overall program plan and create high-level plans to guide detailed planning at the component level.	Portfolio managers create and maintain necessary processes and communication relative to the aggregate portfolio.
Management	Project managers manage the project team to meet the project objectives.	Program managers manage the program staff and the project managers; they provide vision and overall leadership.	Portfolio managers may manage or coordinate portfolio management staff, or program and project staff that may have reporting responsibilities into the aggregate portfolio.
Success	Success is measured by product and project quality, timeliness, budget compliance, and degree of customer satisfaction.	Success is measured by the degree to which the program satisfies the needs and benefits for which it was undertaken.	Success is measured in terms of the aggregate investment performance and benefit realization of the portfolio.
Monitoring	Project managers monitor and control the work of producing the products, services, or results that the project was undertaken to produce.	Program managers monitor the progress of program components to ensure the overall goals, schedules, budget, and benefits of the program will be met.	Portfolio managers monitor strategic changes and aggregate resource allocation, performance results, and risk of the portfolio.

1.5.1 Portfolio Management

A portfolio refers to projects, programs, subportfolios, and operations managed as a group to achieve strategic objectives. The projects or programs of the portfolio may not necessarily be interdependent or directly related. For example, an infrastructure firm that has the strategic objective of "maximizing the return on its investments" may put together a portfolio that includes a mix of projects in oil and gas, power, water, roads, rail, and airports. From this mix, the firm may choose to manage related projects as one program. All of the power projects may be grouped together as a power program. Similarly, all of the water projects may be grouped together as a water program. Thus, the power program and the water program become integral components of the enterprise portfolio of the infrastructure firm.

Portfolio management refers to the centralized management of one or more portfolios to achieve strategic objectives. Portfolio management focuses on ensuring that projects and programs are reviewed to prioritize resource allocation, and that the management of the portfolio is consistent with and aligned to organizational strategies.

1.5.2 Program Management

A program is defined as a group of related projects, subprograms, and program activities managed in a coordinated way to obtain benefits not available from managing them individually. Programs may include elements of related work outside the scope of the discrete projects in the program. A project may or may not be part of a program but a program will always have projects.

Program management is the application of knowledge, skills, tools, and techniques to a program in order to meet the program requirements and to obtain benefits and control not available by managing projects individually.

Projects within a program are related through the common outcome or collective capability. If the relationship between projects is only that of a shared client, seller, technology, or resource, the effort should be managed as a portfolio of projects rather than as a program.

Program management focuses on the project interdependencies and helps to determine the optimal approach for managing them. Actions related to these interdependencies may include:

- Resolving resource constraints and/or conflicts that affect multiple projects within the program,
- Aligning organizational/strategic direction that affects project and program goals and objectives, and
- Resolving issues and change management within a shared governance structure.

An example of a program is a new communications satellite system with projects for design of the satellite and the ground stations, the construction of each, the integration of the system, and the launch of the satellite.

1.5.3 Projects and Strategic Planning

Project management is the application of knowledge, skills, tools, and techniques to project activities to meet the project requirements. Project management is accomplished through the appropriate application and integration of the logically grouped project management processes comprising the following Process Groups: Initiating, Planning, Executing, Monitoring and Controlling, and Closing.

Successful project management starts with selecting and prioritizing projects to support the organizational mission and strategy. This process results in a portfolio of projects that balance threats and opportunities and provides a better utilization of resources.

In customer-driven organizations, the mission statement defines the organization's purpose and serves as the guiding light for the organization and executives. Once formulated, the next step is to create goals, objectives, and strategies. Goals translate the mission into specific, measurable, and tangible terms. The future state of the organization is identified by these goals by setting targets for all levels of the organization. Each level of the organizational objectives supports the higher-level objectives in more detail.

The development of strategies to meet these needs and goals should focus on specific implementation plans of how the organization will achieve their objectives and goals. This requires an extensive analysis of the internal and external environments through the identification of strengths and weaknesses, such as, management, facilities, core competencies, product quality, technology, and financial resources. The deliverable of this analysis is a set of strategies designed to best meet customers' needs. Implementation of these strategies requires actions and completing tasks, and should focus on how to realize these strategies.

1.5.4 Project Management Office

The portfolio, program, or project management office (PMO) is an organizational body assigned with various responsibilities related to the centralized and coordinated management of those projects under its domain. The PMO is the liaison between a company's portfolios, programs, and projects and the corporate measurement systems, such as, the balanced scorecard. A PMO may be delegated with the authority to act as an integral stakeholder and a key decision maker to make recommendations, to terminate projects, or to take other actions, as required, to keep projects and programs consistent with business objectives. Additionally, the PMO may be involved in the selection, management, and deployment of shared or dedicated project resources. A primary function of a PMO is to support project managers in a variety of ways, which may include, but are not limited to:

- Coaching, mentoring, training, and oversight;
- Coordinating communication across projects;
- Developing and managing project policies, procedures, templates, and other project documentation (organizational process assets);
- Identifying and developing project management methodology, best practices, and standards;
- Managing shared resources across all projects administered by the PMO;
- Monitoring compliance with project management standards, policies, procedures, and templates by means of project audits; and
- Providing centralized support for managing changes and tracking risks and issues.

There are various types of PMOs, each varying in the degree of control and influence they have on projects within the organization.

1.5.5 Project-Based Organizations

Organizational structure can influence the organization's ability to deliver successful projects, because the structure of an organization determines the communication requirements, responsibilities, and management reporting structure. There are three organizational structure models: functional, matrix, and projectized.

Project-based organizations (PBO) are fast emerging as a recognized trend of a new form of organization to create a competitive edge. PBOs conduct the majority of their activities as projects rather than functional approaches. PBOs refer to either an entire organization or may be nested within subsidiaries or divisions of larger corporations. PBOs manage portfolios and resources differently than other types of organizations. PBOs provide many advantages, such as a high level of integration, improved communication, and increased project focus.

While executives and organizational managers seek better strategy delivery results, organizations need to understand the various project-based organizational models that can accommodate various situations and address the issues of compartmentalization.

The adoption of an integrated project approach, with horizontal structures that provide integration from business strategy through realization of operational benefits and vertical structures that provide integration between organizational strategy and prioritized portfolios of projects, including a governance-oriented PMO, will enable organizations to promote the implementation of organizational project management.

1.5.6 Organizational Issues and Project Management

In traditional organizations, responsibility for determining and achieving the organizations' goals is assigned to the operations function. Executives, with titles such as chief operations officer (COO), chief technology officer (CTO), chief information officer (CIO), chief financial officer (CFO), strategic planning consultant, etc., establish objectives and goals and develop strategies to achieve them. Executives expect to select from proposed and pending projects to create the mix of projects most likely to support achievement of the organization's goals within the preferred strategies, organizational risk tolerance, and organizational resource (people and funding) constraints.

Project management requires deliberate planning and action to create the conditions for success. This entails implementing strategy, leadership, goals, process, skills, systems, issue resolution, and structure to direct and exploit the dynamic nature of project work. However, when strategy moves from the boardroom to back offices and the marketplace, the ability to deliver utilizing project management is often overlooked. Implementing efficient project management will enable organizations to meet their strategic and operational objectives.

There are several conditions that are essential for project success. These conditions apply to all projects, whether related to top-level strategic business issues or operational ones.

1.5.6.1 Clearly Communicated Strategy

Effective management organizations have a clear, well-communicated strategy and understand how each project supports it. Implementing effective project management includes putting in place a mechanism to evaluate every project for its fit with the strategy prior to implementation. An organization's strategy should provide the boundaries for projects—goals and results should flow from an organization's future direction. Before deciding to embark on a new project and when communicating the goals of that project to the project team, senior management should provide clear answers to the following questions: What are the organization's products and services? Who are its customers and markets? What is its competitive advantage? How will this particular project support the achievement of its strategy?

1.5.6.2 Goals

Effective organizations know which operational goals make a difference in the business strategy and then implement methods for keeping these visible to all. At the beginning of a project, senior management communicates to the project team and provides answers to these important questions: What are the organization's long- and short-term operational goals and budgets? How does the project fit into or support these? Once the project is under way, progress against these goals needs to be evaluated and communicated on an ongoing basis.

1.5.6.3 Leadership

In some organizations, selecting and overseeing the management of projects is directed by the senior management team, allowing them to keep a tight rein on the organization's project portfolio. In other organizations, some of this responsibility is delegated to a project management office, enabling senior management to focus on more strategic tasks and providing more authority to others. Each organization needs to decide how to strike the right balance between control and agility. Whichever method an organization chooses, it needs to be visible and consistent; otherwise it will undermine the system and the organization's goals.

1.5.6.4 Business Processes

Within an organization, the systems used to gather, analyze, and disseminate information are required to support project-based work. This is true regardless of whether the projects are external or internal.

1.5.6.5 Human Capabilities

Effective project management requires the right people with the right skills. A key skill needed by those who are implementing project management is the ability to identify, hire, and retain individuals who are best suited for project work. Some people simply are not suited to the challenges of project management; others enjoy the challenge of working toward a goal and being part of a project team. In addition, each project should enhance existing capabilities and provide new development opportunities in areas such as leadership, problem solving and decision making, human performance management, communication, and portfolio management.

1.5.6.6 Culture and Performance System

An organization's culture consists of its norms, values, and beliefs. These may be explicitly expressed and often remain hidden to form part of the implicit context of organization life that can exercise a gravitational pull on decision making. Unless an organization demonstrates visible, unreserved commitment to sound project management practices, the chances are that project management will be viewed as just another activity. The successful implementation of project management depends on an organization's explicit belief that the manner in which projects are managed is just as important as what they achieve. Project management becomes "the way we do business around here."

1.5.6.7 Information and Business Systems

Project management software is a tool for organizing and representing project information; however, it is not a substitute for project management skills nor the judgment required to apply them. Like any project, new systems and procedures should be aligned and integrated into the business life of an organization to make them relevant to the way business is conducted and to prove value added, resources required, risk, and lessons learned.

1.5.6.8 Team Structure

Implementing project management requires matching the team structure to the project and to the other needs of the organization. Several options exist for organizing people for project work; for example, developing a matrix where reporting responsibility is divided between project and functional managers and the central pool where resources are on call to meet demand. This structure affords the organization the greatest efficiency, provides the greatest range of development opportunities, and fits well with the use of temporary and contract resources. However, it also requires a strong scheduling function with the authority to stand up to demands for specific resources.

1.5.6.9 External Factors

Implementing project management implies emphasis on the internal workings of the organization, but external factors are also at play. Vendors and suppliers need to be aligned to support project work. The right materials need to show up at the right moment. Contracts and procurement processes need to be aligned with project schedules, and rewards should follow both supplier and buyer performance. Also, certain customers and markets may demand that projects be conducted in a special way. External projects with a mission beyond organizational boundaries may require changes in the way the projects are sold, delivered, or reported. Senior management should keep in mind that superior project management skills and innovative practices, processes, and products can be an important competitive differentiator. The organization's skills should be continually benchmarked against those of the competition to make the necessary investment it needs to keep pace or lead the industry.

1.5.6.10 The Future

No organization possesses all of the capabilities needed to face the challenges ahead. However, steps can be taken to prepare for the unpredictable, such as succession planning, continuous training, and the development of future project managers to ensure that the requisite talent will always be available for new projects.

1.6 Business Value

Business value is a concept that is unique to each organization. Business value is defined as the entire value of the business: the total sum of all tangible and intangible elements. Examples of tangible elements include monetary assets, fixtures, stockholder equity, and utility. Examples of intangible elements include good will, brand recognition, public benefit, and trademarks. Depending on the organization, business value scope can be short-, medium-, or long-term. Value may be created through the effective management of ongoing operations. However, through the effective use of portfolio, program, and project management, organizations will possess the ability to employ reliable, established processes to meet strategic objectives and obtain greater business value from their project investments. While not all organizations are business driven, all organizations conduct business-related activities. Whether an organization is a government agency or a nonprofit organization, all organizations focus on attaining business value for their activities.

Successful business value realization begins with comprehensive strategic planning and management. Organizational strategy can be expressed through the organization's mission and vision, including orientation to markets, competition, and other environmental factors. Effective organizational strategy provides defined directions for development and growth, in addition to performance metrics for success. In order to bridge the gap between organizational strategy and successful business value realization, the use of portfolio, program, and project management techniques is essential.

Portfolio management aligns components (projects, programs, or operations) to the organizational strategy, organized into portfolios or subportfolios to optimize project or program objectives, dependencies, costs, timelines, benefits, resources, and risks. This allows organizations to have an overall view of how the strategic goals are reflected in the portfolio, institute appropriate governance management, and authorize human, financial, or material resources to be allocated based on expected performance and benefits.

Using program management, organizations have the ability to align multiple projects for optimized or integrated costs, schedule, effort, and benefits. Program management focuses on project interdependencies and helps to determine the optimal approach for managing and realizing the desired benefits.

With project management, organizations have the ability to apply knowledge, processes, skills, and tools and techniques that enhance the likelihood of success over a wide range of projects. Project management focuses on the successful delivery of products, services, or results. Within programs and portfolios, projects are a means of achieving organizational strategy and objectives.

Organizations can further facilitate the alignment of these portfolio, program, and project management activities by strengthening organizational enablers such as structural, cultural, technological, and human resource practices. By continuously conducting portfolio strategic alignment and optimization, performing business impact analyses, and developing robust organizational enablers, organizations can achieve successful transitions within the portfolio, program, and project domains and attain effective investment management and business value realization.

1.7 Stakeholders

Projects often fail because the key decision makers have not been identified or have not been actively involved in determining the project strategy and direction. Stakeholders are individuals, groups, or organizations who may affect, be affected by, or perceive itself to be affected by a decision, activity, or outcome of a portfolio, program, or project. Many stakeholders provide valuable input and play a critical role in the success of any project or program. They also have the ability to positively or adversely impact the project objectives depending on the benefits or threats they perceive. Therefore, it is essential that key stakeholders be identified and their positions, influence, and source of power be understood. Stakeholders may be internal or external to the organization. Within an organization, internal stakeholders cover all levels of the organization's hierarchy. Updates to the stakeholder list and influence factors should occur on a regular basis.

Key stakeholders of an *OPM3* initiative include, but are not limited to, the following:

- **OPM3 practitioner.** The *OPM3* practitioner is a subject matter expert in organizational project management maturity assessment and improvement who works with organizations to assess project management competency and develop an improvement plan focusing on the Best Practices that the organization should implement based on priorities, attainability, benefits, and cost.
- **Program director.** The individual with executive ownership of the program(s).
- **Program manager.** The individual responsible for managing the program.
- **Project manager.** The individual responsible for managing the individual projects.
- **Sponsor.** A person or group who provides resources and support for the project, program, or portfolio, and is accountable for overall success.
- **Customer.** The individual or organization who promotes the use of the new capabilities and supports the investment.
- **Beneficiary.** The individual or organization who benefits from the use of the new capabilities.
- **Performing organization.** The group that is performing the work.
- **PMO.** The organizational body assigned with various responsibilities related to the centralized and coordinated management of portfolios, programs, and projects as described in Section 1.5.4.
- **Governance board.** The group responsible for ensuring that goals are achieved and providing support for addressing risks and issues.
- **Supplier.** The individual or organization who provides goods and services to the organization.
- **Governmental regulatory agencies.** Agencies imposing policies, laws, rules, or guidance with enforcement authority.
- **Competitors and potential customers.** Competitors and customers who have an interest in the organization's products, services, and performance.
- **Groups.** The groups representing consumer, environmental, or other interests.

1.7.1 *OPM3* Practitioner Knowledge and Skills

In order to be successful in the assessment or improvement of organizations, an *OPM3* practitioner should have expertise in all of the following areas:

- **Knowledge of the latest editions of PMI's portfolio, program and project standards.** An *OPM3* practitioner is required to have expertise in the use of portfolio, program, and project management methods and techniques that include both qualitative and quantitative measures.

- **Process management and continuous process improvement.** The *OPM3* practitioner should be competent in process definition, development, maintenance, control and improvement with respect to the size and complexity of the organization.

- **Strategic alignment.** The *OPM3* practitioner is required to understand the organization's strategic goals and priorities and how the portfolio, program, and project support them.

- **Ability to conduct assessments.** An effective *OPM3* practitioner requires training on how to conduct assessments.

- **Ability to draw conclusions and offer recommendations.** An effective *OPM3* practitioner is required to possess proper training on how to draw conclusions and offer recommendations on the assessments conducted.

- **Ability to engage stakeholders.** An effective *OPM3* practitioner interacts at different levels to understand and influence expectations.

- **Consulting experience.** An *OPM3* practitioner is required to possess business acumen. The *OPM3* practitioner should have knowledge of relevant markets, the customer base, competition, trends, standards, legal and regulatory environments, and appropriate code of conduct. The *OPM3* practitioner is required to be adept at working with executives, managers, project and program managers, and other internal and external stakeholders, as appropriate to the individual and role.

- **Business skills.** An effective *OPM3* practitioner is required to possess skills related to governance, risk and compliance (see Section 3.3.1.1 for greater detail), benefits management, scope management, resource management, and financial management as explained in the areas of expertise in Section 3.3.1. The *OPM3* practitioner is required to possess well-developed skills in communicating, team building, planning, conflict resolution, contract negotiating, meeting facilitating, decision making, and removing organizational barriers to success. This individual is required to be capable of adapting to divergent organizational decision-making models, ranging from autocratic to collegial.

- **Risk management.** An effective *OPM3* practitioner should be well versed in opportunity and threat management.

- **Organizational change management.** An *OPM3* practitioner should have an understanding of how an *OPM3* initiative impacts an organization.

2

2

FOUNDATIONAL CONCEPTS

2.1 Organizational Project Management Described

Organizational project management (OPM) is a strategy execution framework utilizing portfolio, program, and project management as well as organizational-enabling practices to consistently and predictably deliver organizational strategy leading to better performance, better results, and a sustainable competitive advantage. OPM is the integration of people, knowledge, and processes, which are supported by tools across all domains based on the value strategy for the target market. Looking at the description more closely, the word "integration" is used because OPM is the appropriate balance of knowledge, processes, people, and supporting tools.

Figure 2-1 depicts a systematic approach across all domains of organizational project management that encompasses the following:

- **Strategy.** Creating an organizational environment that supports the execution of the organization's strategy.
- **Portfolio: Value decisions.** Decomposing the strategy into initiatives and aligning organizational resources to the initiatives to execute the organization's strategy through a disciplined business value decision process.
- **Programs and projects: Results delivery.** Developing initiatives into the intended business value through a predictable business results delivery system.
- **Operations: Business value realization.** Operationalizing the initiatives and measuring the business value through a business value realization process.
- **Business impact analysis.** Analyzing the impact and value from the business decision process and providing results data from the business.
- **Portfolio review and adjustments.** Reviewing and adjusting the portfolio components based on business value realization and results data.
- **Value performance analysis.** Providing business value realization data from value business fulfillment back to the strategy of the organization.

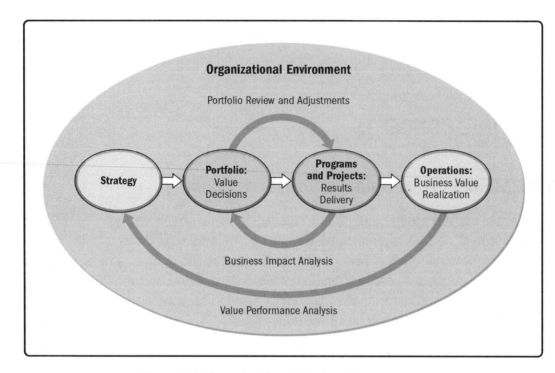

Figure 2-1. Organizational Project Management

The bulleted points mentioned previously describe the capabilities of organizational project management. Each organizational project management domain encompasses multiple processes that translate into specific capabilities that an organization should possess in order to improve its maturity and better succeed with its strategy execution. Additionally, the organization needs an environment with demonstrated capabilities to support this OPM approach in delivering its strategy.

This approach is based on the organization's value strategy for the target market referring to customization and fit. Every organization has a unique vision, mission, and a set of strategies, which communicate the beliefs of the organization—what the organization stands for and what the organization intends to accomplish for its customers and other stakeholders. These elements are the organization's guiding principles and all actions need to align with these principles in order for the organization to be successful.

Because organizational project management describes many capabilities, each organization needs to determine which OPM capabilities are necessary for the organization to fulfill its value strategy within the industry in which it competes. For instance, a bank in one country is not going to need the exact same capabilities as a bank in a different country or as a software development organization in another country.

OPM is an acknowledgment that performing portfolio, program, and project management is not enough to consistently achieve results or sustain competitive advantage. Having well prepared professionals like MBAs, certified accountants, and PMP® credential holders in an organization is not enough to ensure the achievement of better results. The implementation of enabling business practices that support a strategy development framework will not ensure the achievement of better results. Having process improvement in place by itself will not ensure the achievement of better results. Better results come from the execution of strategy with the right people, using the right process, and measuring and controlling the process in order to continuously improve.

To reiterate, organizational project management is a strategy execution framework utilizing portfolio, program, and project management as well as organizational enabling practices to consistently and predictably deliver organizational strategy producing better performance, better results, and a sustainable competitive advantage.

2.2 Investing in OPM

Many times in the past, organizations invested in aspects of project management based on a crisis in the organization. A crisis sparks conversations about project management and leads to small tactical investments to avert the next crisis or to show improvements from the last crisis. These tactical investments include items such as:

- Project management competency development,
- Project management training, and
- Tool implementation.

Although each of these tactical solutions provides some level of improvement, and generates some quick wins, most of the time these solutions do not address the real issues facing an organization. These tactical issues sometimes support individual project success versus project success in delivering the organization's strategy.

Investment in project management requires careful consideration of the organization's strategic objectives and business drivers:

- Organizations seeking an operational efficiency strategy may want to gain control of delivery budgets.
- Organizations that follow a customer intimacy strategy may want to improve the alignment between the marketing and delivery teams.
- Organizations that follow a product innovation strategy may be most concerned with time to market, innovation, and creativity.
- Organizations that seek economic growth tie significantly to value realizations that include growth, increased reputation, market share, and customer retention.

OPM seeks to change the investment approach from crisis investment to proactive investment targeted at value creation for the organization. Organizations need to be patient when making this challenging cultural fit. Organizations that shift to this investment approach reap the benefits of proactive alignment to strategy and better strategic execution than organizations that use traditional investment approaches.

2.3 Organizational Life Cycles

Organizations implement OPM regardless of where they are in their organizational life cycle, as further described below and depicted in Figure 2-2:

- **Birth or startup.** Organizations that have just formed or are starting new lines of business or services are said to be in a birth or startup phase of an organizational life cycle. These organizations utilize organizational project management as a strategy execution framework. They use the *OPM3* Best Practices as a means for determining which domains, processes, and capabilities should be established for successful strategy execution in order to deliver the organizational strategies.

- **Growth.** A growth organization often needs to manage more projects, with more resources, in order to sustain its growth. These organizations use *OPM3* to enhance the maturity of their project delivery systems by developing consistent practices, often led by a PMO.

- **Mature operations.** Organizations that have achieved organizational goals, for example capturing the market share, utilize organizational project management and *OPM3* as a means to sustain their competitive advantage. These organizations are already using *OPM3* and established capabilities to deliver their strategy. They continuously evaluate their capabilities when seeking to sustain this ability because they are often best in class. They use *OPM3* to measure and validate their capabilities while seeking continuous improvement to sustain their competitive edge.

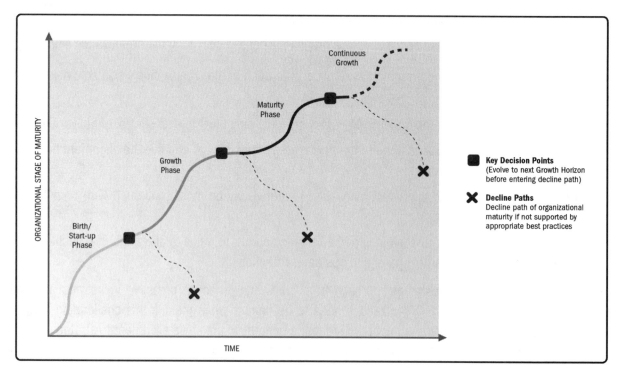

Figure 2-2. Organizational Life Cycle

2

- **Decline or evolution.** Organizations with declining business performance utilize *OPM3* as a diagnostic tool to understand their implementation of organizational project management and how to reverse their downward performance trend. Using *OPM3* as a diagnostic tool is important and should be undertaken as soon as data trends suggest that a decline is approaching.

2.4 Organizational Project Management Maturity Model

2.4.1 What is the Organizational Project Management Maturity Model?

OPM3 consists of many elements which are explained herein and explained in detail in Section 3 of this standard.

2.4.1.1 Domains

Organizational project management consists of three domains: portfolio, program, and project. These domains are explained in detail in the following standards:

- *The Standard for Portfolio Management* – Third Edition. This standard describes the practices of portfolio management. In the context of *OPM3,* portfolio management describes the processes that establish a mechanism that decomposes an organization's strategy into endeavors that, through other business disciplines, deliver the sought-after business values.

- *The Standard for Program Management* – Third Edition. This standard provides guidelines for the management of programs within organizations. It defines program management, performance domains, and related concepts; describes the program management life cycle; and outlines related activities and processes.

- *A Guide to the Project Management Body of Knowledge (PMBOK® Guide)* – Fifth Edition. The *PMBOK® Guide* describes the processes required for a single component to successfully deliver the business values for which it was commissioned.

These standards provide the good practices for each domain. *OPM3* applies quality concepts to these good practices to create Best Practices.

2.4.1.2 Organizational Enablers (OE)

The organizational environment should support the strategy execution framework of organizational project management. This support translates into a series of best practices that describe the capabilities that support OPM. Organizational-enabling best practices have been categorized into 18 groups. There are various types of OE best practices which include, but are not limited to:

- **Structural.** Organizations are structured in many different forms. Some are structured based on function, geography, product, or service line or a combination of these. These structures drive reporting relationships among employees, allocation of resources, and alignment to strategy. Structural enablers help organizations establish strategic alignment and resource allocation based on organizational structures that enable organizational project management.

- **Cultural.** An organization's culture is understood to different degrees by the people within the organization. They understand how people work with each other to get things done. An organization's culture is engrained and takes substantial effort to make changes. In order for OPM to be successful within an organization, its culture needs to embrace portfolio, program, and project management. Executives can build this into the culture by establishing governance, policy, and vision; acting as sponsors rather than just administrators; and supporting communities where OPM best practices can be shared and leveraged.

- **Technological.** Technology helps organizations perform otherwise manual tasks better, faster, and cheaper. It also encourages the reuse of good practices and techniques, improves sharing of knowledge, and allows the organization to gather data for comparison to similar organizations. An organization underpins the success of its projects, programs, and overall portfolio by:

  - Investing in management systems that support effective portfolio, program, and project management;

  - Sharing practices and techniques across projects;

  - Developing a methodology which becomes the way that projects and programs perform work; and

  - Benchmarking portfolio, program, and project performance against comparable organizations.

- **Human resource.** Success in OPM depends on having the right people in place to execute these roles. Human resource enablers, such as competency management, individual performance appraisals, and training investments help ensure successful application of OPM, resulting in higher organizational performance.

Organizational-enabling best practices are further explained in detail in Section 3 of this standard.

2.4.1.3 Process Improvement

For years, businesses have applied process improvement techniques, for example, process reengineering, to operations to improve efficiency and effectiveness. These same techniques apply to OPM to improve efficiency and effectiveness of the entire OPM framework.

The steps of process improvement (see Figure 2-3) include:

- **Standardize.** There are four key steps in standardizing a process:

  - *Governing body overview.* Ensure a process governing body is in place—one that has authority in the organization and can own the process.

  - *Documented process.* Develop and document the process—it may be purchased or written by someone within the organization.

  - *Communicate the process.* Communicate the process to those responsible for executing the process.

  - *Process adherence.* Apply the process consistently across the organization.

Without all four steps, a standardized process is not in place nor is it sustainable.

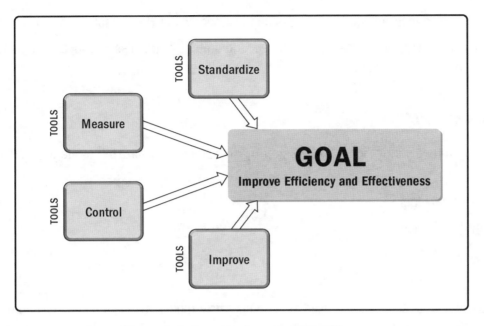

Figure 2-3. Process Improvement Steps

- **Measure.** Once the processes are standardized, select those processes that can be measured to see how effective they are for the organization. The "measure" stage quantifies the quality of the processes and process inputs. There are five key activities involved in the measurement step:
    - o Identify critical process customer-focused measures.
    - o Identify critical process characteristics.
    - o Measure critical process characteristics.
    - o Identify upstream measures.
    - o Measure critical inputs.

- **Control.** Once a process is measured, the organization may gather trending data to determine if it is under control. In order to achieve control of "Best Practices," the organization needs to:
    - o Create a process control plan with upper and lower control limits.
    - o Implement the process control plan.
    - o Observe the process operating within plan boundaries consistently over time.

- **Improve.** Once a process has been standardized, measured, and controlled, organizations can continuously improve them. Continuous improvement is more than making an update to the process. It is based on three key concepts:
    - o Identify process root problems; determine the root cause as to why the process is not performing at the level it should be.

○ Have a focused effort on process improvement with potential solutions.

○ Once a solution has been defined, integrate the process improvement into the way the organization does the work.

2.4.2 How to Use *OPM3*

The *OPM3* Cycle, as depicted in Figure 2-4, is a step-by-step process to utilize this strategy execution framework. The steps are:

- Acquire Knowledge.
- Perform Assessment.
- Manage Improvements.
- Repeat the process.

The *OPM3* Cycle and its steps can be used as a comparative model, a design model, or improvement model. These steps provide easy access to relevant business issues.

- **Comparative model.** For organizations that have adopted some elements of organizational project management, the best approach is comparative. In this approach, organizations use the steps of the model to assess themselves against the model to determine their extent of implementation entering the model at step 1. They use the remaining steps of the model to determine what improvements to make and implement those improvements. Finally, they decide whether they should repeat the process.

- **Design model.** Organizations that are newly formed or are forming their approach to organizational project management use the Best Practices of the model to design their approach and implementation of organizational project management. They enter the cycle at the Manage Improvements step.

- **Improvement model.** Organizations lacking an institutionalized strategy execution framework use the Best Practices of the model to determine which Best Practices should be put into place. They enter the cycle at the Manage Improvements step.

The *OPM3* Cycle depicted in Figure 2-4 is described in more detail in Section 3.

2.4.2.1 Step One—Acquire Knowledge: Prepare for Assessment

In this formative step, the organization prepares for an organizational project management assessment. This is accomplished by:

- Understanding the organization, its mission, vision, and core values;
- Understanding the organization needs, pain points, objectives, and available results; and
- Understanding the *OPM3* model and how assessments are performed.

Refer to Section 4 for more details.

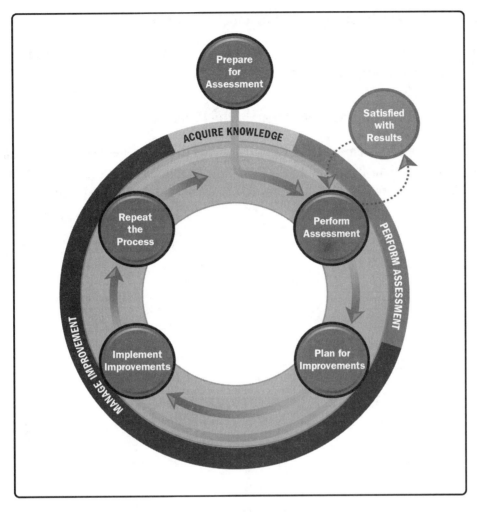

Figure 2-4. *OPM3* **Cycle**

2.4.2.2 Step Two—Perform Assessment

During this step, the capabilities of the organization are compared to the capabilities of the *OPM3* model. Refer to Section 5 for more details.

2.4.2.3 Step Three—Manage Improvement: Plan for Improvements

Once an organization has compared itself against the *OPM3* model, the organization targets which capability improvements are desired. The organization determines these needs and then determines which relevant Best Practices and Capabilities should be implemented to fill those needs. Refer to Section 6 for further details.

2.4.2.4 Step Four—Manage Improvement: Implement Improvements

The organization implements the planned improvements utilizing project management and organizational change methods. Refer to Section 6 for additional details.

2.4.2.5 Step Five—Manage Improvement: Repeat the Process

Upon completion of the improvement cycle, the organization evaluates whether the improvement(s) selected resulted in an organizational capability now available that may impact business results. If more improvement is needed, the organization repeats the *OPM3* Cycle periodically to achieve the desired result.

3

THE ORGANIZATIONAL PROJECT MANAGEMENT MATURITY MODEL (*OPM3*)

3.1 Introduction

This section explains the architecture of *OPM3* in detail, specifically the Best Practices and their constituent components: Capabilities and Outcomes. Dependencies exist between Best Practices and Capabilities and are further explored in this section. Categorization refines the list of Best Practices for practical application. Furthermore, this section describes organizational enabler Best Practices and how they support an organization's improvement plan.

This section introduces the *OPM3* framework, *OPM3* Cycle Elements and Areas of Expertise supported by the associated processes (see Section 3.3). The Cycle Elements include: Acquire Knowledge, Perform Assessment, and Manage Improvement while the Areas of Expertise include: Governance Risk and Compliance, Delivery and Benefits Management, and Change Management.

In order to assist the organization to increase its maturity and consequently achieve better business results, the *OPM3* practitioner needs to understand the entire *OPM3* Context (as illustrated in Figure 3-1) in which the *OPM3* Construct (explained in Section 3.2) represents all the elements that comprise *OPM3*. Knowing and understanding those elements is integral to the success of any *OPM3* initiative. The *OPM3* framework (explained in Section 3.3) represents a number of processes that form an approach that can be utilized to implement the *OPM3* initiative. Both parts of the *OPM3* context along with the skills, knowledge, competencies, and tools and techniques of the *OPM3* practitioner provide the needed business results and enhanced capability for the organization.

3.2 The *OPM3* Construct

The *OPM3* Construct (Figure 3-2) describes the *OPM3* components and their relationships. These components include Domains, Process Improvement Stages, Best Practices, Capabilities, and Outcomes. Once these concepts are presented, categorization and maturity measurement are explored for customized application. The *OPM3* Construct conveys progressively more detail as the reader moves from the higher components to the lower components.

Best Practices are mapped to Process Improvement Stages only for Process Best Practices (Best Practices for Portfolio, Program, and Project Domains). Section 3.2.5 presents a full description of the Process Improvement Stages.

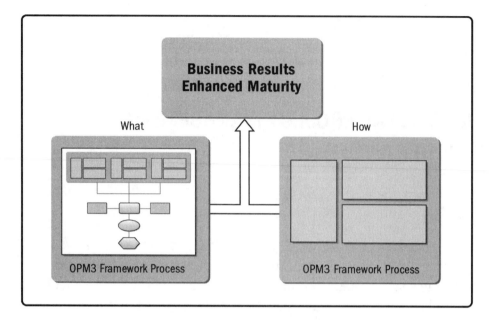

Figure 3-1. The *OPM3* Context

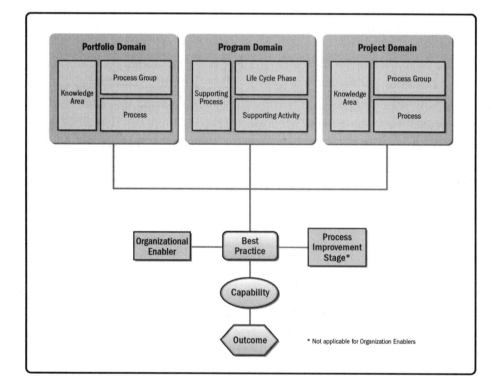

Figure 3-2. The *OPM3* Construct

3.2.1 Best Practice

OPM3 measures organizational project management maturity by assessing the existence of best practices. Best practices refer to the methods, currently recognized within a given industry or discipline, to achieve a stated goal or objective. Industry practitioners from around the globe collaborate periodically on the current trends and practices that make their organizations successful. For example, The *PMBOK® Guide* update team collects project management information and refines it through these established processes. PMI publishes the approved *PMBOK® Guide* processes for industry practitioners to share and apply. *OPM3* brings these *PMBOK® Guide* processes into the *OPM3* framework and applies a quality model to generate Best Practices. This also applies to the portfolio and program standards.

An organization achieves a Best Practice when the organization demonstrates maturity evidenced by successful fulfillment of the Capabilities and Outcomes. For organizational project management, this includes the ability to deliver projects predictably, consistently, and successfully. *OPM3* encourages a culture of improvement, leveraging achieved Best Practices and pursuing desired Best Practices to attain organizational goals.

Figure 3-3 illustrates that each Best Practice contains a set of Capabilities and each Capability contains a set of Outcomes. An organization achieves a Best Practice when it consistently demonstrates all of the supporting Capabilities. An organization attains a Capability when the organization realizes one or more associated Outcomes, as supported by tangible and intangible evidence.

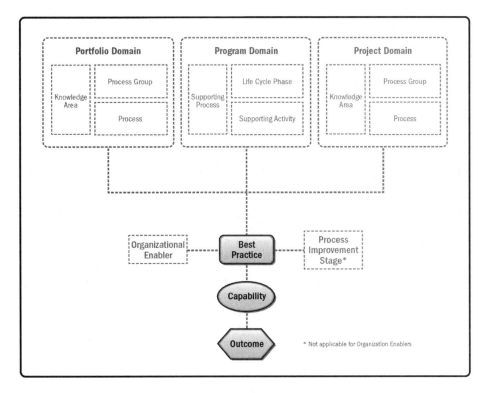

Figure 3-3. The *OPM3* Best Practice

If the organization demonstrates achievement of all the aggregated Capabilities except one, it cannot claim achievement of the Best Practice. Even when an organization does not completely achieve a Best Practice, the organization may still realize benefits that meet the organization's needs. Annex A1 provides a list of all Best Practices within each of the domains.

3.2.2 Capability

A Capability represents the collection of people, process, and technology that enables an organization to deliver organizational project management (OPM). Capabilities are incremental steps leading to the attainment of one or more Best Practices. *OPM3* does not prescribe a sequence for achieving the Capabilities, but all Capabilities are required to be fulfilled to achieve a Best Practice. A Capability from one Best Practice may be a predecessor for achieving another Best Practice. Dependencies may exist whereas certain Best Practices and Capabilities are required to be in place before other Best Practices can be realized. Breaking down each Best Practice into its constituent Capabilities and showing the dependencies among them provides a basis for decisions related to improvement.

3.2.3 Outcome

An Outcome is a result (tangible or intangible) of an organization exhibiting a Capability. An example of a tangible Outcome is a policy for project management. An example of an intangible Outcome is a verbal acknowledgement of a project management policy. A Capability may have multiple outcomes, but a single outcome may be sufficient to satisfy a Capability.

Figure 3-4 illustrates the various components of the *OPM3* Construct.

3.2.4 Domains

Domains represent the three process-based standards (see Figure 3-5): *The Standard for Portfolio Management* – Third Edition, representing the Portfolio Domain; *The Standard for Program Management* – Third Edition, representing the Program Domain; and the *PMBOK Guide®* – Fifth Edition, which represents the Project Domain.

Process-based standards serve as the foundation for Best Practices. When the processes are integrated into *OPM3* to form the Best Practices, the associated details are brought in as well. This information includes: Process Groups and Knowledge Areas for the Project and Portfolio Domains, and Performance Domains for the Program Domain.

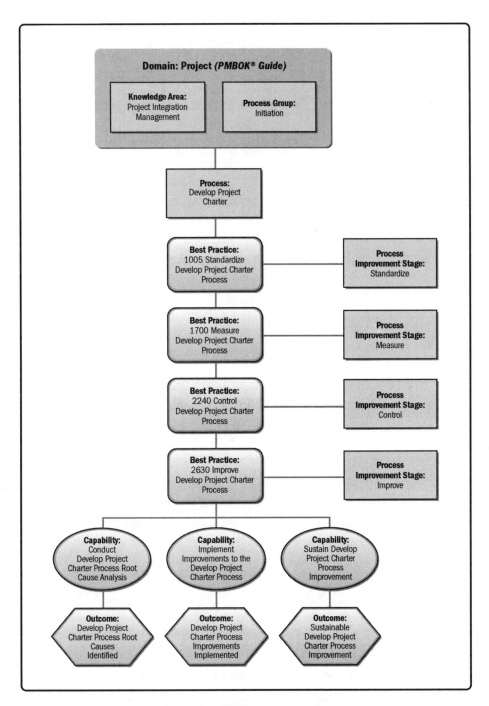

Figure 3-4. The *OPM3* Construct Example

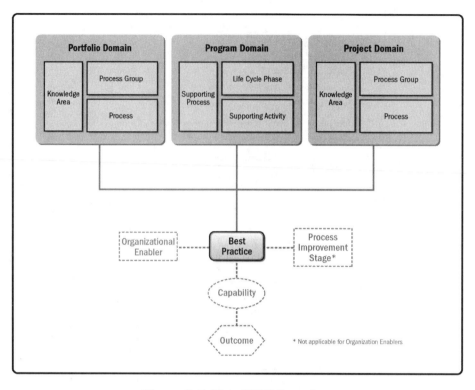

Figure 3-5. The *OPM3* Domains

3.2.4.1 Project

The *PMBOK Guide®*– Fifth Edition identifies five Project Management Process Groups and ten Knowledge Areas. These five Process Groups, which are in line with the project life cycle, are independent of application areas or industry focus. Process Groups and their constituent processes are often repeated prior to completing the project; this is referred to as progressive elaboration.

The five Process Groups are:

- **Initiating.** Defines and authorizes the project or project phase.
- **Planning.** Defines and refines objectives, and plans the course of action required to attain the objectives and scope.
- **Executing.** Integrates people and other resources to carry out the project management plan.
- **Monitoring and Controlling.** Measures and monitors progress to identify variances from the project management plan so that corrective action can be taken when necessary to meet project objectives.
- **Closing.** Formalizes acceptance of the product, service, or result and brings the project or a project phase to an orderly end.

OPM3 provides a flexible approach that encourages organizations to focus on the domains, processes, and Process Groups where the adoption of Best Practices will best support the successful achievement of strategic objectives. Understanding the Process Groups and the processes they support, as well as the organizational enabling Best Practices, helps the organization to determine where they should start the effort to improve their OPM practices.

3.2.4.2 Program

The Standard for Program Management – Third Edition coordinates the management of five interdependent Performance Domains:

- **Program Strategy Alignment.** Identifying opportunities and benefits that achieve the organization's strategic objectives through program implementation.

- **Program Benefits Management.** Defining, creating, maximizing, and sustaining the benefits provided by programs.

- **Program Stakeholder Engagement.** Capturing stakeholder needs and expectations, gaining and maintaining stakeholder support, and mitigating/channeling opposition.

- **Program Governance.** Establishing processes and procedures for maintaining proactive program management oversight and decision-making support for applicable policies and practices throughout the entire program life cycle.

- **Program Life Cycle Management.** Managing all of the program activities related to the program definition, program benefits delivery, and program closure.

The program management supporting processes enable a synergistic approach for the purpose of delivering program benefits. These program supporting processes are:

- Program Communications Management,
- Program Financial Management,
- Program Integration Management,
- Program Procurement Management,
- Program Quality Management,
- Program Resource Management,
- Program Risk Management,
- Program Schedule Management, and
- Program Scope Management.

3.2.4.3 Portfolio

The Standard for Portfolio Management – Third Edition identifies three Portfolio Management Process Groups with five Knowledge Areas. Processes within these Process Groups facilitate informed decision making, strategy translation, and portfolio balancing. These three Process Groups are independent of application area or industry focus.

The three Portfolio Management Process Groups are:

- **Defining Process Group.** Determines how strategic objectives will be implemented in a portfolio; defines and authorizes a portfolio or subportfolio; and develops the portfolio management plan.

- **Aligning Process Group.** Determines how components will be categorized, evaluated, selected for inclusion, and managed in the portfolio.

- **Authorizing and Controlling Process Group.** Determines how to monitor strategic changes, tracks and reviews performance indicators for alignment, authorizes portfolio, and verifies values to the organization from the portfolio.

3.2.5 Process Improvement Stages

OPM3 applies a quality component (See Figure 3-6) referred to as process improvement. The stages are: standardize, measure, control, and improve (SMCI.)

3.2.5.1 Standardize

Standardize, when applied to a process, yields a repeatable and consistent Best Practice. Characteristics of a standardized process include a governing body to manage the process and associated changes, a clearly documented process communicated to those exercising the process, and adherence which is evidenced by the artifacts produced.

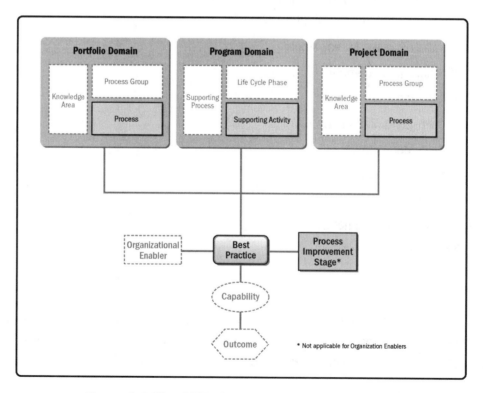

Figure 3-6. The *OPM3* Process Improvement Stages

For example, standardize, when applied to the *PMBOK Guide®* process, Create Project Charter, yields the *OPM3* Best Practice, Standardize Create Project Charter Process.

3.2.5.2 Measure

Measure, when applied to a process, yields a quantified Best Practice. Characteristics of a measured process include customer requirements incorporated in the measurements, identified critical characteristics, measured critical characteristics, inputs related to results, and measured critical parameters. These characteristics clarify the customer requirements and key inputs and outputs.

For example, measure, when applied to the *PMBOK Guide®* process, Create Project Charter, yields the *OPM3* Best Practice, Measure Create Project Charter Process.

3.2.5.3 Control

Control, when applied to a process, yields a managed Best Practice. Characteristics of a controlled process include control plan developed, control plan implemented, and stability achieved.

The control process is the act of comparing actual performance with planned performance, analyzing variances, assessing trends to effect process improvements, evaluating possible alternatives, and recommending appropriate corrective action as needed.

In *OPM3*, the progression of Capabilities includes determining control limits, looking for root causes for processes that are outside the limits, and identifying improvements to bring the process within the control limits.

When used in evaluating Capability maturities, the collective application of control activities constitutes the third stage of the *OPM3* SMCI quality management model.

For example, control, when applied to the *PMBOK Guide®* process, Create Project Charter, yields the *OPM3* Best Practice, Control Create Project Charter Process.

3.2.5.4 Improve

Improve, when applied to a process, yields a continuously improving Best Practice. Characteristics of an improved process include problems identified, improvements implemented, and improvements sustained.

For example, improve, when applied to the *PMBOK Guide®* process, Create Project Charter, yields the *OPM3* Best Practice, Improve Create Project Charter Process, and when applied to Identify Stakeholders, yields the *OPM3* Best Practice, Improve Identify Stakeholders.

Table 3-1 summarizes the complete set of Best Practices for the Develop Project Charter process from the *PMBOK Guide®*. There are four uniquely identified Best Practices created for each process coming into the *OPM3* Portfolio, Program, and Project Domains.

Table 3-1. *PMBOK® Guide* Develop Project Charter Process with SMCI Applied

Best Practice ID	Best Practice Name
1005	Standardize Develop Project Charter Process
1700	Measure Develop Project Charter Process
2240	Control Develop Project Charter Process
2630	Improve Develop Project Charter Process

3.2.6 Organizational Enablers

Organizational enablers (OE) are structural, cultural, technological, and human resource practices that can be leveraged to support and sustain the implementation of Best Practices in portfolios, programs, and projects. The OE Best Practices describe general management processes that should be developed in an organization to support organizational project management. Many systems and cultural factors influence an organization and its business environment. The *OPM3* translates these factors into Best Practices around training, implementing methodologies, and techniques.

The OE Best Practices address the foundational capabilities that an organization needs to support and sustain the process-based standards (see Figure 3-7). The absence of OEs decreases the maturity of process-based Best Practices within an organization.

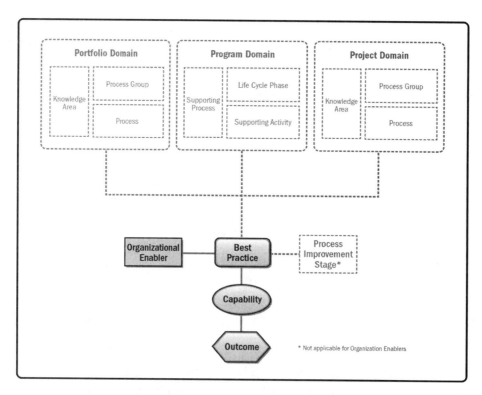

Figure 3-7. The *OPM3* Organizational Enablers (OEs)

Organizational enablers when translated into *OPM3* yield an OE Best Practice. Characteristics of an OE vary according to their category. Organizational enablers are classified into 18 categories as shown in Table 3-2.

Table 3-2. Organizational Enabler Categories

Organizational Enablers
1. Benchmarking
2. Competency Management
3. Governance
4. Individual Performance Appraisals
5. Knowledge Management and PMIS
6. Management Systems
7. Organizational Project Management Communities
8. Organizational Project Management Methodology
9. Organizational Project Management Policy and Vision
10. Organizational Project Management Practices
11. Organizational Project Management Techniques
12. Organizational Structures
13. Project Management Metrics
14. Project Management Training
15. Project Success Criteria
16. Resource Allocation
17. Sponsorship
18. Strategic Alignment

For example, Best Practice 5240, Establish Internal Project Management Communities, relates to OE Category 7, Organizational Project Management Communities. This Best Practice includes the following Capabilities: Facilitate Project Management Activities, Develop Awareness of Project Management Activities, and Sponsor Project Management Activities.

Figure 3-8 shows the example of organizational enabler Best Practice 5240 "Establish Internal Project Management Communities," its Capabilities, and its Outcomes.

3.2.7 Categorization

Categorization segments the *OPM3* Best Practices into manageable groupings (see Figure 3-9).

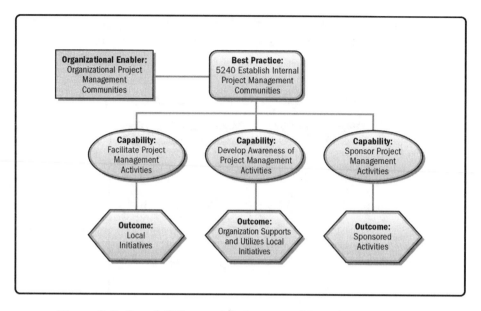

Figure 3-8. Capabilities and Outcomes of Best Practice 5240

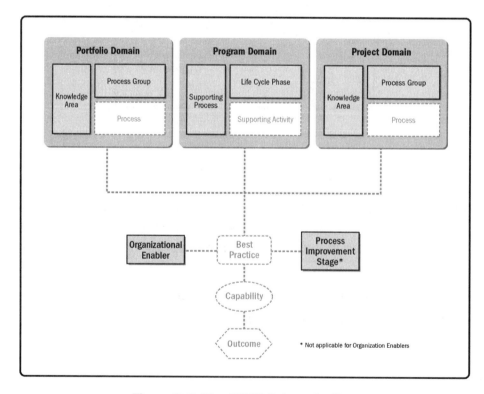

Figure 3-9. The *OPM3* Categorization

There are nine Best Practices categorizations used by organizations:

- **Domain.** This represents the three domains: Portfolio, Program, and Project. Each process, based on SMCI Best Practice, maps to one or more of these domains. This provides an avenue for organizations to focus on single or multiple domains.

- **Process improvement stage (SMCI).** Each Best Practice maps to one of these process improvement stages. This provides organizations with a way to focus on a single process improvement stage.

- **Organizational enabler (OE).** Each organizational enabler maps to one of the 18 OE categories. This provides an organization with the option to clearly focus on a single group of OEs.

- **Process Group.** Each Best Practice from the Project and Portfolio Domain maps to a Process Group: Initiating, Planning, Executing, Controlling, and Closing for the Project Domain; and Defining, Aligning and Authorizing, and Controlling Process Groups for the Portfolio Domain.

- **Performance Domain.** Each Best Practice from the Program Domain maps to a Performance Domain: Strategy Alignment, Benefits Management, Stakeholders Engagement, Governance, and Program Life Cycle Management.

- **Knowledge Area.** Each Best Practice from the Project and Portfolio Domain maps to a Knowledge Area.
  - The Project Domain Knowledge Areas include:
    - Project Integration Management,
    - Project Scope Management,
    - Project Time Management,
    - Project Cost Management,
    - Project Quality Management,
    - Project Human Resource Management,
    - Project Communication Management,
    - Project Risk Management,
    - Project Procurement Management, and
    - Project Stakeholder Management.
  - The Portfolio Domain Knowledge Areas include:
    - Portfolio Strategic Management,
    - Portfolio Governance Management,
    - Portfolio Performance Management,
    - Portfolio Communications Management, and
    - Portfolio Risk Management.

These Knowledge Areas support the processes found in Section 3 of each of these standards by providing inputs, tools and techniques, and outputs. For example, the *PMBOK Guide*® uses the Project Cost Management Knowledge Area to group processes and provide details for training. An organization that desires to decrease cost overruns elects to improve their processes leveraging Best Practices mapped to Project Cost Management.

- **Project predictability.** Each Best Practice that supports an organization's ability to forecast successful project delivery is mapped to project predictability. Organizations want to be aware of any approved work that may be at risk as early in the life cycle as possible.

- **Resource optimization.** Each Best Practice that provides the ability to identify, deploy, and release project resources that deliver customer value maps to resource optimization.

- **Balanced scorecard.** Each Best Practice that supports the development and execution of uniform reporting and tracking mechanisms. One aspect of the balanced scorecard could be that strategy execution is measured consistently and objectively.

Categorization of Best Practices provides an avenue for organizations to assess, design, or improve areas of focus to achieve organizational goals.

3.3. *OPM3* Framework

The *OPM3* framework serves as a guide for organizations that apply *OPM3*. The *OPM3* framework contains Cycle Elements, Areas of Expertise, and *OPM3* processes with inputs, tools and techniques, and outputs as depicted in Figure 3-10.

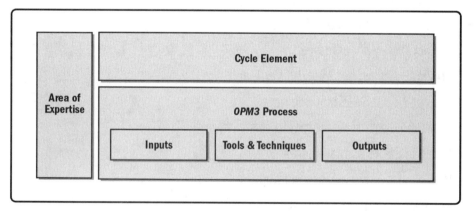

Figure 3-10. The *OPM3* Framework Overview

Key actions required for successful application of the *OPM3* framework include but are not limited to:

- Determine the change impact of implementing selected processes based upon organization needs and *OPM3* practitioner expertise,

- Manage the *OPM3* initiative as a project or a program,

- Obtain stakeholder buy-in,

- Secure the expertise and knowledge outlined in Section 1,

- Understand and select appropriate processes from the *OPM3* framework, and

- Understand differences between Areas of Expertise and the Cycle Elements.

Table 3-3 provides a summary of the twelve *OPM3* processes for the *OPM3* Cycle Elements and Areas of Expertise.

3.3.1 *OPM3* Areas of Expertise

The *OPM3* Areas of Expertise represent the practical knowledge and applied skills required to undertake a successful *OPM3* initiative. The three Areas of Expertise in the *OPM3* framework are outlined below.

3.3.1.1 Governance, Risk, and Compliance (GRC) [6]

Organizations achieve GRC by embracing activities such as corporate governance, enterprise risk management (ERM), and corporate compliance in accordance with applicable laws and regulations. Organizations embrace these areas to ensure proper oversight, manage risk, and address regulatory and corporate compliance.

Table 3-3. The *OPM3* Processes

Area of Expertise \ Cycle Elements	Acquire Knowledge	Perform Assessment	Manage Improvement
Governance, Risk, and Compliance	Understand OPM	Establish Plan	Measure Results
Delivery and Benefits Management	Understand the Organization	Define Scope	Create Recommendations
		Conduct Assessment	Select Initiatives
			Implement Improvements
Organizational Change	Assess Change Readiness	Initiate Change	Manage Change

Within the *OPM3* framework, organizations establish and enforce proper governance over the planning and fulfillment of portfolio, program, and project management. Establishing proper governance helps ensure successful results. This *OPM3* framework area of expertise establishes a plan for, and manages the results of, an *OPM3* assessment that focuses on the practices that affect governance, risk management, and compliance. GRC encompasses three processes: Understand OPM, Establish Plan, and Measure Results.

3.3.1.2 Delivery and Benefits Management

The Delivery and Benefits Management Area of Expertise addresses the execution of *OPM3* throughout the life cycle. It focuses on what is needed to execute a successful *OPM3* initiative. Delivery and Benefits Management encompasses six processes: Understand the Organization, Define the Scope, Conduct Assessment, Create Recommendations, Select Initiatives, and Implement Improvements.

3.3.1.3 Organizational Change

The Organizational Change Area of Expertise focuses on the magnitude of change that accompanies an *OPM3* initiative. To improve the probability of success in sustaining change, leadership should acknowledge and understand the organization's ability to adopt change. This adoption may include multiple variables, such as readiness, awareness, desire, capacity, and willingness. This Area of Expertise encompasses three processes: Assess Change Readiness, Initiate Change, and Manage Change.

Organizations assess change readiness, initiate change, and manage change for initiatives that modify their environment, processes, and tools. Organizations achieve successful change initiatives with a clear understanding of the current state and desired state, coupled with effective management and leadership of the process and human factors.

3.3.2 *OPM3* Cycle Elements

The *OPM3* Cycle Elements are groups of processes required to implement an *OPM3* initiative. The *OPM3* practitioner determines which processes fit the organization based upon the nature of the initiative. The *OPM3* Cycle Elements are: Acquire Knowledge, Perform Assessment, and Manage Improvement.

Sections 4, 5, and 6 provide additional Cycle Element details. The Cycle Elements depicted in Figure 3-11 create a cycle of continuous improvement.

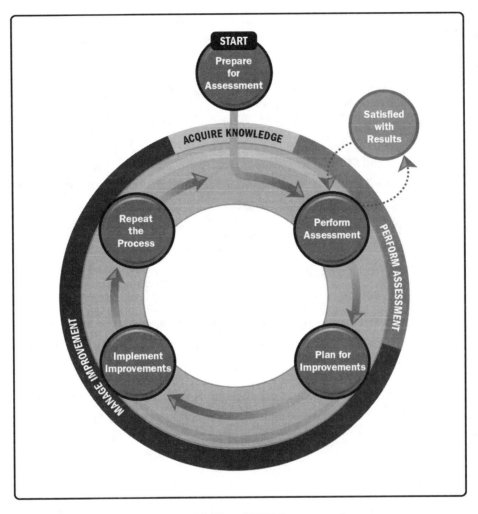

Figure 3-11. The *OPM3* Framework

3.3.2.1 Acquire Knowledge

Stakeholders gain knowledge of *OPM3,* the organization, the industry, and opportunities for *OPM3* initiatives. Acquire Knowledge has three processes, which are summarized below. See Section 4 for further details.

- **Understand OPM.** Prior to starting an *OPM3* initiative, the *OPM3* practitioner and the organization acquire knowledge necessary to apply *OPM3*. This is a due diligence process to gather the following:

  - *People:* This includes, but is not limited to: skilled *OPM3* practitioners, *OPM3* subject matter experts, stakeholders, leadership, general management, facilitators, and researchers.

  - *Process:* This includes, but is not limited to: lean manufacturing process control, process design, organizational enablers, project management processes, program management processes, and portfolio management processes.

  - *Technology:* This includes, but is not limited to: project management information systems and tools.

The Understand *OPM* process builds awareness of the applicability and value of *OPM3*. It is important to understand why organizations undertake an *OPM3* initiative—to improve business results.

- **Understand the Organization.** This process outlines the knowledge an *OPM3* practitioner and the organization acquire to apply *OPM3*. This is a due diligence process to gather the following:

  - *Strategy:* Vision, mission, product, service, desired profits, current performance, regulations, competitive advantage.

  - *People:* Geographic location, skills, organizational structure, vendors, customers, organizational culture, understanding of process and tools, understanding of processes, process design, lean concepts, training, and motivation level.

  - *Process:* Degree of automation, metrics, stability of process, documentation, communication, complexity of processes, process interaction, project management processes, program management processes, portfolio management processes, asset library.

  - *Technology:* Automation tools, project management information system, templates.

The Understand the Organization process combines the right skills, industry knowledge, culture, tools, and strategy for assessment preparation. It is important to understand why organizations undertake an *OPM3* initiative—to improve business results.

- **Assess Change Readiness.** The Assess Change Readiness process captures the organization's willingness to change and readiness for change. The *OPM3* practitioner collects, assesses, and validates the organization's readiness for change based on a variety of factors (e.g., training, culture, equipment).

3.3.2.2 Perform Assessment

The assessment leader plans, executes, and manages the assessment; compiles and analyzes data and documents; and presents results. Perform Assessment has four processes, which are summarized below. Section 5 provides greater details.

- **Establish Plan.** The Establish Plan process produces a plan for conducting an *OPM3* assessment. The *OPM3* practitioner leverages the *PMBOK Guide®* to create this plan and complete this process. The Establish Plan may include subsidiary plans that address the following:

  - Methodology of implementation;

  - Roles and responsibilities;

  - Scope and work breakdown structure (WBS);

  - High-level schedule and milestone list;

  - Success metrics and success factors;

  - Assumptions and constraints;

  - Governance, risk, and compliance;

o Quality management; and

o Budget.

The plan provides an overall view of scope, schedule, cost, and stakeholder buy-in.

- **Define Scope.** The Define Scope process creates an assessment statement of work which includes resources, business units, geographies, deliverables, and acceptance criteria. While conducting the *OPM3* assessment, the *OPM3* practitioner identifies the scope of the assessment in terms of categorization as outlined in Section 3.2.7.

The Define Scope process sets expectations for the assessment work undertaken.

- **Conduct Assessment.** The Conduct Assessment process is the execution of the *OPM3* assessment plan based upon the statement of work. The *OPM3* assessment team gathers, processes, and analyzes organizational information and documents findings in an assessment report.

- **Initiate Change.** The Initiate Change process launches the organizational change management activities that support adoption of the improvement initiatives. Organizations set up mechanisms to identify and evaluate behaviors, attitudes, and environment that may diminish results.

3.3.2.3 Manage Improvement

The improvement leader identifies, selects, and implements improvement initiatives based upon assessment findings and desired organizational business results. Manage Improvements has five processes, which are summarized below. Section 6 provides greater details.

- **Measure Results.** The Measure Results process correlates realized business results with the improvement plans. This process acts as a feedback mechanism that relates the planned improvements to the business results. This reinforces a culture of measurements and effective reporting performance, and serves as the basis for improved estimating.

- **Create Recommendations.** The Create Recommendations process seeks to identify the gaps between the current state and future state of the organization's portfolio, program, and project Best Practices. Analysis of these gaps results in a set of recommendations based upon level of effort, complexity, investment, and organizational impact. The *OPM3* assessment team presents the findings to the stakeholders for consideration.

- **Select Initiatives**. The Select Initiatives process provides the stakeholders with recommendations best suited for implementation, depending on their priority, cost/benefit, and strategic relevance. The recommendations include a sufficient level of detail for decision making. Stakeholders select the improvements from the recommendation list.

- **Implement Improvement Initiatives.** The Implement Improvement initiatives process transforms the selected initiatives into projects, programs, or portfolios. Utilizing the *PMBOK® Guide* – Fifth Edition, *The Standard for Program Management* – Third Edition, or *The Standard for Portfolio Management* – Third Edition, organizations execute the improvement initiatives to realize business benefits.

- **Manage Change.** The Manage Change process leverages the mechanisms put in place during the Initiate Change process to monitor and adjust as appropriate. The *OPM3* assessment team takes into consideration enterprise structure, technology, culture, and process change impacts when organizations undertake an *OPM3* initiative to improve business results.

3.4 *OPM3* Application

The *OPM3* practitioner and the assessment team utilize the *OPM3* Construct and the *OPM3* framework (see Figure 3-12) to ascertain the maturity of an organization and chart a course for improving the desired business results. This continuous improvement cycle provides an organization with the ability to advance the portfolio, program, and project management capabilities through which organizations deliver strategy.

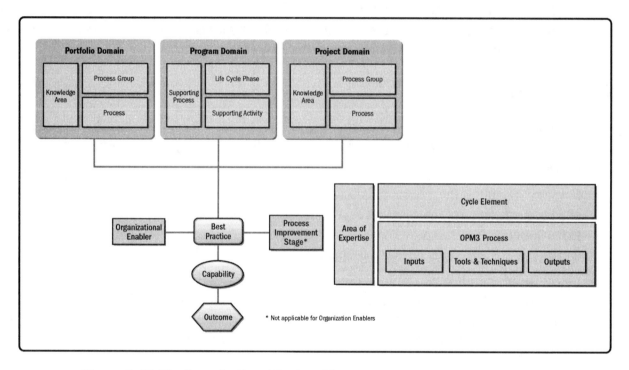

Figure 3-12. The Organizational Project Management Maturity Model (*OPM3*)

3.5 *OPM3* Scoring Methods

The *OPM3* practitioner applies a rigorous scoring method that ascertains whether (binary scoring) or how much/how often (variable measures) each Outcome for a Capability of a Best Practice exists. Additional detail follows on both scoring methods:

- **Binary scoring.** The *OPM3* practitioner awards a (1) for an Outcome that fully exists or a (0) for an Outcome that does not fully exist. The binary scoring method is somewhat simplistic and does not award partial credit.

- **Variable measures.** The *OPM3* practitioner awards a score based on how much and how often the Outcome exists. The variable measures method is more complex and awards for partial credit. Figure 3-13 provides a variable measures scoring method:

```
3 – Fully implemented, consistently, for Outcomes of a Best Practice
2 – Fully implemented, not consistently, for Outcomes of a Best Practice
1 – Partially implemented for Outcomes of a Best Practice
0 – Not implemented for Outcomes of a Best Practice
```

Figure 3-13. OPM3 Variable Measures Scoring Method

3.6 *OPM3* Best Practices List

Best Practices are optimal methods, currently recognized within a given industry or discipline, to achieve a goal or objective. The types of Best Practices are:

- **Domain.** Portfolio, Program, and Project with Process Improvement Stage: Standardize, Measure, Control, and Improve (SMCI).

- **Organizational Enabler.** Non-Domain-based processes, pertaining to environmental and cultural aspects of the organization.

See Annex A1 for a complete list of Best Practices.

ACQUIRE KNOWLEDGE

Acquire Knowledge is a Cycle Element that includes the processes Understand OPM, Understand the Organization, and Assess Change Readiness. Although this Cycle Element discretely defines these three processes, all parties continuously acquire knowledge throughout an *OPM3* initiative. *OPM3* provides information for organizations to understand organizational project management (OPM).

Understanding *OPM3* and how it relates to an organization is vital. Acquiring knowledge assists organizations in achieving business value through portfolio, program, and project management. This section will be of interest to anyone who wants to learn more about OPM and has a desire to improve the business results and/or OPM maturity of their organization. The Acquire Knowledge processes as depicted in Figure 4-1 include:

4.1 **Understand OPM**—In this process, prior to starting an *OPM3* initiative, the *OPM3* practitioner and the organization acquire knowledge necessary to apply *OPM3*.

4.2 **Understand Organization**—This process outlines the knowledge an *OPM3* practitioner and the organization acquire to apply *OPM3*.

4.3 **Assess Change Readiness**—This process captures the organization's willingness to change and readiness for change.

These processes interact with each other and with the processes within the other Cycle Elements. Each process involves effort from individuals or groups depending on their initiative needs. Although the processes presented here are discrete activities with well-defined inputs and outputs, they may overlap and interact while following a different sequence than listed.

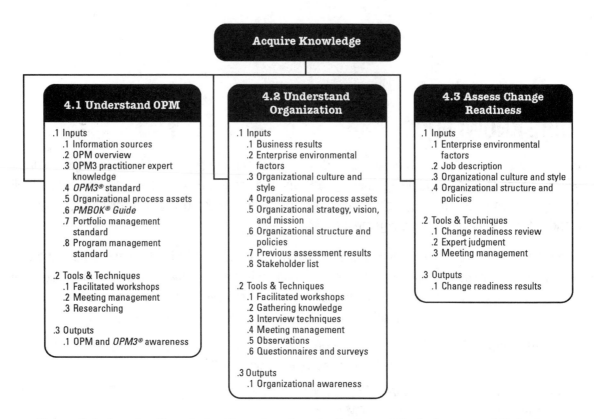

Figure 4-1. Acquire Knowledge Overview: Inputs, Tools and Techniques, and Outputs

4.1 Understand OPM

Prior to starting an *OPM3* initiative, the *OPM3* practitioner and the organization acquire knowledge necessary to apply *OPM3*. This is a due diligence process to gather the following:

- **People.** Skilled *OPM3* practitioner, *OPM3* subject matter experts, *OPM3*-aware stakeholders, leadership, general management, facilitation, and research.

- **Process.** Lean, statistical process control, process design, organizational enablers, project management processes, program management activities, and portfolio management processes.

- **Technology.** Templates and project management information systems.

The Understand OPM process builds awareness of the applicability and value of *OPM3*. It is important to understand why organizations undertake an *OPM3* initiative—to improve business results.

The *OPM3* practitioner understands the *OPM3* Construct, the *OPM3* Cycle Elements, skills, and tools and techniques to apply *OPM3*. Other desirable skillsets for an *OPM3* practitioner include: accounting, finance, change management, organizational development, information technology, project management, human resources, quality management, assessment methods, and process improvement.

The *OPM3* practitioner needs to understand the identified stakeholders or stakeholder groups. Success of an *OPM3* initiative requires that an *OPM3* practitioner engages the appropriate stakeholders during the *OPM3* initiative. Frequent communication promotes stakeholder awareness through the following types of activities:

- Orientation for an *OPM3* initiative,
- Workshops,
- Training sessions,
- Literature, and
- Personal coaching.

The *OPM3* practitioner needs to understand enterprise environmental factors during communication with stakeholders.

Understand OPM is the process of conveying strategic, financial, and operational information about the organization desiring to improve business results to the organization and *OPM3* initiative team. See Figure 4-2 for a list of inputs, tools and techniques, and outputs.

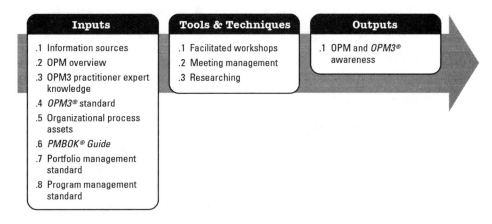

Figure 4-2. Understand OPM: Inputs, Tools and Techniques, and Outputs

4.1.1 Understand OPM: Inputs

4.1.1.1 Information Sources

Information sources, such as case studies, seminars, training, white papers, and articles, are collected from various sources to aid with the understanding of the organization and OPM.

4.1.1.2 OPM Overview

The OPM overview is conducted so that stakeholders have an opportunity to gain a high-level understanding of OPM and how it improves business results. This may include presentation material.

4.1.1.3 *OPM3* Practitioner Expert Knowledge

As outlined in Section 1.7.1, in order to be successful in the assessment or improvement of organizations, an *OPM3* practitioner should have expertise in all of the following areas:

- **Knowledge of the latest editions of PMI's portfolio, program, and project standards.** An *OPM3* practitioner is required to have expertise in the use of portfolio, program, and project management methods and techniques that include both qualitative and quantitative measures.

- **Process management and continuous process improvement.** The *OPM3* practitioner should be competent in process definition, development, maintenance, control, and improvement with respect to the size and complexity of the organization.

- **Strategic alignment.** The *OPM3* practitioner is required to understand the organization's strategic goals and priorities and how the portfolio, program, and project support them.

- **Ability to conduct assessments.** An effective *OPM3* practitioner requires training on how to conduct assessments.

- **Ability to draw conclusions and offer recommendations.** An effective *OPM3* practitioner is required to possess proper training on how to draw conclusions and offer recommendations on the assessments conducted.

- **Ability to engage stakeholders.** An effective *OPM3* practitioner interacts at different levels to understand and influence expectations.

- **Consulting experience.** An *OPM3* practitioner is required to possess business acumen. The *OPM3* practitioner should have knowledge of relevant markets, the customer base, competition, trends, standards, legal and regulatory environments, and appropriate code of conduct. The *OPM3* practitioner needs to be adept at working with executives, managers, project and program managers, and other internal and external stakeholders, as appropriate to the individual and role.

- **Business skills.** An effective *OPM3* practitioner should possess skills related to governance, risk and compliance (see Section 3.3.1.1 for greater detail), benefits management, scope management, resource management and financial management as explained in Section 3.3.1 (Areas of Expertise). The *OPM3* practitioner is required to possess well-developed skills in communicating, team building, planning, conflict resolution, contract negotiating, meeting facilitation, decision making, and removing organizational barriers to success. This individual is required to be capable of adapting to divergent organizational decision-making models, ranging from autocratic to collegial.

- **Risk management.** An effective *OPM3* practitioner should be well versed in opportunity and threat management.

- **Organizational change management.** An *OPM3* practitioner should have an understanding of how an *OPM3* initiative impacts an organization.

4.1.1.4 *OPM3* Standard

The *OPM3* standard represents a best practice model applied to PMI process-based and activity-based standards plus organizational enablers that help establish and mature portfolio, program, and project management in an organization.

4.1.1.5 Organizational Process Assets

The organizational process assets encompass policies, procedures, guidelines, templates, checklists, and methodologies. These assets include the organization's knowledge base such as lessons learned and historical process information as the organization improves.

4.1.1.6 *PMBOK® Guide*

As covered in Section 3, *OPM3* contains the processes from the *PMBOK Guide®*.

4.1.1.7 Portfolio Management Standard

The Standard for Portfolio Management describes the processes of the centralized management of one or more portfolios to achieve specific strategic business objectives. As covered in Section 3, *OPM3* contains the processes from *The Standard for Portfolio Management*.

4.1.1.8 Program Management Standard

The Standard for Program Management describes the activities of centralized and coordinated management of a group of related projects to achieve the organization's strategic objectives and benefits. As covered in Section 3, *OPM3* contains the performance domains from *The Standard for Program Management*.

4.1.2 Understand OPM: Tools and Techniques

4.1.2.1 Facilitated Workshops

Facilitated workshops bring together key cross-functional stakeholders, experts, and both internal and external consultants to understand OPM. Workshops are a technique for eliciting information in order to understand OPM. Facilitated sessions build trust, foster relationships, and improve communication among the participants or increase stakeholder understanding.

4.1.2.2 Meeting Management

Meeting management includes planning, scheduling, conducting, documenting, and following up on meetings pertaining to OPM.

4.1.2.3 Researching

Researching is the systematic investigation into new or existing knowledge. White papers, industry courses, articles, books, research papers and other materials are available to ascertain a broader knowledge of OPM.

4.1.3 Understand OPM: Outputs

4.1.3.1 OPM *and OPM3* Awareness

OPM awareness grows through a variety of activities throughout the Understand OPM process. OPM is ever evolving which makes it challenging to synthesize the vast amount of available information. Gaining *OPM3* knowledge is essential when an organization seeks to mature portfolio, program, and project management. Although the results of OPM and *OPM3* awareness are not used as a discrete input to any of the following processes, the knowledge gained constitutes the basis for all the processes outlined in Sections 4 and 5.

4.2 Understand Organization

This process outlines the knowledge that an *OPM3* practitioner and the organization acquire to apply *OPM3*. This is a due diligence process to gather the following:

- **Strategy.** Vision, mission, product, service, desired profits, current performance, regulations, strategy metrics, measures, and key performance indicators (KPIs), department strategies (e.g., human resource strategy, marketing strategy, IT strategy, etc.), studies or assessments conducted on current weaknesses, threats, or areas of improvement.

- **People.** Geographic location; skills; tenure; organization structure; vendors; customers; organizational culture; understanding of process and tools; and understanding of processes, process design, lean concepts, and training.

- **Process.** Degree of automation, metrics, stability of process, documentation, communication, complexity of processes, process interaction, project management processes, program management processes, portfolio management processes, asset library.

- **Technology.** Automation tools, project management information system, templates.

The Understand Organization process combines the right skills, industry knowledge, culture, tools, and strategy for assessment preparation. It is important to understand why organizations undertake an *OPM3* initiative—to improve business results. This process includes the *OPM3* team conducting meetings with senior executives to understand the strategic direction of the organization. See Figure 4-3 for a list of inputs, tools and techniques, and outputs.

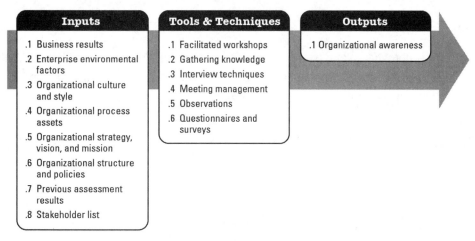

Figure 4-3. Understand Organization: Inputs, Tools and Techniques, and Outputs

4.2.1 Understand Organization: Inputs

4.2.1.1 Business Results

Business results include the income statement, balance sheet, cash flow statements, government-required reports for publicly traded companies, annual reports, and other internally or externally published information. The *OPM3* practitioner gathers operations data to support improving business results. Business results also include department budgets, department operational information, and department goals that assist with identifying measures pre- and post-improvement.

4.2.1.2 Enterprise Environmental Factors

Enterprise environmental factors refer to both internal and external environmental factors that surround or influence an organization's business success. Enterprise environmental factors may enhance or constrain *OPM3* initiative options. Enterprise environmental factors include, but are not limited to, the following:

- Cultural factors,
- Existing human resources,
- Market conditions,
- Organization's communications channels,
- Organizational processes,

- Personnel administration,
- Political climate, and
- Project management information systems.

4.2.1.3 Organizational Culture and Style

Organizational culture and style play an important part in understanding the environment landscape in which the people, process, and tools described earlier reside. Different approaches and activities need to be employed for the Acquire Knowledge Cycle Element processes to be effective.

4.2.1.4 Organizational Process Assets

Described in Section 4.1.1.5.

4.2.1.5 Organizational Strategy, Vision, and Mission

The organizational strategy, vision, mission, values, and purpose help shape strategic objectives and include the mission, vision, values, and purpose. Mission and vision statements convey the organization's intent to shape the culture and inspire employees. The *OPM3* practitioner should be sensitive to the organization's core values.

4.2.1.6 Organizational Structure and Policies

Organizational structure and policies provide insight on the management style, reporting channel, and span of control. Policies impact how OPM is adopted and need to be considered for each individual organization.

4.2.1.7 Previous Assessment Results

For follow-up assessments (second or later iterations), previous assessment results provide background on the prior state of the organization. These historical results provide awareness of what had previously been done, the reaction to prior assessments if applicable, and what potential opportunities exist.

4.2.1.8 Stakeholder List

The stakeholder list includes key stakeholders that provide oversight and influence with a vested interest in improving business results. Stakeholders are individuals, groups, or organizations who may affect, be affected by, or perceive itself to be affected by a decision, activity, or outcome of a portfolio, program, or project. Many stakeholders provide valuable input and play a critical role in the success of any project or program.

4.2.2 Understand Organization: Tools and Techniques

4.2.2.1 Facilitated Workshops

Described in Section 4.1.2.1.

4.2.2.2 Gathering Knowledge

This process involves gathering knowledge from key stakeholders. Four steps guide the gathering of this knowledge:

- **Elicit organizational knowledge.** Traditional elicitation techniques include interviews and workshops. Knowledge gathered may address organizational questions such as:

    o What is the organization's business area?

    o What is the organization's business need?

    o What is the organization's business goal?

- **Analyze organizational knowledge.** Extract the real state of the organization by analyzing elicited knowledge. There may be a difference between stated and real state of the organization.

- **Document organizational knowledge.** Document elicited knowledge for stakeholder review, understanding, and confirmation.

- **Validate documented organizational knowledge.** By reviewing and inspecting the documented knowledge, confirm the documented knowledge is unambiguous and consistent throughout the document.

4.2.2.3 Interview Techniques

An interview is a formal or informal approach to gather information from stakeholders. An *OPM3* practitioner conducts interviews by asking prepared questions and recording the responses. Interview scenarios include:

- One interviewer—one interviewee,
- One interviewer—many interviewees,
- Many interviewers—one interviewee, and
- Many interviewers—many interviewees.

The *OPM3* practitioner establishes an atmosphere of trust, exchanges information, gives and receives feedback, and sometimes performs a follow-up interview. Interview preparation and planning include:

- Utilizing appropriate methods (face-to-face, telephone, email, chat messaging, etc.),
- Incorporating critical thinking, and
- Identifying problems.

4.2.2.4 Meeting Management

Described in Section 4.1.2.2.

4.2.2.5 Observations

Observations provide a direct way of viewing individuals in their organization and how they perform their jobs or tasks and execute processes. Observers witness how activities performed in an environment impact a process. Observers glean direct or indirect evidence resulting from work being performed. Observers draw conclusions regarding the environment and the state of people, processes, and tools within that environment.

4.2.2.6 Questionnaires and Surveys

Questionnaires and surveys are written sets of questions designed to quickly accumulate information from a wide number of respondents. The *OPM3* practitioner uses questionnaires and surveys to rapidly gather information. Figure 4-4 contains some sample questions for a questionnaire or survey.

Topic	Question
Organization's strategic plan	What are the main goals in your strategic plan for the next 5 years?
Customer expectations	What product/service standards do you think your customers are expecting to receive from you?
Political environment	What legislative changes are expected to affect your operations?
Social environment	What kind of social activities does your HR department arrange for your staff?
Economic environment	Are the current economic conditions in the market enabling your future growth targets?
Technical environment	What kind of technologies are you relying upon for performing your operations?
Strength of the organization	What are your main competitive advantages in the market?
Weakness of the organization	What are the organization's most painful weakness points that you would like to address?
Organizational structure	How are organizational power and decision-making authorities granted in the organization?
Other data	Do you work with offshore suppliers?

Figure 4-4. Sample Questionnaire and Survey Topics

4.2.3 Understand Organization: Outputs

4.2.3.1 Organizational Awareness

Organizational awareness grows through a variety of activities throughout the Understand Organization process. Organizations continually evolve and can be complex to understand. Gaining organizational knowledge is essential as an organization seeks to mature portfolio, program, and project management.

Although the results of organizational awareness are not used as a discrete input to any of the processes included in Sections 4 and 5, the knowledge obtained constitutes the basis for all of these processes.

4.3 Assess Change Readiness

Assess Change Readiness is the process that establishes the organization's willingness or ability to change. If the organization has a very low propensity to change, resistance is likely to be experienced when undertaking an *OPM3* initiative. Assess the change readiness of individuals and the overall organization.

Readiness reflects the individuals' ability to change and that of the environment within which they operate. Extensive research and literature exist regarding this topic. The organization facilitates adoption and broad acceptance by the community when improvements are made to the enterprise structure, technology, and culture. Process change impact needs to consider readiness of the target population, change agents, and sponsors. See Figure 4-5 for a list of inputs, tools and techniques, and outputs.

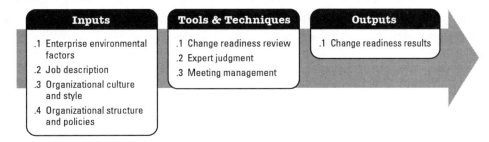

Figure 4-5. Assess Change Readiness: Inputs, Tools and Techniques, and Outputs

4.3.1 Assess Change Readiness: Inputs

4.3.1.1 Enterprise Environmental Factors

Described in Section 4.2.1.2.

4.3.1.2 Job Description

The job description outlines the job function performed by individuals in the organization. Job descriptions are classified as one of the organization's assets and serve as an input to the Assess Change Readiness process. By reviewing job descriptions, the organization determines whether skills required to change the organization exist.

4.3.1.3 Organizational Culture and Style

Described in Section 4.2.1.3.

4.3.1.4 Organizational Structure and Policies

Described in Section 4.2.1.6.

4.3.2 Assess Change Readiness: Tools and Techniques

4.3.2.1 Change Readiness Review

Change readiness review reveals preliminary findings based on insights gained from the Understanding OPM and Understanding Organization processes. This review serves as a general gauge of the organization's preparedness for change and potential obstacles.

4.3.2.2 Expert Judgment

Expert judgment is a tool or technique demonstrated by knowledgeable parties associated with the organization. Qualified individuals demonstrate expert judgment by providing information and data used to solve problems or make decisions through specialized education, knowledge, skill, experience, or training.

4.3.2.3 Meeting Management

Described in Section 4.1.2.2.

4.3.3 Assess Change Readiness: Outputs

4.3.3.1 Change Readiness Results

The change readiness results convey the organization's readiness for change in the following areas:

- Attitude and expectations of the key stakeholders are understood.
- Sponsor is defined to deploy resources to understand OPM and its fit for organizational culture and environment.
- Organization/department is assigned and accepts responsibility for improvement initiatives.
- OPM is understood among stakeholders.
- Organization's strategic plan is clear, understood, and accepted by the stakeholders.
- Organization's vision and mission are clear and understood among stakeholders.
- Organization's structure and policies are clear and understood among stakeholders.

5

PERFORM ASSESSMENT

This section describes the processes required to successfully plan, scope, and conduct an *OPM3* assessment. It is structured such that Perform Assessment delivers a framework consistent with the *OPM3* Areas of Expertise and Cycle Elements. Within the Perform Assessment Cycle Element, there are four processes that are discrete and not necessarily sequential. Practitioners often perform the four interwoven and possibly iterative processes concurrently.

The Perform Assessment Cycle Element is comprised of four processes as depicted in Figure 5-1:

5.1 **Establish Plan**—An *OPM3* practitioner and the organizational leaders work together to establish a plan prior to starting an *OPM3* initiative.

5.2 **Define Scope**—The Define Scope process identifies the breadth and depth of the planned assessment. Scoping includes skills, resources, funding, and other preparations that flow into the Establish Plan process.

5.3 **Conduct Assessment**—The Conduct Assessment process is where the organization executes the assessment plan based upon the Define Scope process.

5.4 **Initiate Change**—The Initiate Change process provides change management information to the team throughout the Perform Assessment Cycle Element. An *OPM3* practitioner tailors the approach based on the organizational environment in which OPM is being assessed.

In summary, these four processes interact to produce assessment findings. These findings quantitatively drive OPM initiatives that correlate to desired business results.

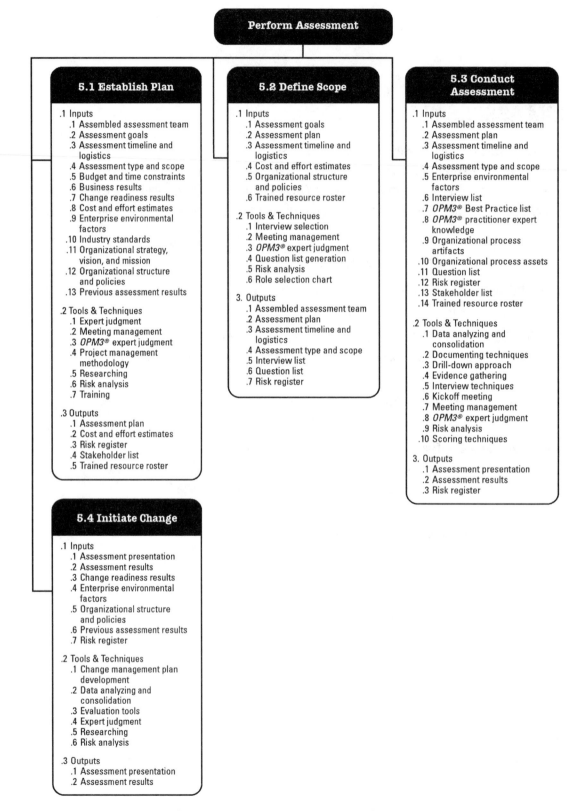

Figure 5-1. Perform Assessment Overview

5.1 Establish Plan

The Establish Plan process transforms goals, organizational performance, market position, and other information into an assessment plan. An *OPM3* practitioner focuses on preparing for an assessment and how it relates to improving business performance. When available, the *OPM3* practitioner leverages the organization's project management methodology to manage the initiative. An external *OPM3* practitioner may employ other available methodologies. This process also yields cost estimates, risks, key stakeholders, and an assessment team. See Figure 5-2 for a list of inputs, tools and techniques, and outputs.

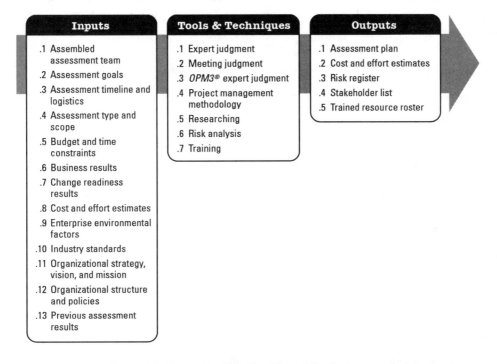

Figure 5-2. Establish Plan: Inputs, Tools and Techniques, and Outputs

5.1.1 Establish Plan: Inputs

5.1.1.1 Assembled Assessment Team

The assembled assessment team addresses the skills, abilities, training, and industry knowledge needed for an OPM initiative. Assessment team roles include the *OPM3* practitioner, organizational process owner, key stakeholders, industry subject matter experts (SMEs), and process SMEs.

5.1.1.2 Assessment Goals

Assessment goals cover why an organization wants to undertake an OPM initiative. The *OPM3* practitioner strives to align the assessment goals to improve business performance. Examples of goals include, but are not limited to, greater benefits realization, reduced project cycle time, better cost estimating, standardized processes across several departments, improved metrics, and faster improvements, etc.

5.1.1.3 Assessment Timeline and Logistics

Assessment timeline and logistics provide the Establish Plan process with time frames acceptable to the organization. Logistical information includes, but is not limited to, the physical building locations, conference rooms, dates, time frames, equipment, and catering.

5.1.1.4 Assessment Type and Scope

Assessment type and scope address the method of the assessment, whether it will be document-based or interview-based, or both, and includes portfolio, program, and project management. Organizational enablers are typically in scope for all assessments regardless of industry, size, or complexity.

Types of assessments include, but are not limited to, the following:

- Evidence-based/interview-based,
- High-level/detailed,
- Remote/local, and
- Single user and multiusers.

Scope options include, but are not limited to, the following:

- By business result,
- By Knowledge Area,
- By Process Group,
- By SMCI (standardize, measure, control, and improve),
- Complete assessment,
- Domain-based (portfolio, program, and project), and
- Organizational enablers only.

5.1.1.5 Budget and Time Constraints

Budget and time constraints bound the OPM initiative. Examples of constraints include, but are not limited to: the number of interviews, duration of the interviews, participant availability, geographic challenges, and associated costs.

5.1.1.6 Business Results

Business results include the income statement, balance sheet, cash flow statements, government-required reports for publicly traded companies, annual reports, and other internally or externally published information. The *OPM3* practitioner gathers operations data to support improving business results. Business results also include department budgets, department operational information, and department goals that assist with identifying measures pre- and post-improvement.

5.1.1.7 Change Readiness Results

Change readiness results convey the organization's readiness for change in the following areas:

- Attitude and expectations of the key stakeholders are understood.
- Sponsor is defined to deploy resources to understand OPM and its fit for organizational culture and environment.
- Organization/department is assigned and accepts responsibility for improvement initiatives.
- OPM is understood among stakeholders.
- Organization's strategic plan is clear, understood, and accepted by the stakeholders.
- Organization's vision and mission are clear and understood among stakeholders.
- Organization's structure and policies are clear and understood among stakeholders.

5.1.1.8 Cost and Effort Estimates

Cost and effort estimates capture the resources projected to be consumed by the OPM initiative. Examples of cost and effort include number of days, number of people, resource rates, travel costs, facility costs, etc.

5.1.1.9 Enterprise Environmental Factors

Enterprise environmental factors refer to both internal and external environmental factors that surround or influence an organization's business success. Enterprise environmental factors may enhance or constrain *OPM3* initiative options. Enterprise environmental factors include, but are not limited to, the following:

- Cultural factors,
- Existing human resources,
- Market conditions,
- Organization's communications channels
- Organizational processes,
- Personnel administration,
- Political climate, and
- Project management information systems.

5.1.1.10 Industry Standards

It is beneficial to be cognizant of industry standards that govern or influence organizations. This domain knowledge helps guide the team during discussions, interviews, assessments, and improvements.

5.1.1.11 Organizational Strategy, Vision, and Mission

The organizational strategy, vision, mission, values, and purpose help shape strategic objectives and include the mission, vision, values, and purpose. Mission and vision statements convey the organization's intent to shape the culture and inspire employees. The *OPM3* practitioner should be sensitive to the organization's core values.

5.1.1.12 Organizational Structure and Policies

Organizational structure and policies provide insight on the management style, reporting channel, and span of control. Policies impact how OPM is adopted and should be considered for each individual organization.

5.1.1.13 Previous Assessment Results

For follow-up assessments (second or later iterations), previous results provide background on the prior state of the organization. These historical results provide awareness of what has previously been done, the reaction to prior assessments if applicable, and what potential opportunities exist.

5.1.2 Establish Plan: Tools and Techniques

5.1.2.1 Expert Judgment

Expert judgment is a tool or technique demonstrated by knowledgeable parties associated with the organization. Qualified individuals demonstrate expert judgment by providing information and data used to solve problems or make decisions through specialized education, knowledge, skill, experience, or training.

5.1.2.2 Meeting Management

Meeting management includes planning, scheduling, conducting, documenting, and following-up on meetings pertaining to *OPM3*.

5.1.2.3 *OPM3* Expert Judgment

OPM3 expert judgment is a tool or technique leveraging OPM knowledgeable parties associated with the organization. *OPM3* expertise is provided by any group or person with specialized education, knowledge, skill experience, or training. Qualified individuals demonstrate *OPM3* expert judgment by providing information and data from PMI standards (*PMBOK® Guide* – Fifth Edition, *The Standard for Program Management* – Third Edition, *The Standard for Portfolio Management* – Third Edition, and *Project Manager Competency Development Framework* – Second Edition) to solve problems or make decisions.

5.1.2.4 Project Management Methodology

Project management methodology is a collection of methods and rules followed in the science or discipline of project management. Artifacts generated by a methodology include project charter, schedule, templates, procedures, training materials, etc.

5.1.2.5 Researching

Researching is the systematic investigation into new or existing knowledge. White papers, industry courses, articles, books, research papers, and other materials are available to ascertain broader knowledge of *OPM3*.

5.1.2.6 Risk Analysis

Risk analysis is a technique applied to systematically assess potential barriers and opportunities to improve success. Steps for risk analysis include:

- Identifying risks to expose uncertainty, which requires an intimate knowledge of the industry, legal, social, political, and cultural environment;
- Evaluating risks and assigning classifications;
- Determining and managing impacts on the assessment project; and
- Developing a response plan.

5.1.2.7 Training

Training is the acquisition of knowledge, skills, and competencies through instruction. The change readiness process identifies any party affiliated with the OPM initiative that needs training. The *OPM3* practitioner creates training plans to address training needs. *OPM3* practitioners attend training to develop mastery of translating organizational capability to *OPM3* Best Practices.

5.1.3 Establish Plan: Outputs

5.1.3.1 Assessment Plan

The assessment plan output is a culmination of defining, preparing, integrating, and coordinating all aspects of planning.

The assessment plan identifies:

- People responsible for the assessment process;
- Mission, goals, and outcomes of the initiative;

- Outcome targets; and
- Performance measures.

5.1.3.2 Cost and Effort Estimates

The cost and effort estimates output captures the revised amount of resources projected to be consumed by the OPM initiative. Examples of cost and effort include number of days, number of people, resource rates, travel costs, and facility costs, etc.

5.1.3.3 Risk Register

The risk register documents all identified risks throughout the life cycle of an OPM initiative. It quantifies risk in terms of the likelihood of occurrence and impact, initial plan for responding to each high-level risk, and cost and responsibility of mitigation. Refer to the *PMBOK® Guide* for details on the management of a risk register.

5.1.3.4 Stakeholder List

The stakeholder list includes key stakeholders that provide oversight and influence with a vested interest in improving business results. Key stakeholders are individuals, groups, or organizations who may affect, be affected by, or perceive itself to be affected by a decision, activity, or outcome of a project, program, or portfolio. Many stakeholders provide valuable input and play a critical role in the success of any project or program.

5.1.3.5 Trained Resource Roster

The trained resource roster output includes those individuals who acquire OPM knowledge, skills, and competencies through instruction. The *OPM3* practitioner includes training plans as part of the assessment plan to address team member training needs.

5.2 Define Scope

The Define Scope process outlines who, what, where, and how much boundary is needed for the *OPM3* initiative. Defining the scope develops a common understanding of what is included in, and excluded from, the initiative. This scope provides the foundation for building the schedule, budget, and staffing plans. See Figure 5-3 for a list of inputs, tools and techniques, and outputs.

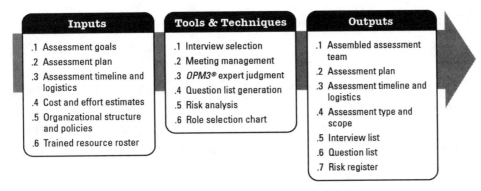

Inputs	Tools & Techniques	Outputs
.1 Assessment goals .2 Assessment plan .3 Assessment timeline and logistics .4 Cost and effort estimates .5 Organizational structure and policies .6 Trained resource roster	.1 Interview selection .2 Meeting management .3 *OPM3®* expert judgment .4 Question list generation .5 Risk analysis .6 Role selection chart	.1 Assembled assessment team .2 Assessment plan .3 Assessment timeline and logistics .4 Assessment type and scope .5 Interview list .6 Question list .7 Risk register

Figure 5-3. Define Scope: Inputs, Tools and Techniques, and Outputs

5.2.1 Define Scope: Inputs

5.2.1.1 Assessment Goals

Described in Section 5.1.1.2.

5.2.1.2 Assessment Plan

Described in Section 5.1.3.1.

5.2.1.3 Assessment Timeline and Logistics

Described in Section 5.1.1.3.

5.2.1.4 Cost and Effort Estimates

Described in Section 5.1.1.8.

5.2.1.5 Organizational Structure and Policies

Described in Section 5.1.1.12.

5.2.1.6 Trained Resource Roster

Described in Section 5.1.3.5.

5.2.2 Define Scope: Tools and Techniques

5.2.2.1 Interview Selection

The interview selection technique provides the *OPM3* practitioner with a way to efficiently and effectively gather evidence from the organization through interviews. Practitioners seek important information from a number of resources within the organization to confirm Best Practices. The *OPM3* practitioner selects a sample of roles across the organization to document findings and draw conclusions about the entire population. Valid conclusions require statistically significant sample size selection.

5.2.2.2 Meeting Management

Described in Section 5.1.2.2.

5.2.2.3 *OPM3* Expert Judgment

Described in Section 5.1.2.3.

5.2.2.4 Question List Generation

The question list generation technique is used by the *OPM3* practitioner to compile an appropriate set of questions for the scoped initiative. Questions typically address each role selected for an interview.

5.2.2.5 Risk Analysis

Described in Section 5.1.2.6.

5.2.2.6 Role Selection Chart

The role selection chart technique provides the *OPM3* practitioner with a way to quickly determine the roles that participate in an initiative. As the initiative scope varies, the *OPM3* practitioner selects different roles for the interview process. High-quality assessment results include an appropriate range of roles from across the organization. The *OPM3* practitioner considers these roles:

- Corporate leadership,
- Director of PMO,
- Functional leaders,
- Human resources leaders,
- Portfolio manager (person or committee),
- Process owners,
- Project and program managers,

- Subject matter experts (SMEs), and
- Team members.

5.2.3 Define Scope: Outputs

5.2.3.1 Assembled Assessment Team

Described in Section 5.1.1.1.

5.2.3.2 Assessment Plan

Described in Section 5.1.3.1.

5.2.3.3 Assessment Timeline and Logistics

Described in Section 5.1.1.3.

5.2.3.4 Assessment Type and Scope

Described in Section 5.1.1.4.

5.2.3.5 Interview List

The interview list output documents the set of individuals selected for interview. The *OPM3* practitioner schedules and adjusts interviews during the Conduct Assessment process using the interview list.

5.2.3.6 Question List

The question list output documents the set of questions administered to the interviewees from the interview list. Questions are typically grouped by role and Knowledge Area.

5.2.3.7 Risk Register

Described in Section 5.1.3.3.

5.3 Conduct Assessment

The Conduct Assessment process is applicable when the assessment team evaluates the organization against the specified scope. This includes a kick-off meeting, document reviews, interviews, documenting findings, gathering evidence, analyzing data, and creating the final report. The *OPM3* practitioner records evidence and is continually translating the collected evidence into the *OPM3* Best Practice to determine the degree to which it exists. The *OPM3* practitioner analyzes and validates results to report back to the organization. See Figure 5-4 for a list of inputs, tools and techniques, and outputs.

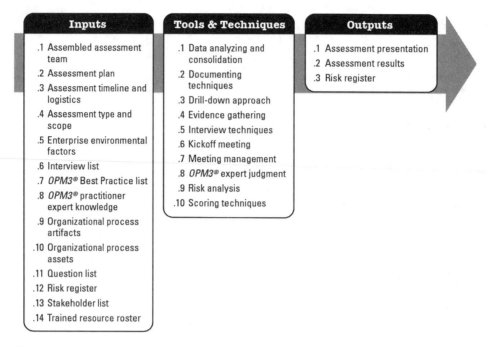

Figure 5-4. Conduct Assessment: Inputs, Tools and Techniques, and Outputs

5.3.1 Conduct Assessment: Inputs

5.3.1.1 Assembled Assessment Team

Described in Section 5.1.1.1.

5.3.1.2 Assessment Plan

Described in Section 5.1.3.1.

5.3.1.3 Assessment Timeline and Logistics

Described in Section 5.1.1.3.

5.3.1.4 Assessment Type and Scope

Described in Section 5.1.1.4.

5.3.1.5 Enterprise Environmental Factors

Described in Section 5.1.1.9.

5.3.1.6 Interview List

Described in Section 5.2.3.5.

5.3.1.7 *OPM3* Best Practices List

The *OPM3* Best Practices list, found in Annex A1, represents methods currently recognized within a given industry or discipline to achieve a goal or objective. An organization demonstrates achievement of an *OPM3* Best Practice by consistently demonstrating all of the supporting capabilities and realizing the Outcomes associated with each Capability.

5.3.1.8 *OPM3* Practitioner Expert Knowledge

The *OPM3* practitioner expert knowledge input addresses a broad spectrum of topics encompassing the *OPM3* multidimensional model. Organizations seek external consulting services to translate the organization's business needs into the model when in-house *OPM3* expertise is unavailable.

5.3.1.9 Organizational Process Artifacts

Organizational process artifacts are outputs created by the execution of a process. These artifacts include things such as a project charter, schedule, meeting minutes, risk register, etc. Practitioners use these artifacts to evaluate the health of an organization's processes.

5.3.1.10 Organizational Process Assets

The organizational process assets encompass policies, procedures, guidelines, templates, checklists, and methodologies. These assets include the organization's knowledge base such as lessons learned and historical process information as the organization improves.

5.3.1.11 Question List

Described in Section 5.2.3.6.

5.3.1.12 Risk Register

Described in Section 5.1.3.3.

5.3.1.13 Stakeholder List

Described in Section 5.1.3.4.

5.3.1.14 Trained Resource Roster

Described in Section 5.1.3.5.

5.3.2 Conduct Assessment: Tools and Techniques

5.3.2.1 Data Analyzing and Consolidation

The data analyzing and consolidation technique enables the *OPM3* practitioner to analyze information collected during the assessment process. The *OPM3* practitioner gains greater insight by applying multivariate, bivariate, and univariate techniques to data from the interviews. Steps for analysis include the following:

- Aggregate and group similar information;
- Avoid drawing false conclusions;
- Be objective, accurate, and truthful;
- Corroborate process artifacts with interview findings;
- Separate fact from opinion; and
- Support findings with data.

Data consolidation reveals patterns, common themes, trends, and highlights outliers.

5.3.2.2 Documenting Techniques

Documenting techniques ensure a full, clear, and accurate account of the site, all field operations, and observation details. Capturing the assessment inputs with pen and paper encourages open communication during interviews. Depending on the culture and receptiveness of the organization, other documenting techniques may be appropriate. The *OPM3* practitioner employs non-attribution in the collection of the assessment information. This means that all documented information is not associated with a specific project or person.

5.3.2.3 Drill-Down Approach

The drill-down approach technique involves progressively drilling into more detail. The drill-down approach is an analytical method that compares and contrasts scenarios in relation to specific conditions and situations.

5.3.2.4 Evidence Gathering

The evidence gathering technique assists the *OPM3* practitioner with accumulating evidence to support assessment findings. The *OPM3* practitioner collects evidence to validate the existence of Best Practices. There should be a balance between available evidence and sufficient evidence for the assessment to avoid analysis paralysis. The assessment team ensures that access to the systems or PMIS are available for gathering the evidence identified in the assessment plan.

5.3.2.5 Interview Techniques

An interview is a formal or informal approach to discover information from stakeholders. An *OPM3* practitioner conducts interviews by asking prepared questions and recording the responses. Interview scenarios include:

- One interviewer—one interviewee,
- One interviewer—many interviewees,
- Many interviewers—one interviewee, and
- Many interviewers—many interviewees.

The *OPM3* practitioner establishes an atmosphere of trust, exchanges information, gives and receives feedback, and sometimes performs a follow-up interview. Preparation and planning include:

- Identifying problems;
- Incorporating critical thinking, and
- Utilizing appropriate methods (face-to-face, telephone, email, chat messaging, etc.).

5.3.2.6 Kickoff Meeting

The kickoff meeting technique outlines the purpose, sets the tone, clarifies expectations, plans for logistics, reinforces scope, discusses the timeline, describes the resource needs of the assessment, and describes how the assessment results will be handled. Allow time for answering questions and ensure that participants feel comfortable with the upcoming assessment interviews.

5.3.2.7 Meeting Management

Described in Section 5.1.2.2.

5.3.2.8 *OPM3* Expert Judgment

Described in Section 5.1.2.3.

5.3.2.9 Risk Analysis

Described in Section 5.1.2.6.

5.3.2.10 Scoring Techniques

Scoring techniques assign a numeric value to findings and include:

- Ordinal scale,
- Conditional distribution (yes or no), and
- Dimensional matrix (low, mid, high).

Scoring techniques quantify the collected assessment data in a consistent and structured manner.

5.3.3 Conduct Assessment: Outputs

5.3.3.1 Assessment Presentation

The assessment presentation output is a culmination of the Conduct Assessment process. The *OPM3* practitioner summarizes the primary findings of the assessment results and sets the baseline for the organization. The presentation balances the strengths and opportunities for improvement. To gain buy-in, the *OPM3* practitioner socializes the presentation with sponsors and key stakeholders prior to delivery. It is important to be attentive to difficult team members and stakeholders who are typically vocal in public forums. Delivery of the assessment presentation and assessment results brings closure to the Cycle Element Perform Assessment.

5.3.3.2 Assessment Results

The assessment results output is the written report summarizing the Conduct Assessment process. Elements to consider when structuring the assessment results include, but are not limited to, using executive language, graphics to pictorially convey messages, and a writing style to fit the organization.

5.3.3.3 Risk Register

Described in Section 5.1.3.3.

5.4 Initiate Change

The Initiate Change process begins with an analysis of the current state of affairs to identify where the organization is in need of change. This analysis gives team members and stakeholders a clear purpose in making the changes and what they hope to achieve. To increase the probability of success, a change management process turns intention into action to achieve benefits realization.

The *OPM3* practitioner analyzes inputs such as change readiness results to understand the organization's readiness for change. The Initiate Change process runs concurrently with the other processes in the Perform Assessment Cycle Element to evaluate the organization, culture, processes, tools, and technologies as an enterprise solution. The *OPM3* practitioner makes adjustments as the Establish Plan and Define Scope processes ebb and flow. Throughout the Conduct Assessment process, the *OPM3* practitioner makes periodic adjustments and leverages every opportunity to pace change at an acceptable rate for the organization. Pacing change at a rate higher than an organization can absorb has a negative impact on people and processes. See Figure 5-5 for a list of inputs, tools and techniques, and outputs.

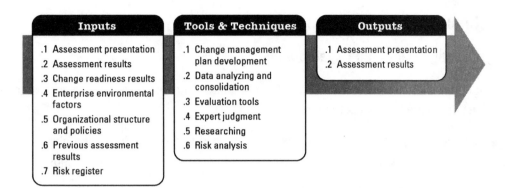

Figure 5-5. Initiate Change: Inputs, Tools and Techniques, and Outputs

5.4.1 Initiate Change: Inputs

5.4.1.1 Assessment Presentation

Described in Section 5.3.3.1.

5.4.1.2 Assessment Results

Described in Section 5.3.3.2.

5.4.1.3 Change Readiness Results

Described in Section 5.1.1.7.

5.4.1.4 Enterprise Environmental Factors

Described in Section 5.1.1.9.

5.4.1.5 Organizational Structure and Policies

Described in Section 5.1.1.12.

5.4.1.6 Previous Assessment Results

Described in Section 5.1.1.13.

5.4.1.7 Risk Register

Described in Section 5.1.3.3.

5.4.2 Initiate Change: Tools and Techniques

5.4.2.1 Change Management Plan Development

Change management plan development involves the management of organizational change activities related to the *OPM3* initiative and desired business results.

The change management plan development technique is used to gather information about the organizational environment, its training style, leadership style, agility, desire to change, and ability to change.

The *OPM3* practitioner applies different methods, depending on the complexity of the change initiatives. A special focus when developing the change management plan is to plan measures to handle possible concerns and resistance that could appear during the change process of the organization.

Key components of creating a change management plan include but are not limited to:

- Evaluating the change management methodology to fit the culture,
- Reviewing the communications plan for effectiveness,
- Engaging managers and supervisors to support tactical measures,
- Considering proactive and reactive resistance to change measures,
- Establishing feedback and measure processes to promote change adoption, and
- Implementing reward systems.

5.4.2.2 Data Analyzing and Consolidation

Described in Section 5.3.2.1.

5.4.2.3 Evaluation Tools

Evaluation tools compare the organization's ability to change and desire to change against the scope defined for the assessment. The assessment team gains an understanding of the probability that the change will be accepted, adopted, and sustained.

5.4.2.4 Expert Judgment

Described in Section 5.1.2.1.

5.4.2.5 Researching

Described in Section 5.1.2.5.

5.4.2.6 Risk Analysis

Described in Section 5.1.2.6.

5.4.3 Initiate Change: Outputs

5.4.3.1 Assessment Presentation

Described in Section 5.3.3.1.

5.4.3.2 Assessment Results

Described in Section 5.3.3.2.

5

6

MANAGE IMPROVEMENT

This section describes the processes to transform the assessment results into an improvement plan within the context of the organization. The difficulty of selecting a single improvement path stems from understanding the complex organizational variables (e.g., strategy, process, technology, communication channels, change readiness, culture, and style). The *OPM3* practitioner guides the selection of improvements by translating the art of the possible into the science of the practical. Once selection is complete, the organization executes the improvement plan by leveraging project and program management methodologies. Linking organizational metrics to the improvement activity improves the odds of success by engaging management and resources. The *OPM3* practitioner anticipates organizational responses and fosters acceptance throughout the Manage Improvement Cycle Element.

Within the Manage Improvement Cycle Element, there are five processes that are discrete and not necessarily sequential. The Manage Improvement processes as depicted in Figure 6-1 are:

6.1 Create Recommendations. The process of identifying the linkage of the Best Practices and Capabilities to the desired business results of the organization.

6.2 Select Initiatives. The process of prioritizing the Best Practices and deciding which improvements to implement or defer, based on cost, timing, change readiness, and resource availability.

6.3 Implement Improvement Initiatives. The process of executing improvement plans to obtain better business results.

6.4 Measure Results. The process of quantifying the impact of improvement activities against historical and target performance.

6.5 Manage Change. The process of synthesizing organizational information such as structure, processes, tools, skills, culture, and style that promote or hinder improvement.

In summary, the Manage Improvement Cycle Element enables the organization to do the right things in the right order to realize improved business results.

Figure 6-1. Manage Improvement Overview

6.1 Create Recommendations

The Create Recommendations process produces cost and effort estimates and identifies areas of improvement for the organization. The *OPM3* practitioner creates recommendations by leveraging results from the Perform Assessment Cycle Element and utilizing appropriate techniques. The *OPM3* practitioner clarifies what to improve, why it should be improved, and how much investment the improvement needs. See Figure 6-2 for a list of inputs, tools and techniques, and outputs.

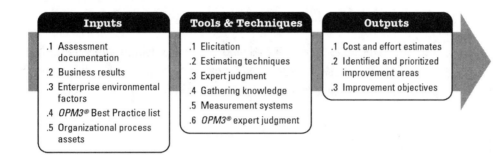

Inputs	Tools & Techniques	Outputs
.1 Assessment documentation	.1 Elicitation	.1 Cost and effort estimates
.2 Business results	.2 Estimating techniques	.2 Identified and prioritized improvement areas
.3 Enterprise environmental factors	.3 Expert judgment	.3 Improvement objectives
.4 *OPM3®* Best Practice list	.4 Gathering knowledge	
.5 Organizational process assets	.5 Measurement systems	
	.6 *OPM3®* expert judgment	

Figure 6-2. Create Recommendations: Inputs, Tools and Techniques, and Outputs

6.1.1 Create Recommendations: Inputs

6.1.1.1 Assessment Documentation

The assessment documentation input describes assessment deliverables that the *OPM3* practitioner synthesizes while creating improvement recommendations. These include:

- **Assessment presentation.** The assessment presentation output is a culmination of the Conduct Assessment process. The *OPM3* practitioner summarizes the primary findings of the assessment results and sets the baseline for the organization. The presentation balances the strengths and opportunities for improvement. To gain buy-in, the *OPM3* practitioner socializes the presentation with sponsors and key stakeholders prior to delivery. It is important to be attentive to difficult team members and stakeholders who are typically vocal in public forums. Delivery of the assessment presentation and assessment results brings closure to the Cycle Element Perform Assessment.

- **Assessment results.** The assessment results output is the written report summarizing the Conduct Assessment process. Elements to consider when structuring the assessment results include, but are not limited to, using executive language, graphics to pictorially convey messages, and a writing style to fit the organization.

6.1.1.2 Business Results

Business results include the income statement, balance sheet, cash flow statements, government-required reports for publicly traded companies, annual reports, and other internally or externally published information. The *OPM3* practitioner gathers operations data to support improving business results. Business results also include department budgets, department operational information, and department goals that assist with identifying measures pre- and post-improvement.

6.1.1.3 Enterprise Environmental Factors

Enterprise environmental factors refer to both internal and external environmental factors that surround or influence an organization's business success. Enterprise environmental factors may enhance or constrain *OPM3* initiative options. Enterprise environmental factors include, but are not limited to, the following:

- Cultural factors,
- Existing human resources,
- Market conditions,
- Organization's communications channels,
- Organizational processes,
- Personnel administration,
- Political climate, and
- Project management information systems.

6.1.1.4 *OPM3* Best Practices List

The *OPM3* Best Practices list, found in Annex A1, represents methods currently recognized within a given industry or discipline to achieve a goal or objective. An organization demonstrates achievement of an *OPM3* Best Practice by consistently demonstrating all of the supporting capabilities and realizing the Outcomes associated with each Capability.

6.1.1.5 Organizational Process Assets

The organizational process assets encompass policies, procedures, guidelines, templates, checklists, and methodologies. These assets include the organization's knowledge base such as lessons learned and historical process information as the organization improves.

6.1.2 Create Recommendations: Tools and Techniques

6.1.2.1 Elicitation

The *OPM3* practitioner uses elicitation to draw out improvement recommendations. These techniques include:

- **Facilitated workshops.** Facilitated workshops bring together key cross-functional stakeholders, experts, and both internal and external consultants to understand the OPM. Workshops are a technique for eliciting information in order to understand OPM. Facilitated sessions build trust, foster relationships, and improve communication among the participants or increase stakeholder understanding.

- **Focus groups.** Focus groups bring together key cross-functional stakeholders and subject matter experts to create recommendations for improvement. A trained moderator guides the group through an interactive discussion, designed to be more conversational than a one-on-one interview.

- **Group creativity techniques.** The *OPM3* practitioner organizes group activities to identify improvement recommendations. Creativity techniques include, but are not limited to:
  - *Brainstorming*—A technique used to generate and collect multiple ideas related to recommendations.
  - *Nominal group technique*—This technique enhances brainstorming with a voting process used to rank the most useful ideas for further brainstorming or prioritization.
  - *Idea/mind mapping*—This technique consolidates ideas created through individual brainstorming sessions into a single map to reflect commonality and differences in understanding and stimulates new ideas.
  - *Affinity diagram*—This technique allows large numbers of ideas to be sorted into groups for review and analysis.
  - *Multicriteria decision analysis*—This technique utilizes a decision matrix to provide a systematic analytical approach for establishing criteria, such as risk levels, uncertainty, and valuation for evaluating and ranking many ideas.

- **Group decision-making techniques.** Group decision making is an assessment process of multiple alternatives with an expected outcome in the form of future actions resolution. These techniques generate, classify, and prioritize recommendations.

  There are multiple methods of reaching a group decision, for example:
  - *Unanimity*—Everyone in the group collaboratively agrees on a single course of action.
  - *Majority*—Support exists from more than 50% of the collaborating members of the group.
  - *Plurality*—The largest block in a collaborating group decides even when a majority is not achieved.
  - *Dictatorship*—One individual makes the decision for the group.

- **Interview techniques.** An interview is a formal or informal approach to discover information from stakeholders. An *OPM3* practitioner conducts interviews by asking prepared questions and recording the responses. Interview scenarios include:

  o One interviewer—one interviewee,

  o One interviewer—many interviewees,

  o Many interviewers—one interviewee, and

  o Many interviewers—many interviewees.

The *OPM3* practitioner establishes an atmosphere of trust, exchanges information, gives and receives feedback, and sometimes performs a follow-up interview.

Preparation and planning include:

- Identifying problems,

- Incorporating critical thinking, and

- Utilizing appropriate methods (face-to-face, telephone, email, chat messaging, etc.).

6.1.2.2 Estimating Techniques

Estimating techniques quantify the magnitude of a recommendation for an organizational culture, process, skill set, or other applicable entity. When little information is available and decisions on general directions are made, estimation techniques are applied. There are a number of different techniques that can be applied for quantifying and classifying the possible influence of recommendations on the different dimensions and dependencies, including process improvement and costs, processes improvement and skill set, cost and skill set, etc. The *OPM3* practitioner selects the appropriate estimation technique, including, but not limited to:

- Analogous estimating,

- Parametric estimating,

- Bottom-up estimating,

- Three-points estimates,

- Influence diagrams,

- SWOT (strengths, weaknesses, opportunities and threats) analysis,

- Cost of quality, and

- Vendor bid analysis.

6.1.2.3 Expert Judgment

Expert judgment is a tool or technique demonstrated by knowledgeable parties associated with the organization. Qualified individuals demonstrate expert judgment by providing information and data used to solve problems or make decisions through specialized education, knowledge, skill, experience, or training.

6.1.2.4 Gathering Knowledge

This process involves gathering knowledge from key stakeholders. Four steps guide the gathering of this knowledge:

- **Elicit organizational knowledge.** Traditional elicitation techniques include interviews and workshops. Knowledge gathered may address organizational questions such as:
    - What is the organization's business area?
    - What is the organization's business need?
    - What is the organization's business goal?
- **Analyze organizational knowledge.** Extract the real state of the organization by analyzing elicited knowledge. There may be a difference between the stated and real state of the organization.
- **Document organizational knowledge.** Document elicited knowledge for stakeholder review, understanding, and confirmation.
- **Validate documented organizational knowledge.** By reviewing and inspecting the documented knowledge, confirm the documented knowledge is unambiguous and consistent throughout the document.

6.1.2.5 Measurement Systems

Measurement systems deliver concrete metrics to make decisions. These metrics are often called key performance indicators (KPI). The measurements systems are any IT or manual system used to track the status or health of a key performance indicator.

6.1.2.6 *OPM3* Expert Judgment

Based on the assessment results, the *OPM3* practitioner decides which areas of improvement the organization should focus. In most cases, time or financial restrictions do not allow detailed analysis of the cost and benefits regarding the implementation of each Best Practice. On a high level, quick decisions are made to do the right things in the right order to reach strategic goals. *OPM3* expert judgment is a tool or technique demonstrated by knowledgeable parties associated with the organization. Qualified individuals demonstrate expert judgment by providing information and data used to solve problems or make decisions through specialized education, knowledge, skill experience, or training. When analyzing candidate recommendations, current organizational capability (maturity) is a factor.

Like the maturity of an organization, the OPM maturity of an organization also changes over time, as shown in Figure 6-3. The organization progresses through the different stages of maturity over time, with the maturity growing or declining. Organizations move from birth or startup to death. The *OPM3* practitioner leverages *OPM3* to identify the current maturity of the organization. Figure 6-4 depicts a current and future state of an organization. On each maturity level, different Best Practices are applied or implemented for the three domains portfolio, program, and project management, as well as for the organizational enablers. The *OPM3* practitioner pursues implementation of the corresponding Best Practices, depending on the desired *OPM3* maturity level.

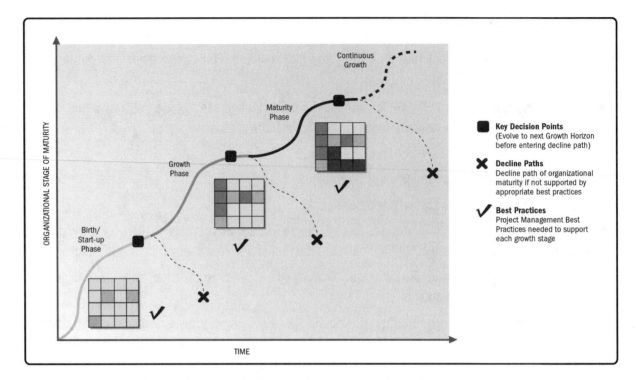

Figure 6-3. Maturity Stages of an Organization

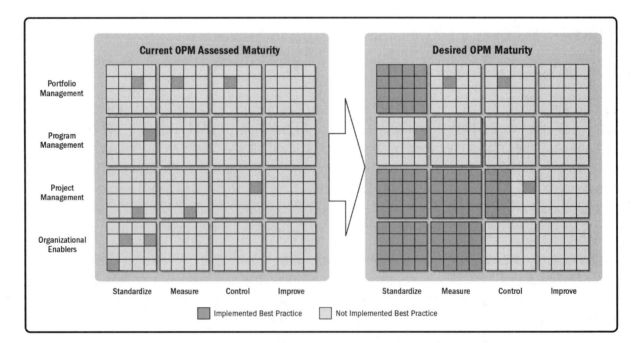

Figure 6-4. High-Level Schema of Current versus Desired OPM Maturity

The focus of increasing maturity depends on the strategic and tactical targets of the organization. Organizations improve business results by increasing the maturity in:

- Certain domains;
- OE categories;
- Process groups of portfolio, program and project management; and
- Business processes.

The *OPM3* practitioner applies expert judgment to the assessment results shown in the example in Figure 6-5 by identifying gaps and relevant areas of improvement.

Based on the identified high-level areas for improvement (see Figure 6-4) and the assessment results (see Figure 6-5), the related Best Practices can be identified. Depending on the desired *OPM3* maturity level and the implementation status of single Best Practices, the *OPM3* practitioner gets a recommendation which measures should be considered (see Figure 6-6).

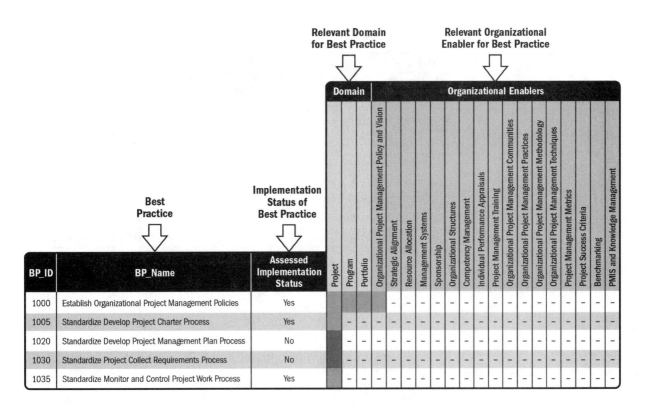

Figure 6-5. Example of *OPM3* Assessment Results

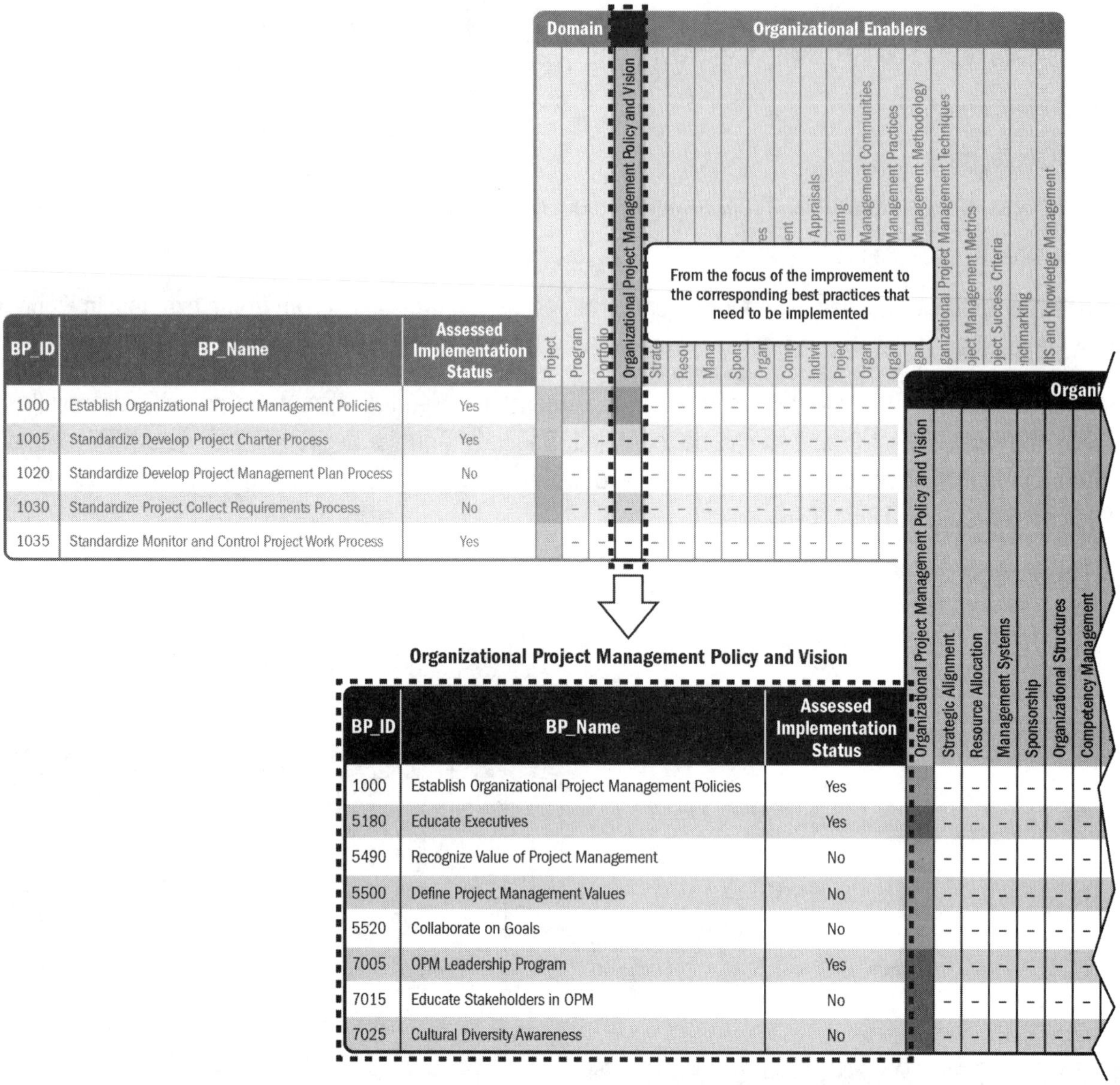

Figure 6-6. Selection of Best Practice Based on the Desired Maturity Level

The overview of the implementation status of each Best Practice and the Best Practices that need to be implemented to reach the desired *OPM3* maturity level (see Figure 6-7) is the basis for the further evaluation process.

For each Best Practice that is in focus for improvement, the *OPM3* team and the relevant stakeholders decide whether the Best Practice should be implemented. The determination of the relative impact of each Best Practice can be assessed by using the elicitation techniques described in 6.1.2.1.

Organizational Project Management Policy and Vision		Current Maturity ⬇	Desired Maturity ⬇
BP	**BP Name**	**Assessed Implementation Status**	**Desired Implementation Status**
1000	Establish Organizational Project Management Policies	Yes	Yes
5180	Educate Executives	Yes	Yes
5490	Recognize Value of Project Management	No	Yes
5520	Collaborate on Goals	No	Yes
7015	Educate Stakeholders in OPM	No	Yes
7025	Cultural Diversity Awareness	Yes	Yes
7005	OPM Leadership Program	No	Yes
5500	Define Project Management Values	No	No

Figure 6-7. Example of Implementation Status for Desired Maturity Level on Best Practice Level

6.1.3 Create Recommendations: Outputs

6.1.3.1 Cost and Effort Estimates

The cost and effort estimates output captures the rough amount of resources projected to be consumed by the *OPM3* initiative; for example, number of days, number of people, resource rates, travel costs, facility costs, etc.

6.1.3.2 Identified and Prioritized Improvement Areas

The identified and prioritized improvement areas output captures the requirements of the organization's relevant stakeholders pertaining to the desired areas to improve. The *OPM3* practitioner defines a list of *OPM3* Best Practices aligning with the business results sought by stakeholders.

6.1.3.3 Improvement Objectives

The improvement objectives output records the business result sought by the organization's stakeholders. The *OPM3* practitioner translates this business result into an improvement objective associated with *OPM3* Best Practices.

6.2 Select Initiatives

The select initiatives process outlines a set of initiatives, grouping relevant Best Practices for implementation to meet the improvement objectives. The *OPM3* practitioner leverages a variety of tools and techniques to document the initiatives. See Figure 6-8 for a list of inputs, tools and techniques, and outputs.

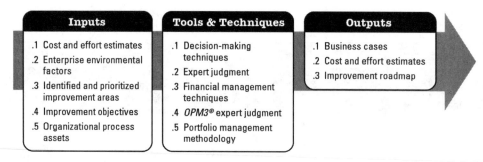

Figure 6-8. Select Initiatives: Inputs, Tools and Techniques, and Outputs

6.2.1 Select Initiatives: Inputs

6.2.1.1 Cost and Effort Estimates

Described in Section 6.1.3.1.

6.2.1.2 Enterprise Environmental Factors

Described in Section 6.1.1.3.

6.2.1.3 Identified and Prioritized Improvement Areas

Described in Section 6.1.3.2.

6.2.1.4 Improvement Objectives

Described in Section 6.1.3.3.

6.2.1.5 Organizational Process Assets

Described in Section 6.1.1.5.

6.2.2 Select Initiatives: Tools and Techniques

6.2.2.1 Decision-Making Techniques

Decision-making techniques are rational processes/systematic procedures for applying critical thinking to information, data, and experience in order to make a balanced decision when the choice between alternatives is unclear. These techniques provide organized ways of applying critical thinking skills developed around accumulating answers to questions about the problem. Steps include clarifying purpose, evaluating alternatives, assessing risks and benefits, and making a decision. These steps usually involve scoring criteria and alternatives. Scoring (a systematic method for handling and communicating information) provides a common language and approach that removes decision making from the realm of personal preference or idiosyncratic behavior. The decision-making techniques provide tools to gain consensus on complex topics. These techniques include:

- **Pros and cons analysis.** Pros and cons analysis is a qualitative comparison method in which good things (pros) and bad things (cons) are identified about each alternative. Lists of the pros and cons, based on the input of subject matter experts, are compared for each alternative.

- **Kepner-Tregoe (K-T) decision analysis.** K-T is a quantitative comparison method in which a team of experts numerically scores criteria and alternatives based on individual judgments/assessments. The size of the team needed tends to be inversely proportional to the quality of the data available— the more intangible and qualitative the data, the greater the number of people that should be involved.

- **Analytic hierarchy process (AHP).** AHP is a quantitative comparison method used to select a preferred alternative by using pair-wise comparisons of the alternatives based on their relative performance against the criteria. The basis of this technique is that humans are more capable of making relative judgments than absolute judgments.

- **Facilitated workshops.** Facilitated workshops bring together key cross-functional stakeholders, experts, and external consultants to create recommendations. Workshops are a technique to elicit information to create these recommendations. Facilitated sessions build trust, foster relationships, and improve communication among the participants or increase stakeholder understanding.

- **Group decision-making techniques.** Group decision-making techniques involve multiple individuals analyzing a problem or situation. The group evaluates different options and identifies appropriate courses of action. The group employs structured and unstructured problem-solving activities.

6.2.2.2 Expert Judgment

Described in Section 6.1.2.3.

6.2.2.3 Financial Management Techniques

Financial management techniques assist the *OPM3* practitioner with selecting the appropriate organizational improvement initiatives. These techniques include but are not limited to:

- **Estimating technique.** Described in Section 6.1.2.2.

- **Financial asset analysis.** The financial asset analysis technique seeks to understand the organization's physical needs to support selecting the appropriate Best Practices. This technique considers types of assets (equipment, buildings, etc.) to identify constraints. The resulting analysis reveals the range of Best Practices an organization implements in a certain period.

- **Cost-benefit analysis.** The cost-benefit analysis technique is a systematic process for calculating and comparing benefits and costs of initiatives. This technique has two purposes:
  - To determine if it is a sound investment/decision by applying methods such as return on investment (ROI), cost-benefit ratio, and payback; and
  - To provide a basis for comparing projects by applying methods such as net present value (NPV), discounted cash flow (DCF), and internal rate of return (IRR). The analysis involves comparing the total expected cost of each option against the total expected benefits to see whether the benefits outweigh the costs, and if so, by how much.

- **Financial capacity analysis.** The improvement team conducts a financial resource capacity analysis to understand the capacity of the organization to finance the implementation of the selected Best Practices. The analysis utilizes the financial and/or budget process of the organization. The *OPM3* practitioner measures internal financial capacity, coupled with external financial resource availability, to compile a broad financial landscape. The financial resource capacity constrains the number of Best Practices an organization undertakes in a given timeframe.

6.2.2.4 *OPM3* Expert Judgment

Based on the selected initiatives, the *OPM3* practitioner selects which areas of improvement upon which the organization should focus. The *OPM3* practitioner takes into account the current *OPM3* maturity when analyzing candidate recommendations.

The Best Practices, which were grouped into initiatives during the Create Recommendations process, provide the *OPM3* practitioner with enough information to identify which initiatives require a business case (see Figure 6-9). The business case provides stakeholders with information to decide if the improvement initiative is worth the investment.

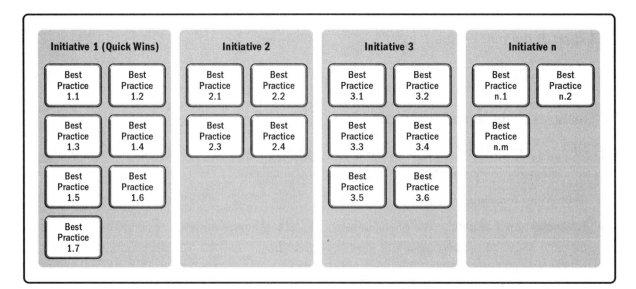

Figure 6-9: Grouping of Best Practices to Improvement Initiatives

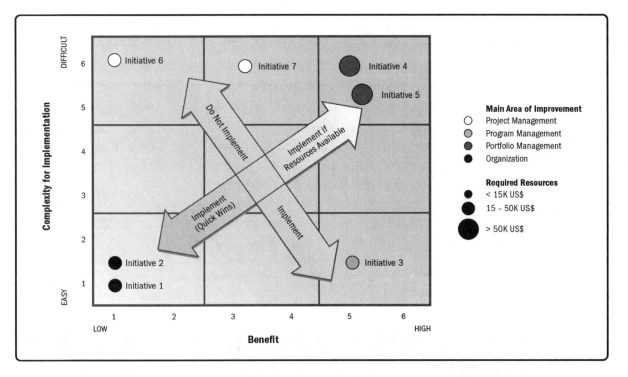

Figure 6-10. Portfolio Diagram for Prioritization and Identification

A portfolio diagram, as Figure 6-10 illustrates, uses the dimensions "complexity of implementation" and "benefit" to rank each initiative in relation to the others.

The main purpose of using the portfolio diagram is to reach a common understanding of the scope of initiatives (see Figure 6-9) and to get a common agreement on priorities. Under consideration of limited resources, the prioritization process results in a list of recommended Best Practices that should be implemented as a first step to meet the improvement objectives. As shown in Figure 6-11, most organizations allocate resources for daily operation and resources available for other projects such as, an *OPM3* improvement project. Each selected improvement initiative reduces the available resources for projects. Realistic planning reveals that only a limited number of initiatives can be implemented within a certain period of time.

Initiative selection, tempered by resource availability, yields candidate improvement objectives. The different options for an improvement maturity path (see Figure 6-12) convey to the relevant stakeholders the improvement initiatives to be implemented and their expected business value realization. Different maturity scores (for measuring *OPM3* maturity, see Section 3.5 on *OPM3* Scoring Methods) can be reached by implementing the different improvement options. The organization decides, on the basis of its strategic objectives and resource restrictions, which improvement option is the most appropriate.

Transforming the selected improvement initiatives into a high-level timeline generates an improvement roadmap for the stakeholders (see Figure 6-13).

Lastly, the *OPM3* practitioner garners approval for the recommended improvement roadmap from relevant stakeholders. Upon final approval of projects and programs, stakeholders assign required resources.

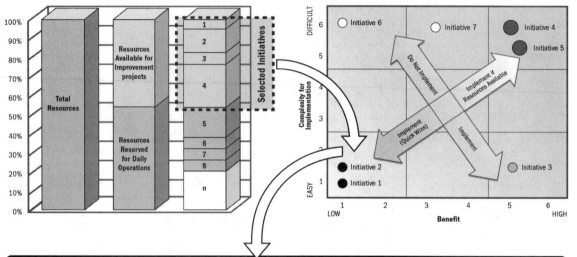

BP_ID	BP_Name	Duration and Effort in Days			Cost in T$			Benefits	
		Internal Effort	External Effort	Duration	Investments	OTC	Cost P.A.	Quantitative	Qualitative
Initiative 1									
1000	Establish Organizational Project Management Policies	20	15		30		5000		
5490	Recognize Value of Project Management		40						
Initiative 2									
5500	Define Project Management Values	65	20						
5520	Collaborate on Goals	70	30						
Initiative 3									
6960	Create an Organizational Maturity Development Program	30	25		50				
7005	OPM Leadership Program								
Initiative 4									
7015	Educate Stakeholders in OPM	40				60			
7025	Cultural Diversity Awareness	40			20	30			

Figure 6-11. Prioritization of Selected Initiatives under Constraints of Limited Resources

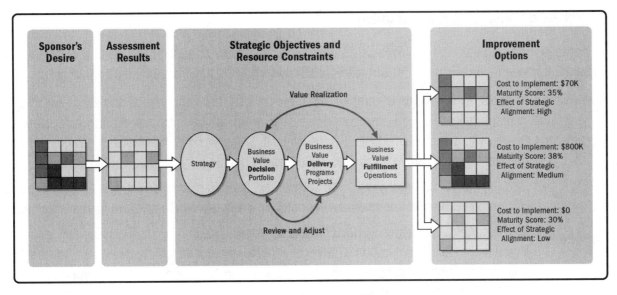

Figure 6-12. Sample Maturity Improvement Path

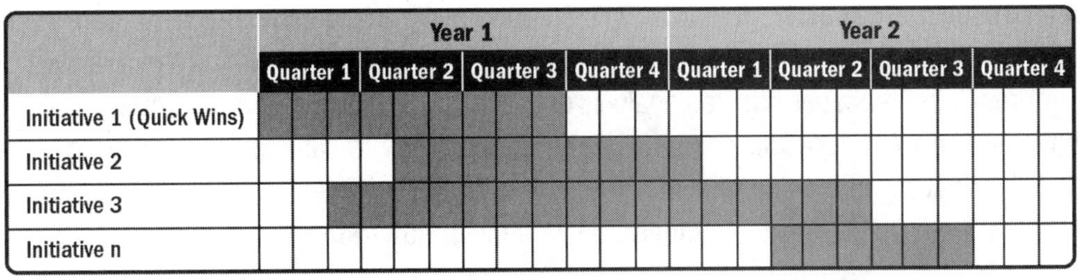

	Year 1				Year 2			
	Quarter 1	Quarter 2	Quarter 3	Quarter 4	Quarter 1	Quarter 2	Quarter 3	Quarter 4
Initiative 1 (Quick Wins)								
Initiative 2								
Initiative 3								
Initiative n								

Figure 6-13. Sample OPM Improvement Roadmap for Increasing OPM

6.2.2.5 Portfolio Management Methodology

The portfolio management methodology assists with selecting, prioritizing, and resourcing the initiatives that best meet the improvement objectives. These techniques include, but are not limited to, the following:

- **Evaluation tools.** Evaluation tools compare the organization's ability to change and its desire to change against the scope defined for the assessment. The assessment team gains an understanding of the probability that the change will be accepted, adopted, and sustained. The *OPM3* practitioner selects evaluation tools to support the selection of initiatives. Evaluation tools include, but are not limited to the following:

  - *Scoring model comprising weighted key criteria.* Scoring models assign points to Best Practices according to potential improvement impact. This method evaluates and compares Best Practices.

  - *Graphical representations.* Various graphical representations facilitate comparison among Best Practices under consideration. Graphical representations include histograms, pie charts, line charts, and bubble charts. Two-criterion grids are among the most utilized and most effective graphical tools for comparison.

- **Prioritization tools.** Prioritization tools provide a classification and ranking framework to evaluate Best Practices. The *OPM3* practitioner compares the Best Practices, ensuring optimal alignment with the strategic plan and the expectations of the relevant stakeholders. Prioritization tools include weighted rankings and scoring techniques.

- **Human resource capacity analysis.** The improvement team conducts a human resource capacity analysis to understand the organization's capacity to source and implement the selected Best Practices. The improvement team performs an analysis of organizational skill sets to determine the resource skill set limitations. The *OPM3* practitioner measures internal resource capacity, coupled with external resource availability, to compile a broad resource landscape. The human resource capacity constrains the number of Best Practices an organization undertakes in a given timeframe.

6.2.3 Select Initiatives: Outputs

6.2.3.1 Business Cases

Business cases provide the necessary information from a business standpoint to determine whether or not the initiative is worth the required investment. Business cases contain the business need and the cost-benefit analysis that justifies the initiatives.

6.2.3.2 Cost and Effort Estimates

Described in Section 6.1.3.1.

6.2.3.3 Improvement Roadmap

The improvement roadmap defines the timing and focus of the Best Practice improvement initiatives. The roadmap includes initiatives that represent a significant output for the maturity improvement project/program or are interdependent with other initiatives. The *OPM3* practitioner refines the improvement roadmap schedule, based on collected feedback.

6.3 Implement Improvement Initiatives

The Implement Improvement Initiatives process represents the execution aspect of Best Practice improvements. See Figure 6-14 for a list of inputs, tools and techniques, and outputs.

Organizations often spend 90% of their total effort in the improvement phase of an *OPM3* Cycle. The *OPM3* practitioner balances level-of-effort and complexity when executing improvement initiatives. The organization implements the initiative as a series of individual projects, a program, or a portfolio. Figure 6-15 depicts how the *OPM3* practitioner considers grouping the projects.

Figure 6-14. Implement Improvement Initiatives: Inputs, Tools and Techniques, and Outputs

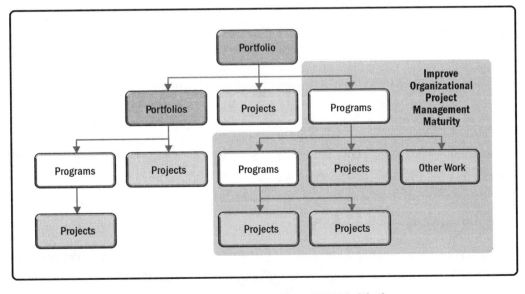

Figure 6-15. Structure of an *OPM3* Initiative

The *OPM3* practitioner leverages the following standards to create a plan for the *OPM3* initiative:

- **Project Management.** *A Guide to the Project Management Body of Knowledge (PMBOK® Guide)* – Fifth Edition.
- **Program Management.** T*he Standard for Program Management* – Third Edition.
- **Portfolio Management.** *The Standard for Portfolio Management* – Third Edition.

6.3.1 Implement Improvement Initiatives: Inputs

6.3.1.1 Business Cases

Described in Section 6.2.3.1.

6.3.1.2 Cost and Effort Estimates

Described in Section 6.1.3.1.

6.3.1.3 Enterprise Environmental Factors

Described in Section 6.1.1.3.

6.3.1.4 Improvement Roadmap

Described in Section 6.2.3.3.

6.3.1.5 Organizational Process Assets

Described in Section 6.1.1.5.

6.3.2 Implement Improvement Initiatives: Tools and Techniques

6.3.2.1 Program Management Methodology

Program management methodology contains processes manage an improvement initiative according to defined improvement objectives.

6.3.2.2 Project Management Methodology

Project management methodology is a collection of methods and rules followed in the science or discipline of project management. Artifacts generated by a methodology include project charter, schedule, templates, procedures, training materials, etc.

6.3.3 Implement Improvement Initiatives: Outputs

6.3.3.1 Business Results

The business results output captures the business results originally targeted for post-improvement implementation. These results may be lagging type metrics that require thirty days, sixty days, and sometimes longer to realize. It is important to be cognizant of the stability of the business result being targeted and its associated cycle time.

6.3.3.2 Improvement Roadmap

The improvement roadmap documents completed and revised work. Figure 6-16 shows the growth of organizational project management maturity and improved value realization achieved by implementing the clusters of Best Practices with the most benefit.

After completing an improvement activity, the *OPM3* practitioner reassesses where the organization is on the continuum of organizational project management maturity. By repeating the assessment or tackling other Best Practices improvement initiatives, the organization gains greater insights where to apply resources for other Best Practice improvement initiatives.

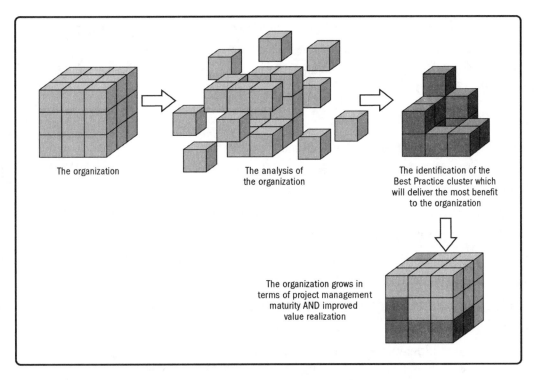

The organization

The analysis of the organization

The identification of the Best Practice cluster which will deliver the most benefit to the organization

The organization grows in terms of project management maturity AND improved value realization

Figure 6-16. Maturity Growth of the Organization

6.3.3.3 Organizational Process Assets

Described in Section 6.1.1.5.

6.4 Measure Results

The Measure Results process addresses the overall status and progress monitoring and measuring associated with improvement objectives. The *OPM3* practitioner collects and consolidates data for the respective initiatives. Monitoring requires interfacing with the governance structure of the *OPM3* initiative to ensure the stakeholders have a clear picture of the current benefit delivery and expected future benefits. See Figure 6-17 for a list of inputs, tools and techniques, and outputs.

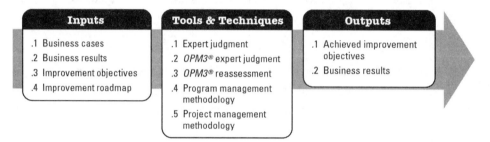

Inputs	Tools & Techniques	Outputs
.1 Business cases	.1 Expert judgment	.1 Achieved improvement objectives
.2 Business results	.2 *OPM3®* expert judgment	.2 Business results
.3 Improvement objectives	.3 *OPM3®* reassessment	
.4 Improvement roadmap	.4 Program management methodology	
	.5 Project management methodology	

Figure 6-17. Measure Results: Inputs, Tools and Techniques, and Outputs

Effective management of results supports appropriate preventive and corrective actions at the top level of the *OPM3* initiative, especially during the improvement phase of the *OPM3* Cycle. An integrated change control process involves redirecting or modifying the *OPM3* initiatives as needed, based on feedback from individual project work on implementing Best Practices.

The process of measuring results includes:

- **Monitor and control performance.** Monitor and control performance of the activities in all *OPM3* initiatives, ensuring that the execution of the *OPM3* initiatives occurs according to the approved *OPM3* roadmap.

- **Monitor and control scope of the *OPM3* Cycle**. Monitor and control the overall scope as well as the major changes resulting from individual initiatives that impact the desired maturity status.

- **Monitor and control *OPM3* roadmap.** Ensure the on-time delivery of all initiatives by tracking the actual start and finish of initiatives against the approved roadmap.

- **Monitor and control financials.** Analyze actual cost, compare actual costs against planned costs, and conduct trend analysis.

- **Manage stakeholder expectations**. Ensure that stakeholders' expectations are identified and that stakeholders are kept informed about the status of *OPM3* initiatives.

- **Monitor and control risks**. Track known risks, identify new risks, execute risk response plans, and evaluate effectiveness of risk response actions.

- **Manage program benefits**. Ensure there is a defined set of reports and metrics communicated to the stakeholders.

OPM3 practitioners constantly monitor and report benefits to stakeholders, who can then assess the overall health of the *OPM3* initiative, and take action as required ensuring successful benefit delivery.

6.4.1 Measure Results: Inputs

6.4.1.1 Business Cases

Described in Section 6.2.3.1.

6.4.1.2 Business Results

Described in Section 6.1.1.2.

6.4.1.3 Improvement Objectives

Described in Section 6.1.3.3.

6.4.1.4 Improvement Roadmap

Described in Section 6.3.3.2.

6.4.2 Measure Results: Tools and Techniques

6.4.2.1 Expert Judgment

Described in Section 6.1.2.3.

6.4.2.2 *OPM3* Expert Judgment

Described in Section 6.1.2.6.

6.4.2.3 *OPM3* Reassessment

As the organization continues to implement improvement initiatives and monitor and control that work, the organization decides to conduct another *OPM3* assessment to gauge the achievement of Best Practices that contribute to the improvement objectives.

6.4.2.4 Program Management Methodology

Described in Section 6.3.2.1.

6.4.2.5 Project Management Methodology

Described in Section 6.3.2.2.

6.4.3 Measure Results: Outputs

6.4.3.1 Achieved Improvement Objectives

The achieved improvement objectives output reflects historical performance compared to current performance post-improvements. One example is the reduction of project cycle time from 18 months to 15 months.

6.4.3.2 Business Results

Described in Section 6.3.3.1.

6.5 Manage Change

The ability to manage change, driven by external or internal demands, is important for organizations. Whenever people are involved, change does not only mean to implement tools and technology and define processes and policies, but also to involve individuals throughout the entire *OPM3* improvement cycle. See Figure 6-18 for a list of inputs, tools and techniques, and outputs.

Organizations can change only if the people affected by the change embrace it. No matter how large the endeavor, its success ultimately lies with changing how and what each individual does. Effective change management requires an understanding and appreciation of not only the as-is and to-be states, but also of how one person successfully makes a change.

Figure 6-18. Manage Change: Inputs, Tools and Techniques, and Outputs

Leaders of change in an organization need to recognize the following:

- People don't like change,
- People resist what they don't like, and
- People respond differently to change.

Achieving the goal of organizational transformation starts with a plan for initiating and managing change. Implementing change exposes aspects of organizations and systems that hinder the ability to achieve better results. Addressing these hindrances promotes positive transformation. People directly involved in change processes learn new skills and acquire experience. Transformation is not a goal but a sustainable capacity for change—a continuing process of reassessment and renewal focused on measurable improvement.

In larger systems and organizations, sometimes change has to happen all at once. However, in many cases, introducing change on a smaller scale is less risky and success can come in smaller steps. Thus, it can be introduced to a portion of the organization such as a region, an agency, or some specific targeted part of a system or group; in the case of *OPM3*, it can be introduced in a set of related Best Practices and appropriate prerequisites.

6.5.1 Manage Change: Inputs

6.5.1.1 Assessment Documentation

Described in Section 6.1.1.1.

6.5.1.2 Business Results

Described in Section 6.1.1.2.

6.5.1.3 Change Readiness Results

The change readiness results input conveys the organization's readiness for change in the following areas:

- Attitude and expectations of the key stakeholders are understood.
- Sponsor is defined to deploy resources to understand OPM and its fit for organizational culture and environment.
- Organization/department is assigned and accepts responsibility for improvement initiatives.
- OPM is understood among stakeholders.
- Organization's strategic plan is clear, understood, and accepted by the stakeholders.
- Organization's vision and mission is clear and understood among stakeholders.
- Organization's structure and policies are clear and understood among stakeholders.

6.5.1.4 Enterprise Environmental Factors

Described in Section 6.1.1.3.

6.5.1.5 Improvement Roadmap

Described in Section 6.2.3.3.

6.5.2 Manage Change: Tools and Techniques

6.5.2.1 Change Management Plan Development

Change management plan development involves the management of organizational change activities related to the *OPM3* initiative and desired business results.

The change management plan development technique is used to gather information about the organizational environment, its training style, leadership style, agility, desire to change, and ability to change.

The *OPM3* practitioner applies different methods, depending on the complexity of the change initiatives. A special focus when developing the change management plan is to plan measures to handle possible concerns and resistance that could appear during the change process of the organization.

Key components of creating a change management plan includes but are not limited to:

- Evaluating the change management methodology to fit the culture,
- Reviewing the communications plan for effectiveness,
- Engaging managers and supervisors to support tactical measures,
- Considering proactive and reactive resistance to change measures,
- Establishing feedback and measure processes to promote change adoption, and
- Implementing reward systems.

6.5.2.2 Facilitated Workshops

Facilitated workshops bring together key cross-functional stakeholders, experts, and external consultants to create recommendations. Workshops are a technique to elicit information to create these recommendations. Facilitated sessions build trust, foster relationships, and improve communication among the participants or increase stakeholder understanding.

6.5.2.3 Interview Techniques

An interview is a formal or informal approach to discover information from stakeholders. An *OPM3* practitioner conducts interviews by asking prepared questions and recording the responses. Interview scenarios include:

- One interviewer—one interviewee,
- One interviewer—many interviewees,
- Many interviewers—one interviewee, and
- Many interviewers—many interviewees.

The *OPM3* practitioner establishes an atmosphere of trust, exchanges information, gives and receives feedback, and sometimes performs a follow-up interview.

Preparation and planning include:

- Identifying problems,
- Incorporating critical thinking, and
- Utilizing appropriate methods (face-to-face, telephone, email, chat messaging, etc.).

6.5.3 Manage Change: Outputs

6.5.3.1 Change Management Plan

The change management plan describes the initiatives for supporting the implementation of the *OPM3* initiatives and the measures to handle the identified concerns and possible resistance from individuals or groups.

6.5.3.2 Communications Plan

The communications plan describes the communication needs and expectations for the change initiative, how and in what format information will be communicated, when and where each communication will be made, and who is responsible for providing each type of communication.

6.5.3.3 Training and Coaching Needs

Training and coaching needs is a document that describes which training and coaching initiatives will be executed in order to increase the acceptance of the change initiatives.

REFERENCES

[1]   Project Management Institute. (2013). *A Guide to the Project Management Body of Knowledge* (*PMBOK® Guide*) – Fifth Edition. Newtown Square, PA: Author.

[2]   Project Management Institute. (2013). *The Standard for Portfolio Management* – Third Edition. Newtown Square, PA: Author.

[3]   Project Management Institute. (2013). *The Standard for Program Management* – Third Edition. Newtown Square, PA: Author.

[4]   Project Management Institute. (2012). *PMI's Lexicon of Project Management Terms*. Newtown Square, PA: Author.

[5]   Project Management Institute. (2007). *Project Manager Competency Development Framework* (*PMCDF*) — Second Edition. Newtown Square, PA: Author.

[6]   Tarantino, A. (2008). *The Governance, Risk, and Compliance Handbook: Technology, Finance, Environmental, and International Guidance and Best Practices*. Hoboken, NJ: Wiley Publishing.

ANNEX A1
OPM3 BEST PRACTICES LIST

Best practices are optimal methods, currently recognized within a given industry or discipline, to achieve a goal or objective. The types of best practices are:

- **Domain.** Project, program, and portfolio, with process improvement stage: standardize measure, control, and improve (SMCI).

- **Organizational Enabler.** Non-domain-based processes, pertaining to environmental and cultural aspects of the organization.

Table A1-1 provides the name and a brief description of each Best Practice and maps each Best Practice to the appropriate *OPM3* categories. This mapping allows the organization to focus on those Best Practices related to the categories important to them. Utilizing a scoring method previously described, an organization conducts an assessment based upon the *OPM3* Framework and scores the following Best Practices as appropriate.

Continuous improvement is a total quality management concept based on theories developed by Edward Deming and Walter Shewart. The Capabilities supporting an SMCI Best Practice aligned with key principles of continuous improvement.

Table A1-1. *OPM3* Best Practices List

Best Practice ID	Best Practice Name	Best Practice Description	Portfolio Domain	Program Domain	Project Domain	Organizational Enabler	Process Improvement Stage
1000	Establish Organizational Project Management Policies	The organization has policies describing the standardization, measurement, control, and continuous improvement of organizational project management processes.	Portfolio	Program	Project	Organizational Project Management Policy and Vision	
1005	Standardize Develop Project Charter Process	Develop Project Charter Process standards are established.			Project		Standardize
1020	Standardize Develop Project Management Plan Process	Develop Project Management Plan Process standards are established.			Project		Standardize
1030	Standardize Project Collect Requirements Process	Collect Requirements Process standards are established.			Project		Standardize
1035	Standardize Monitor and Control Project Work Process	Monitor and Control Project Work Process standards are established.			Project		Standardize
1040	Standardize Project Define Scope Process	Define Scope Process standards are established.			Project		Standardize
1045	Measure Monitor and Control Project Work Process	Monitor and Control Project Work Process measures are established, assembled, and analyzed.			Project		Measure
1050	Standardize Project Define Activities Process	Define Activities Process standards are established.			Project		Standardize
1055	Control Monitor and Control Project Work Process	Monitor and Control Project Work Process controls are established and executed to control the stability of the process.			Project		Control

Best Practice ID	Best Practice Name	Best Practice Description	Portfolio Domain	Program Domain	Project Domain	Organizational Enabler	Process Improvement Stage
1060	Standardize Project Sequence Activities Process	Sequence Activities Process standards are established.			Project		Standardize
1065	Improve Monitor and Control Project Work Process	Monitor and Control Project Work Process problem areas are assessed, root causes are identified, process improvement recommendations are collected, and process improvements are implemented.			Project		Improve
1070	Standardize Project Estimate Activity Durations Process	Estimate Activity Durations Process standards are established.			Project		Standardize
1075	Standardize Project Create WBS Process	Create WBS Process standards are established.			Project		Standardize
1080	Standardize Project Develop Schedule Process	Develop Schedule Process standards are established.			Project		Standardize
1085	Measure Project Create WBS Process	Create WBS Process measures are established, assembled, and analyzed.			Project		Measure
1090	Standardize Project Plan Human Resource Management Process	Plan Human Resource Management Process standards are established.			Project		Standardize
1095	Control Project Create WBS Process	Create WBS Process controls are established and executed to control the stability of the process.			Project		Control
1100	Standardize Project Estimate Costs Process	Estimate Costs Process standards are established.			Project		Standardize

Best Practice ID	Best Practice Name	Best Practice Description	Portfolio Domain	Program Domain	Project Domain	Organizational Enabler	Process Improvement Stage
1105	Improve Project Create WBS Process	Create WBS Process problem areas are assessed, root causes are identified, process improvement recommendations are collected, and process improvements are implemented.			Project		Improve
1110	Standardize Project Determine Budget Process	Determine Budget Process standards are established.			Project		Standardize
1115	Standardize Project Estimate Activity Resources Process	Estimate Activity Resources Process standards are established.			Project		Standardize
1120	Standardize Project Plan Risk Management Process	Plan Risk Management Process standards are established.			Project		Standardize
1125	Measure Project Estimate Activity Resources Process	Estimate Activity Resources Process measures are established, assembled, and analyzed.			Project		Measure
1130	Standardize Project Plan Quality Management Process	Plan Quality Management Process standards are established.			Project		Standardize
1135	Control Project Estimate Activity Resources Process	Estimate Activity Resources Process controls are established and executed to control the stability of the process.			Project		Control
1145	Improve Project Estimate Activity Resources Process	Estimate Activity Resources Process problem areas are assessed, root causes are identified, process improvement recommendations are collected, and process improvements are implemented.			Project		Improve

Best Practice ID	Best Practice Name	Best Practice Description	Portfolio Domain	Program Domain	Project Domain	Organizational Enabler	Process Improvement Stage
1150	Standardize Acquire Project Team Process	Acquire Project Team Process standards are established.			Project		Standardize
1155	Standardize Manage Project Team Process	Manage Project Team Process standards are established.			Project		Standardize
1160	Standardize Project Plan Communications Management Process	Plan Communications Management Process standards are established.			Project		Standardize
1165	Measure Manage Project Team Process	Manage Project Team Process measures are established, assembled, and analyzed.			Project		Measure
1170	Standardize Project Identify Risks Process	Identify Risks Process standards are established.			Project		Standardize
1175	Control Manage Project Team Process	Manage Project Team Process controls are established and executed to control the stability of the process.			Project		Control
1180	Standardize Project Perform Qualitative Risk Analysis Process	Perform Qualitative Risk Analysis Process standards are established.			Project		Standardize
1185	Improve Manage Project Team Process	Manage Project Team Process problem areas are assessed, root causes are identified, process improvement recommendations are collected, and process improvements are implemented.			Project		Improve
1190	Standardize Project Perform Quantitative Risk Analysis Process	Perform Quantitative Risk Analysis Process standards are established.			Project		Standardize
1195	Standardize Project Identify Stakeholders Process	Identify Stakeholders Process standards are established.			Project		Standardize
1200	Standardize Project Plan Risk Responses Process	Plan Risk Responses Process standards are established.			Project		Standardize

Best Practice ID	Best Practice Name	Best Practice Description	Portfolio Domain	Program Domain	Project Domain	Organizational Enabler	Process Improvement Stage
1210	Standardize Project Plan Procurement Management Process	Plan Procurement Management Process standards are established.			Project		Standardize
1230	Standardize Direct and Manage Project Work Process	Direct and Manage Project Work Process standards are established.			Project		Standardize
1240	Standardize Project Perform Quality Assurance Process	Perform Quality Assurance Process standards are established.			Project		Standardize
1250	Standardize Develop Project Team Process	Develop Project Team Process standards are established.			Project		Standardize
1260	Standardize Project Manage Communications Process	Manage Communications Process standards are established.			Project		Standardize
1270	Standardize Project Conduct Procurements Process	Conduct Procurements Process standards are established.			Project		Standardize
1290	Standardize Project Control Procurements Process	Control Procurements Process standards are established.			Project		Standardize
1300	Standardize Project Control Communications Process	Control Communications Process standards are established.			Project		Standardize
1310	Standardize Project Perform Integrated Change Control Process	Perform Integrated Change Control Process standards are established.			Project		Standardize
1320	Standardize Project Validate Scope Process	Validate Scope Process standards are established.			Project		Standardize
1330	Standardize Project Control Scope Process	Control Scope Process standards are established.			Project		Standardize
1340	Standardize Project Control Schedule Process	Control Schedule Process standards are established.			Project		Standardize
1350	Standardize Project Control Costs Process	Control Costs Process standards are established.			Project		Standardize

Best Practice ID	Best Practice Name	Best Practice Description	Portfolio Domain	Program Domain	Project Domain	Organizational Enabler	Process Improvement Stage
1360	Standardize Project Control Quality Process	Control Quality Process standards are established.			Project		Standardize
1370	Standardize Project Control Risks Process	Control Risks Process standards are established.			Project		Standardize
1380	Standardize Project Close Procurements Process	Close Procurements Process standards are established.			Project		Standardize
1390	Standardize Close Project or Phase Process	Close Project or Phase Process standards are established.			Project		Standardize
1400	Staff Organizational Project Management With Competent Resources	The organization provides organizational project management with an adequate workforce with the right level of competence for each project-related role.	Portfolio	Program	Project	Competency Management	
1430	Establish Project Manager Competency Processes	The organization establishes a process to ensure project managers have sufficient knowledge and experience.			Project	Competency Management	
1450	Establish Strong Sponsorship	Sponsors actively participate in supporting the project.	Portfolio	Program	Project	Sponsorship	
1460	Tailor Project Management Processes Flexibly	The organization applies processes in a manner that is relevant to each project.	Portfolio	Program	Project	Organizational Project Management Methodology	
1530	Use Formal Individual Performance Assessment	The organization integrates PM performance in their formal processes and procedures to assess performance.	Portfolio			Individual Performance Appraisals	
1540	Include Strategic Goals Into Project Objectives	Objectives of projects include explicit strategic goals in addition to time, cost, and quality.			Project	Project Success Criteria	

Best Practice ID	Best Practice Name	Best Practice Description	Portfolio Domain	Program Domain	Project Domain	Organizational Enabler	Process Improvement Stage
1590	Record Project Resource Assignments	The organization has a formal process for assigning resources to projects and recording assignments.	Portfolio	Program	Project	Resource Allocation	
1670	Know Inter-Project Plan	Project Managers know the goals and plans of all projects related to their own projects. This allows them to explore alternative ways to avoid conflicts while still satisfying goals.			Project	Organizational Project Management Practices	
1700	Measure Develop Project Charter Process	Develop Project Charter Process measures are established, assembled, and analyzed.			Project		Measure
1710	Measure Develop Project Management Plan Process	Develop Project Management Plan Process measures are established, assembled, and analyzed.			Project		Measure
1720	Measure Project Collect Requirements Process	Collect Requirements Process measures are established, assembled, and analyzed.			Project		Measure
1730	Measure Project Define Scope Process	Define Scope Process measures are established, assembled, and analyzed.			Project		Measure
1740	Measure Project Define Activities Process	Define Activities Process measures are established, assembled, and analyzed.			Project		Measure
1750	Measure Project Sequence Activities Process	Sequence Activities Process measures are established, assembled, and analyzed.			Project		Measure

Best Practice ID	Best Practice Name	Best Practice Description	Portfolio Domain	Program Domain	Project Domain	Organizational Enabler	Process Improvement Stage
1760	Measure Project Estimate Activity Durations Process	Estimate Activity Durations Process measures are established, assembled, and analyzed.			Project		Measure
1770	Measure Project Develop Schedule Process	Develop Schedule Process measures are established, assembled, and analyzed.			Project		Measure
1780	Measure Project Plan Human Resource Management Process	Plan Human Resource Management Process measures are established, assembled, and analyzed.			Project		Measure
1790	Measure Project Estimate Costs Process	Estimate Costs Process measures are established, assembled, and analyzed.			Project		Measure
1800	Measure Project Determine Budget Process	Determine Budget Process measures are established, assembled, and analyzed.			Project		Measure
1810	Measure Project Plan Risk Management Process	Plan Risk Management Process measures are established, assembled, and analyzed.			Project		Measure
1820	Measure Project Plan Quality Management Process	Plan Quality Management Process measures are established, assembled, and analyzed.			Project		Measure
1840	Measure Acquire Project Team Process	Acquire Project Team Process measures are established, assembled, and analyzed.			Project		Measure

Best Practice ID	Best Practice Name	Best Practice Description	Portfolio Domain	Program Domain	Project Domain	Organizational Enabler	Process Improvement Stage
1850	Measure Project Plan Communications Management Process	Plan Communications Management Process measures are established, assembled, and analyzed.			Project		Measure
1860	Measure Project Identify Risks Process	Identify Risks Process measures are established, assembled, and analyzed.			Project		Measure
1870	Measure Project Perform Qualitative Risk Analysis Process	Perform Qualitative Risk Analysis Process measures are established, assembled, and analyzed.			Project		Measure
1880	Measure Project Perform Quantitative Risk Analysis Process	Perform Quantitative Risk Analysis Process measures are established, assembled, and analyzed.			Project		Measure
1890	Measure Project Plan Risk Responses Process	Plan Risk Responses Process measures are established, assembled, and analyzed.			Project		Measure
1900	Measure Project Plan Procurement Management Process	Plan Procurement Management Process measures are established, assembled, and analyzed.			Project		Measure
1920	Measure Direct and Manage Project Work Process	Direct and Manage Project Work Process measures are established, assembled, and analyzed.			Project		Measure
1930	Measure Project Perform Quality Assurance Process	Perform Quality Assurance Process measures are established, assembled, and analyzed.			Project		Measure

Best Practice ID	Best Practice Name	Best Practice Description	Portfolio Domain	Program Domain	Project Domain	Organizational Enabler	Process Improvement Stage
1940	Measure Develop Project Team Process	Develop Project Team Process measures are established, assembled, and analyzed.			Project		Measure
1950	Measure Project Manage Communications Process	Manage Communications Process measures are established, assembled, and analyzed.			Project		Measure
1960	Measure Project Conduct Procurements Process	Conduct Procurements Process measures are established, assembled, and analyzed.			Project		Measure
1980	Measure Project Control Procurements Process	Control Procurements Process measures are established, assembled, and analyzed.			Project		Measure
1990	Measure Project Control Communications Process	Control Communications Process measures are established, assembled, and analyzed.			Project		Measure
2000	Measure Project Perform Integrated Change Control Process	Perform Integrated Change Control Process measures are established, assembled, and analyzed.			Project		Measure
2005	Measure Project Identify Stakeholders Process	Identify Stakeholders Process measures are established, assembled, and analyzed.			Project		Measure
2010	Measure Project Validate Scope Process	Validate Scope Process measures are established, assembled, and analyzed.			Project		Measure

Best Practice ID	Best Practice Name	Best Practice Description	Portfolio Domain	Program Domain	Project Domain	Organizational Enabler	Process Improvement Stage
2015	Control Project Identify Stakeholders Process	Identify Stakeholders Process controls are established and executed to control the stability of the process.			Project		Control
2020	Measure Project Control Scope Process	Control Scope Process measures are established, assembled, and analyzed.			Project		Measure
2025	Improve Project Identify Stakeholders Process	Identify Stakeholders Process problem areas are assessed, root causes are identified, process improvement recommendations are collected, and process improvements are implemented.			Project		Improve
2030	Measure Project Control Schedule Process	Control Schedule Process measures are established, assembled, and analyzed.			Project		Measure
2035	Standardize Project Manage Stakeholder Engagement Process	Manage Stakeholder Engagement Process standards are established.			Project		Standardize
2040	Measure Project Control Costs Process	Control Costs Process measures are established, assembled, and analyzed.			Project		Measure
2045	Measure Project Manage Stakeholder Engagement Process	Manage Stakeholder Engagement Process measures are established, assembled, and analyzed.			Project		Measure
2050	Measure Project Control Quality Process	Control Quality Process measures are established, assembled, and analyzed.			Project		Measure

Best Practice ID	Best Practice Name	Best Practice Description	Portfolio Domain	Program Domain	Project Domain	Organizational Enabler	Process Improvement Stage
2055	Control Project Manage Stakeholder Engagement Process	Manage Stakeholder Engagement Process controls are established and executed to control the stability of the process.			Project		Control
2060	Measure Project Control Risks Process	Control Risks Process measures are established, assembled, and analyzed.			Project		Measure
2065	Improve Project Manage Stakeholder Engagement Process	Manage Stakeholder Engagement Process problem areas are assessed, root causes are identified, process improvement recommendations are collected, and process improvements are implemented.			Project		Improve
2070	Measure Project Close Procurements Process	Close Procurements Process measures are established, assembled, and analyzed.			Project		Measure
2080	Measure Close Project or Phase Process	Close Project or Phase Process measures are established, assembled, and analyzed.			Project		Measure
2090	Adhere to Project Management Techniques	The organization selects a core set of project management techniques to which it adapts and evolves over time. The organization also permits these techniques to be tailored based upon the specific needs of the project.			Project	Organizational Project Management Techniques	

Best Practice ID	Best Practice Name	Best Practice Description	Portfolio Domain	Program Domain	Project Domain	Organizational Enabler	Process Improvement Stage
2190	Benchmark Organizational Project Management Performance Against Industry Standards	The organization identifies external standards against which they measure organizational project management performance.	Portfolio	Program	Project	Benchmarking	
2240	Control Develop Project Charter Process	Develop Project Charter Process controls are established and executed to control the stability of the process.			Project		Control
2250	Control Develop Project Management Plan Process	Develop Project Management Plan Process controls are established and executed to control the stability of the process.			Project		Control
2260	Control Project Collect Requirements Process	Collect Requirements Process controls are established and executed to control the stability of the process.			Project		Control
2270	Control Project Define Scope Process	Define Scope Process controls are established and executed to control the stability of the process.			Project		Control
2280	Control Project Define Activities Process	Define Activities Process controls are established and executed to control the stability of the process.			Project		Control
2290	Control Project Sequence Activities Process	Sequence Activities Process controls are established and executed to control the stability of the process.			Project		Control

Best Practice ID	Best Practice Name	Best Practice Description	Portfolio Domain	Program Domain	Project Domain	Organizational Enabler	Process Improvement Stage
2300	Control Project Estimate Activity Durations Process	Estimate Activity Durations Process controls are established and executed to control the stability of the process.			Project		Control
2310	Control Project Develop Schedule Process	Develop Schedule Process controls are established and executed to control the stability of the process.			Project		Control
2320	Control Project Plan Human Resource Management Process	Plan Human Resource Management Process controls are established and executed to control the stability of the process.			Project		Control
2330	Control Project Estimate Costs Process	Estimate Costs Process controls are established and executed to control the stability of the process.			Project		Control
2340	Control Project Determine Budget Process	Determine Budget Process controls are established and executed to control the stability of the process.			Project		Control
2350	Control Project Plan Risk Management Process	Plan Risk Management Process controls are established and executed to control the stability of the process.			Project		Control
2360	Control Project Plan Quality Management Process	Plan Quality Management Process controls are established and executed to control the stability of the process.			Project		Control

Best Practice ID	Best Practice Name	Best Practice Description	Portfolio Domain	Program Domain	Project Domain	Organizational Enabler	Process Improvement Stage
2380	Control Acquire Project Team Process	Acquire Project Team Process controls are established and executed to control the stability of the process.			Project		Control
2390	Control Project Plan Communications Management Process	Plan Communications Management Process controls are established and executed to control the stability of the process.			Project		Control
2400	Control Project Identify Risks Process	Identify Risks Process controls are established and executed to control the stability of the process.			Project		Control
2410	Control Project Perform Qualitative Risk Analysis Process	Perform Qualitative Risk Analysis Process controls are established and executed to control the stability of the process.			Project		Control
2420	Control Project Perform Quantitative Risk Analysis Process	Perform Quantitative Risk Analysis Process controls are established and executed to control the stability of the process.			Project		Control
2430	Control Project Plan Risk Responses Process	Plan Risk Responses Process controls are established and executed to control the stability of the process.			Project		Control
2440	Control Project Plan Procurement Management Process	Plan Procurement Management Process controls are established and executed to control the stability of the process.			Project		Control

Best Practice ID	Best Practice Name	Best Practice Description	Portfolio Domain	Program Domain	Project Domain	Organizational Enabler	Process Improvement Stage
2460	Control Direct and Manage Project Work Process	Direct and Manage Project Work Process controls are established and executed to control the stability of the process.			Project		Control
2470	Control Project Perform Quality Assurance Process	Perform Quality Assurance Process controls are established and executed to control the stability of the process.			Project		Control
2480	Control Develop Project Team Process	Develop Project Team Process controls are established and executed to control the stability of the process.			Project		Control
2490	Control Project Manage Communications Process	Manage Communications Process controls are established and executed to control the stability of the process.			Project		Control
2500	Control Project Conduct Procurements Process	Conduct Procurements Process controls are established and executed to control the stability of the process.			Project		Control
2520	Control Project Control Procurements Process	Control Procurements Process controls are established and executed to control the stability of the process.			Project		Control
2530	Control Project Control Communications Process	Control Communications Process controls are established and executed to control the stability of the process.			Project		Control

Best Practice ID	Best Practice Name	Best Practice Description	Portfolio Domain	Program Domain	Project Domain	Organizational Enabler	Process Improvement Stage
2540	Control Project Perform Integrated Change Control Process	Perform Integrated Change Control Process controls are established and executed to control the stability of the process.			Project		Control
2550	Control Project Validate Scope Process	Validate Scope Process controls are established and executed to control the stability of the process.			Project		Control
2560	Control Project Control Scope Process	Control Scope Process controls are established and executed to control the stability of the process.			Project		Control
2570	Control Project Control Schedule Process	Control Schedule Process controls are established and executed to control the stability of the process.			Project		Control
2580	Control Project Control Costs Process	Control Costs Process controls are established and executed to control the stability of the process.			Project		Control
2590	Control Project Control Quality Process	Control Quality Process controls are established and executed to control the stability of the process.			Project		Control
2600	Control Project Control Risks Process	Control Risks Process controls are established and executed to control the stability of the process.			Project		Control

Best Practice ID	Best Practice Name	Best Practice Description	Portfolio Domain	Program Domain	Project Domain	Organizational Enabler	Process Improvement Stage
2610	Control Project Close Procurements Process	Close Procurements Process controls are established and executed to control the stability of the process.			Project		Control
2620	Control Close Project or Phase Process	Close Project or Phase Process controls are established and executed to control the stability of the process.			Project		Control
2630	Improve Develop Project Charter Process	Develop Project Charter Process problem areas are assessed, root causes are identified, process improvement recommendations are collected, and process improvements are implemented.			Project		Improve
2640	Improve Develop Project Management Plan Process	Develop Project Management Plan Process problem areas are assessed, root causes are identified, process improvement recommendations are collected, and process improvements are implemented.			Project		Improve
2650	Improve Project Collect Requirements Process	Collect Requirements Process problem areas are assessed, root causes are identified, process improvement recommendations are collected, and process improvements are implemented.			Project		Improve

Best Practice ID	Best Practice Name	Best Practice Description	Portfolio Domain	Program Domain	Project Domain	Organizational Enabler	Process Improvement Stage
2660	Improve Project Define Scope Process	Define Scope Process problem areas are assessed, root causes are identified, process improvement recommendations are collected, and process improvements are implemented.			Project		Improve
2670	Improve Project Define Activities Process	Define Activities Process problem areas are assessed, root causes are identified, process improvement recommendations are collected, and process improvements are implemented.			Project		Improve
2680	Improve Project Sequence Activities Process	Sequence Activities Process problem areas are assessed, root causes are identified, process improvement recommendations are collected, and process improvements are implemented.			Project		Improve
2690	Improve Project Estimate Activity Durations Process	Estimate Activity Durations Process problem areas are assessed, root causes are identified, process improvement recommendations are collected, and process improvements are implemented.			Project		Improve
2700	Improve Project Develop Schedule Process	Develop Schedule Process problem areas are assessed, root causes are identified, process improvement recommendations are collected, and process improvements are implemented.			Project		Improve

Best Practice ID	Best Practice Name	Best Practice Description	Portfolio Domain	Program Domain	Project Domain	Organizational Enabler	Process Improvement Stage
2710	Improve Project Plan Human Resource Management Process	Plan Human Resource Management Process problem areas are assessed, root causes are identified, process improvement recommendations are collected, and process improvements are implemented.			Project		Improve
2720	Improve Project Estimate Costs Process	Estimate Costs Process problem areas are assessed, root causes are identified, process improvement recommendations are collected, and process improvements are implemented.			Project		Improve
2730	Improve Project Determine Budget Process	Determine Budget Process problem areas are assessed, root causes are identified, process improvement recommendations are collected, and process improvements are implemented.			Project		Improve
2740	Improve Project Plan Risk Management Process	Plan Risk Management Process problem areas are assessed, root causes are identified, process improvement recommendations are collected, and process improvements are implemented.			Project		Improve
2750	Improve Project Plan Quality Management Process	Plan Quality Management Process problem areas are assessed, root causes are identified, process improvement recommendations are collected, and process improvements are implemented.			Project		Improve

Best Practice ID	Best Practice Name	Best Practice Description	Portfolio Domain	Program Domain	Project Domain	Organizational Enabler	Process Improvement Stage
2770	Improve Acquire Project Team Process	Acquire Project Team Process problem areas are assessed, root causes are identified, process improvement recommendations are collected, and process improvements are implemented.			Project		Improve
2780	Improve Project Plan Communications Management Process	Plan Communications Management Process problem areas are assessed, root causes are identified, process improvement recommendations are collected, and process improvements are implemented.			Project		Improve
2790	Improve Project Identify Risks Process	Identify Risks Process problem areas are assessed, root causes are identified, process improvement recommendations are collected, and process improvements are implemented.			Project		Improve
2800	Improve Project Perform Qualitative Risk Analysis Process	Perform Qualitative Risk Analysis Process problem areas are assessed, root causes are identified, process improvement recommendations are collected, and process improvements are implemented.			Project		Improve
2810	Improve Project Perform Quantitative Risk Analysis Process	Perform Quantitative Risk Analysis Process problem areas are assessed, root causes are identified, process improvement recommendations are collected, and process improvements are implemented.			Project		Improve

Best Practice ID	Best Practice Name	Best Practice Description	Portfolio Domain	Program Domain	Project Domain	Organizational Enabler	Process Improvement Stage
2820	Improve Project Plan Risk Responses Process	Plan Risk Responses Process problem areas are assessed, root causes are identified, process improvement recommendations are collected, and process improvements are implemented.			Project		Improve
2830	Improve Project Plan Procurement Management Process	Plan Procurement Management Process problem areas are assessed, root causes are identified, process improvement recommendations are collected, and process improvements are implemented.			Project		Improve
2850	Improve Direct and Manage Project Work Process	Direct and Manage Project Work Process problem areas are assessed, root causes are identified, process improvement recommendations are collected, and process improvements are implemented.			Project		Improve
2860	Improve Project Perform Quality Assurance Process	Perform Quality Assurance Process problem areas are assessed, root causes are identified, process improvement recommendations are collected, and process improvements are implemented.			Project		Improve
2870	Improve Develop Project Team Process	Develop Project Team Process problem areas are assessed, root causes are identified, process improvement recommendations are collected, and process improvements are implemented.			Project		Improve

Best Practice ID	Best Practice Name	Best Practice Description	Portfolio Domain	Program Domain	Project Domain	Organizational Enabler	Process Improvement Stage
2880	Improve Project Manage Communications Process	Manage Communications Process problem areas are assessed, root causes are identified, process improvement recommendations are collected, and process improvements are implemented.			Project		Improve
2890	Improve Project Conduct Procurements Process	Conduct Procurements Process problem areas are assessed, root causes are identified, process improvement recommendations are collected, and process improvements are implemented.			Project		Improve
2910	Improve Project Control Procurements Process	Control Procurements Process problem areas are assessed, root causes are identified, process improvement recommendations are collected, and process improvements are implemented.			Project		Improve
2920	Improve Project Control Communications Process	Control Communications Process problem areas are assessed, root causes are identified, process improvement recommendations are collected, and process improvements are implemented.			Project		Improve
2930	Improve Project Perform Integrated Change Control Process	Perform Integrated Change Control Process problem areas are assessed, root causes are identified, process improvement recommendations are collected, and process improvements are implemented.			Project		Improve

Best Practice ID	Best Practice Name	Best Practice Description	Portfolio Domain	Program Domain	Project Domain	Organizational Enabler	Process Improvement Stage
2940	Improve Project Validate Scope Process	Validate Scope Process problem areas are assessed, root causes are identified, process improvement recommendations are collected, and process improvements are implemented.			Project		Improve
2950	Improve Project Control Scope Process	Control Scope Process problem areas are assessed, root causes are identified, process improvement recommendations are collected, and process improvements are implemented.			Project		Improve
2960	Improve Project Control Schedule Process	Control Schedule Process problem areas are assessed, root causes are identified, process improvement recommendations are collected, and process improvements are implemented.			Project		Improve
2970	Improve Project Control Costs Process	Control Costs Process problem areas are assessed, root causes are identified, process improvement recommendations are collected, and process improvements are implemented.			Project		Improve
2980	Improve Project Control Quality Process	Control Quality Process problem areas are assessed, root causes are identified, process improvement recommendations are collected, and process improvements are implemented.			Project		Improve

Best Practice ID	Best Practice Name	Best Practice Description	Portfolio Domain	Program Domain	Project Domain	Organizational Enabler	Process Improvement Stage
2990	Improve Project Control Risks Process	Control Risks Process problem areas are assessed, root causes are identified, process improvement recommendations are collected, and process improvements are implemented.			Project		Improve
3000	Improve Project Close Procurements Process	Close Procurements Process problem areas are assessed, root causes are identified, process improvement recommendations are collected, and process improvements are implemented.			Project		Improve
3010	Improve Close Project or Phase Process	Close Project or Phase Process problem areas are assessed, root causes are identified, process improvement recommendations are collected, and process improvements are implemented.			Project		Improve
3030	Capture and Share Lessons Learned	The organization collects and shares lessons learned from projects, programs, and portfolios.	Portfolio	Program	Project	Knowledge Management and PMIS	
3070	Encourage Risk Taking	The organization encourages project teams to take calculated risks that enhance project performance.			Project	Organizational Project Management Techniques	
3120	Standardize Program Initiation Process	Program Initiation Process standards are established.		Program			Standardize
3130	Standardize Program Management Plan Development Process	Program Management Plan Development Process standards are established.		Program			Standardize

Best Practice ID	Best Practice Name	Best Practice Description	Portfolio Domain	Program Domain	Project Domain	Organizational Enabler	Process Improvement Stage
3140	Standardize Program Scope Planning Process	Program Scope Planning Process standards are established.		Program			Standardize
3155	Standardize Program Infrastructure Development Process	Program Infrastructure Development Process standards are established.		Program			Standardize
3165	Measure Program Infrastructure Development Process	Program Infrastructure Development Process measures are established, assembled, and analyzed.		Program			Measure
3175	Control Program Infrastructure Development Process	Program Infrastructure Development Process controls are established and executed to control the stability of the process.		Program			Control
3185	Improve Program Infrastructure Development Process	Program Infrastructure Development Process problem areas are assessed, root causes are identified, process improvement recommendations are collected, and process improvements are implemented.		Program			Improve
3190	Standardize Program Schedule Planning Process	Program Schedule Planning Process standards are established.		Program			Standardize
3210	Standardize Program Cost Estimation Process	Program Cost Estimation Process standards are established.		Program			Standardize
3215	Standardize Program Performance Monitoring and Control Process	Program Performance Monitoring and Control Process standards are established.		Program			Standardize

Best Practice ID	Best Practice Name	Best Practice Description	Portfolio Domain	Program Domain	Project Domain	Organizational Enabler	Process Improvement Stage
3220	Standardize Program Cost Budgeting Process	Program Cost Budgeting Process standards are established.		Program			Standardize
3225	Measure Program Performance Monitoring and Control Process	Program Performance Monitoring and Control Process measures are established, assembled, and analyzed.		Program			Measure
3230	Standardize Program Risk Management Planning Process	Program Risk Management Planning Process standards are established.		Program			Standardize
3235	Control Program Performance Monitoring and Control Process	Program Performance Monitoring and Control Process controls are established and executed to control the stability of the process.		Program			Control
3240	Standardize Program Quality Planning Process	Program Quality Planning Process standards are established.		Program			Standardize
3245	Improve Program Performance Monitoring and Control Process	Program Performance Monitoring and Control Process problem areas are assessed, root causes are identified, process improvement recommendations are collected, and process improvements are implemented.		Program			Improve
3270	Standardize Program Communications Planning Process	Communications Planning Process standards are established.		Program			Standardize
3280	Standardize Program Risk Identification Process	Program Risk Identification Process standards are established.		Program			Standardize
3310	Standardize Program Risk Response Planning Process	Program Risk Response Planning Process standards are established.		Program			Standardize

Best Practice ID	Best Practice Name	Best Practice Description	Portfolio Domain	Program Domain	Project Domain	Organizational Enabler	Process Improvement Stage
3320	Standardize Program Procurement Planning Process	Program Procurement Planning Process standards are established.		Program			Standardize
3340	Standardize Program Execution Management Process	Program Execution Management Process standards are established.		Program			Standardize
3370	Standardize Program Information Distribution Process	Information Distribution Process standards are established.		Program			Standardize
3400	Standardize Program Procurement Administration Process	Program Procurement Administration Process standards are established.		Program			Standardize
3410	Standardize Program Performance Reporting Process	Program Performance Reporting Process standards are established.		Program			Standardize
3440	Standardize Program Scope Control Process	Program Scope Control Process standards are established.		Program			Standardize
3450	Standardize Program Schedule Control Process	Program Schedule Control Process standards are established.		Program			Standardize
3480	Standardize Program Risk Monitoring and Control Process	Program Risk Monitoring and Control Process standards are established.		Program			Standardize
3490	Standardize Program Procurement Closure Process	Program Procurement Closure Process standards are established.		Program			Standardize
3500	Standardize Program Closure Process	Program Closure Process standards are established.		Program			Standardize
3590	Measure Program Initiation Process	Program Initiation Process measures are established, assembled, and analyzed.		Program			Measure

Best Practice ID	Best Practice Name	Best Practice Description	Portfolio Domain	Program Domain	Project Domain	Organizational Enabler	Process Improvement Stage
3600	Measure Program Management Plan Development Process	Program Management Plan Development Process measures are established, assembled, and analyzed.		Program			Measure
3605	Standardize Program Risk Analysis Process	Program Risk Analysis Process standards are established.		Program			Standardize
3610	Measure Program Scope Planning Process	Program Scope Planning Process measures are established, assembled, and analyzed.		Program			Measure
3615	Measure Program Risk Analysis Process	Program Risk Analysis Process measures are established, assembled, and analyzed.		Program			Measure
3625	Control Program Risk Analysis Process	Program Risk Analysis Process controls are established and executed to control the stability of the process.		Program			Control
3635	Improve Program Risk Analysis Process	Program Risk Analysis Process problem areas are assessed, root causes are identified, process improvement recommendations are collected, and process improvements are implemented.		Program			Improve
3655	Standardize Program Procurement Process	Program Procurement Process standards are established.		Program			Standardize
3660	Measure Program Schedule Planning Process	Program Schedule Planning Process measures are established, assembled, and analyzed.		Program			Measure

Best Practice ID	Best Practice Name	Best Practice Description	Portfolio Domain	Program Domain	Project Domain	Organizational Enabler	Process Improvement Stage
3665	Measure Program Procurement Process	Program Procurement Process measures are established, assembled, and analyzed.		Program			Measure
3675	Control Program Procurement Process	Program Procurement Process controls are established and executed to control the stability of the process.		Program			Control
3680	Measure Program Cost Estimation Process	Program Cost Estimation Process measures are established, assembled, and analyzed.		Program			Measure
3685	Improve Program Procurement Process	Program Procurement Process problem areas are assessed, root causes are identified, process improvement recommendations are collected, and process improvements are implemented.		Program			Improve
3690	Measure Program Cost Budgeting Process	Program Cost Budgeting Process measures are established, assembled, and analyzed.		Program			Measure
3700	Measure Program Risk Management Planning Process	Program Risk Management Planning Process measures are established, assembled, and analyzed.		Program			Measure
3705	Standardize Program Financial Framework Establishment Process	Program Financial Framework Establishment Process standards are established.		Program			Standardize

Best Practice ID	Best Practice Name	Best Practice Description	Portfolio Domain	Program Domain	Project Domain	Organizational Enabler	Process Improvement Stage
3710	Measure Program Quality Planning Process	Program Quality Planning Process measures are established, assembled, and analyzed.		Program			Measure
3715	Measure Program Financial Framework Establishment Process	Program Financial Framework Establishment Process measures are established, assembled, and analyzed.		Program			Measure
3725	Control Program Financial Framework Establishment Process	Program Financial Framework Establishment Process controls are established and executed to control the stability of the process.		Program			Control
3735	Improve Program Financial Framework Establishment Process	Program Financial Framework Establishment Process problem areas are assessed, root causes are identified, process improvement recommendations are collected, and process improvements are implemented.		Program			Improve
3740	Measure Program Communications Planning Process	Communications Planning Process measures are established, assembled, and analyzed.		Program			Measure
3745	Standardize Program Financial Management Plan Development Process	Program Financial Management Plan Development Process standards are established.		Program			Standardize

Best Practice ID	Best Practice Name	Best Practice Description	Portfolio Domain	Program Domain	Project Domain	Organizational Enabler	Process Improvement Stage
3750	Measure Program Risk Identification Process	Program Risk Identification Process measures are established, assembled, and analyzed.		Program			Measure
3755	Measure Program Financial Management Plan Development Process	Program Financial Management Plan Development Process measures are established, assembled, and analyzed.		Program			Measure
3765	Control Program Financial Management Plan Development Process	Program Financial Management Plan Development Process controls are established and executed to control the stability of the process.		Program			Control
3775	Improve Program Financial Management Plan Development Process	Program Financial Management Plan Development Process problem areas are assessed, root causes are identified, process improvement recommendations are collected, and process improvements are implemented.		Program			Improve
3780	Measure Program Risk Response Planning Process	Program Risk Response Planning Process measures are established, assembled, and analyzed.		Program			Measure
3790	Measure Program Procurement Planning Process	Program Procurement Planning Process measures are established, assembled, and analyzed.		Program			Measure

Best Practice ID	Best Practice Name	Best Practice Description	Portfolio Domain	Program Domain	Project Domain	Organizational Enabler	Process Improvement Stage
3805	Standardize Program Financial Monitoring and Control Process	Program Financial Monitoring and Control Process standards are established.		Program			Standardize
3810	Measure Program Execution Management Process	Program Execution Management Process measures are established, assembled, and analyzed.		Program			Measure
3815	Measure Program Financial Monitoring and Control Process	Program Financial Monitoring and Control Process measures are established, assembled, and analyzed.		Program			Measure
3825	Control Program Financial Monitoring and Control Process	Program Financial Monitoring and Control Process controls are established and executed to control the stability of the process.		Program			Control
3835	Improve Program Financial Monitoring and Control Process	Program Financial Monitoring and Control Process problem areas are assessed, root causes are identified, process improvement recommendations are collected, and process improvements are implemented.		Program			Improve
3840	Measure Program Information Distribution Process	Information Distribution Process measures are established, assembled, and analyzed.		Program			Measure
3870	Measure Program Procurement Administration Process	Program Procurement Administration Process measures are established, assembled, and analyzed.		Program			Measure

Best Practice ID	Best Practice Name	Best Practice Description	Portfolio Domain	Program Domain	Project Domain	Organizational Enabler	Process Improvement Stage
3880	Measure Program Performance Reporting Process	Program Performance Reporting Process measures are established, assembled, and analyzed.		Program			Measure
3910	Measure Program Scope Control Process	Program Scope Control Process measures are established, assembled, and analyzed.		Program			Measure
3920	Measure Program Schedule Control Process	Program Schedule Control Process measures are established, assembled, and analyzed.		Program			Measure
3950	Measure Program Risk Monitoring and Control Process	Program Risk Monitoring and Control Process measures are established, assembled, and analyzed.		Program			Measure
3960	Measure Program Procurement Closure Process	Program Procurement Closure Process measures are established, assembled, and analyzed.		Program			Measure
3970	Measure Program Closure Process	Program Closure Process measures are established, assembled, and analyzed.		Program			Measure
4000	Control Program Initiation Process	Program Initiation Process controls are established and executed to control the stability of the process.		Program			Control
4010	Control Program Management Plan Development Process	Program Management Plan Development Process controls are established and executed to control the stability of the process.		Program			Control

Best Practice ID	Best Practice Name	Best Practice Description	Portfolio Domain	Program Domain	Project Domain	Organizational Enabler	Process Improvement Stage
4020	Control Program Scope Planning Process	Program Scope Planning Process controls are established and executed to control the stability of the process.		Program			Control
4070	Control Program Schedule Planning Process	Program Schedule Planning Process controls are established and executed to control the stability of the process.		Program			Control
4090	Control Program Cost Estimation Process	Program Cost Estimation Process controls are established and executed to control the stability of the process.		Program			Control
4100	Control Program Cost Budgeting Process	Program Cost Budgeting Process controls are established and executed to control the stability of the process.		Program			Control
4110	Control Program Risk Management Planning Process	Program Risk Management Planning Process controls are established and executed to control the stability of the process.		Program			Control
4120	Control Program Quality Planning Process	Program Quality Planning Process controls are established and executed to control the stability of the process.		Program			Control
4150	Control Program Communications Planning Process	Communications Planning Process controls are established and executed to control the stability of the process.		Program			Control

Best Practice ID	Best Practice Name	Best Practice Description	Portfolio Domain	Program Domain	Project Domain	Organizational Enabler	Process Improvement Stage
4160	Control Program Risk Identification Process	Program Risk Identification Process controls are established and executed to control the stability of the process.		Program			Control
4190	Control Program Risk Response Planning Process	Program Risk Response Planning Process controls are established and executed to control the stability of the process.		Program			Control
4200	Control Program Procurement Planning Process	Program Procurement Planning Process controls are established and executed to control the stability of the process.		Program			Control
4220	Control Program Execution Management Process	Program Execution Management Process controls are established and executed to control the stability of the process.		Program			Control
4250	Control Program Information Distribution Process	Information Distribution Process controls are established and executed to control the stability of the process.		Program			Control
4280	Control Program Procurement Administration Process	Program Procurement Administration Process controls are established and executed to control the stability of the process.		Program			Control
4290	Control Program Performance Reporting Process	Program Performance Reporting Process controls are established and executed to control the stability of the process.		Program			Control

Best Practice ID	Best Practice Name	Best Practice Description	Portfolio Domain	Program Domain	Project Domain	Organizational Enabler	Process Improvement Stage
4320	Control Program Scope Control Process	Program Scope Control Process controls are established and executed to control the stability of the process.		Program			Control
4330	Control Program Schedule Control Process	Program Schedule Control Process controls are established and executed to control the stability of the process.		Program			Control
4355	Standardize Program Transition and Benefits Sustainment Process	Program Transition and Benefits Sustainment Process standards are established.		Program			Standardize
4360	Control Program Risk Monitoring and Control Process	Program Risk Monitoring and Control Process controls are established and executed to control the stability of the process.		Program			Control
4365	Measure Program Transition and Benefits Sustainment Process	Program Transition and Benefits Sustainment Process measures are established, assembled, and analyzed.		Program			Measure
4370	Control Program Procurement Closure Process	Program Procurement Closure Process controls are established and executed to control the stability of the process.		Program			Control
4375	Control Program Transition and Benefits Sustainment Process	Program Transition and Benefits Sustainment Process controls are established and executed to control the stability of the process.		Program			Control

Best Practice ID	Best Practice Name	Best Practice Description	Portfolio Domain	Program Domain	Project Domain	Organizational Enabler	Process Improvement Stage
4380	Control Program Closure Process	Program Closure Process controls are established and executed to control the stability of the process.		Program			Control
4385	Improve Program Transition and Benefits Sustainment Process	Program Transition and Benefits Sustainment Process problem areas are assessed, root causes are identified, process improvement recommendations are collected, and process improvements are implemented.		Program			Improve
4390	Improve Program Initiation Process	Program Initiation Process problem areas are assessed, root causes are identified, process improvement recommendations are collected, and process improvements are implemented.		Program			Improve
4405	Improve Program Management Plan Development Process	Program Management Plan Development Process problem areas are assessed, root causes are identified, process improvement recommendations are collected, and process improvements are implemented.		Program			Improve
4410	Improve Program Scope Planning Process	Program Scope Planning Process problem areas are assessed, root causes are identified, process improvement recommendations are collected, and process improvements are implemented.		Program			Improve

Best Practice ID	Best Practice Name	Best Practice Description	Portfolio Domain	Program Domain	Project Domain	Organizational Enabler	Process Improvement Stage
4460	Improve Program Schedule Planning Process	Program Schedule Planning Process problem areas are assessed, root causes are identified, process improvement recommendations are collected, and process improvements are implemented.		Program			Improve
4480	Improve Program Cost Estimation Process	Program Cost Estimation Process problem areas are assessed, root causes are identified, process improvement recommendations are collected, and process improvements are implemented.		Program			Improve
4490	Improve Program Cost Budgeting Process	Program Cost Budgeting Process problem areas are assessed, root causes are identified, process improvement recommendations are collected, and process improvements are implemented.		Program			Improve
4500	Improve Program Risk Management Planning Process	Program Risk Management Planning Process problem areas are assessed, root causes are identified, process improvement recommendations are collected, and process improvements are implemented.		Program			Improve
4510	Improve Program Quality Planning Process	Program Quality Planning Process problem areas are assessed, root causes are identified, process improvement recommendations are collected, and process improvements are implemented.		Program			Improve

Best Practice ID	Best Practice Name	Best Practice Description	Portfolio Domain	Program Domain	Project Domain	Organizational Enabler	Process Improvement Stage
4540	Improve Program Communications Planning Process	Communications Planning Process problem areas are assessed, root causes are identified, process improvement recommendations are collected, and process improvements are implemented.		Program			Improve
4550	Improve Program Risk Identification Process	Program Risk Identification Process problem areas are assessed, root causes are identified, process improvement recommendations are collected, and process improvements are implemented.		Program			Improve
4580	Improve Program Risk Response Planning Process	Program Risk Response Planning Process problem areas are assessed, root causes are identified, process improvement recommendations are collected, and process improvements are implemented.		Program			Improve
4590	Improve Program Procurement Planning Process	Program Procurement Planning Process problem areas are assessed, root causes are identified, process improvement recommendations are collected, and process improvements are implemented.		Program			Improve
4610	Improve Program Execution Management Process	Program Execution Management Process problem areas are assessed, root causes are identified, process improvement recommendations are collected, and process improvements are implemented.		Program			Improve

Best Practice ID	Best Practice Name	Best Practice Description	Portfolio Domain	Program Domain	Project Domain	Organizational Enabler	Process Improvement Stage
4640	Improve Program Information Distribution Process	Information Distribution Process problem areas are assessed, root causes are identified, process improvement recommendations are collected, and process improvements are implemented.		Program			Improve
4670	Improve Program Procurement Administration Process	Program Procurement Administration Process problem areas are assessed, root causes are identified, process improvement recommendations are collected, and process improvements are implemented.		Program			Improve
4680	Improve Program Performance Reporting Process	Program Performance Reporting Process problem areas are assessed, root causes are identified, process improvement recommendations are collected, and process improvements are implemented.		Program			Improve
4710	Improve Program Scope Control Process	Program Scope Control Process problem areas are assessed, root causes are identified, process improvement recommendations are collected, and process improvements are implemented.		Program			Improve
4720	Improve Program Schedule Control Process	Program Schedule Control Process problem areas are assessed, root causes are identified, process improvement recommendations are collected, and process improvements are implemented.		Program			Improve

Best Practice ID	Best Practice Name	Best Practice Description	Portfolio Domain	Program Domain	Project Domain	Organizational Enabler	Process Improvement Stage
4750	Improve Program Risk Monitoring and Control Process	Program Risk Monitoring and Control Process problem areas are assessed, root causes are identified, process improvement recommendations are collected, and process improvements are implemented.		Program			Improve
4760	Improve Program Procurement Closure Process	Program Procurement Closure Process problem areas are assessed, root causes are identified, process improvement recommendations are collected, and process improvements are implemented.		Program			Improve
4770	Improve Program Closure Process	Program Closure Process problem areas are assessed, root causes are identified, process improvement recommendations are collected, and process improvements are implemented.		Program			Improve
4945	Standardize Define Portfolio Process	Define Portfolio Process standards are established.	Portfolio				Standardize
4955	Measure Define Portfolio Process	Define Portfolio Process measures are established, assembled, and analyzed.	Portfolio				Measure
4965	Control Define Portfolio Process	Define Portfolio Process controls are established and executed to control the stability of the process.	Portfolio				Control

Best Practice ID	Best Practice Name	Best Practice Description	Portfolio Domain	Program Domain	Project Domain	Organizational Enabler	Process Improvement Stage
4975	Improve Define Portfolio Process	Define Portfolio Process problem areas are assessed, root causes are identified, process improvement recommendations are collected, and process improvements are implemented.	Portfolio				Improve
4985	Standardize Optimize Portfolio Process	Optimize Portfolio Process standards are established.	Portfolio				Standardize
4995	Measure Optimize Portfolio Process	Optimize Portfolio Process measures are established, assembled, and analyzed.	Portfolio				Measure
5005	Control Optimize Portfolio Process	Optimize Portfolio Process controls are established and executed to control the stability of the process.	Portfolio				Control
5015	Improve Optimize Portfolio Process	Optimize Portfolio Process problem areas are assessed, root causes are identified, process improvement recommendations are collected, and process improvements are implemented.	Portfolio				Improve
5025	Standardize Authorize Portfolio Process	Authorize Portfolio Process standards are established.	Portfolio				Standardize
5030	Standardize Develop Portfolio Communication Management Plan Process	Develop Portfolio Communication Management Plan Process standards are established.	Portfolio				Standardize
5035	Measure Authorize Portfolio Process	Authorize Portfolio Process measures are established, assembled, and analyzed.	Portfolio				Measure
5045	Control Authorize Portfolio Process	Authorize Portfolio Process controls are established and executed to control the stability of the process.	Portfolio				Control

Best Practice ID	Best Practice Name	Best Practice Description	Portfolio Domain	Program Domain	Project Domain	Organizational Enabler	Process Improvement Stage
5055	Improve Authorize Portfolio Process	Authorize Portfolio Process problem areas are assessed, root causes are identified, process improvement recommendations are collected, and process improvements are implemented.	Portfolio				Improve
5070	Standardize Manage Portfolio Information Process	Manage Portfolio Information Process standards are established.	Portfolio				Standardize
5080	Standardize Portfolio Manage Strategic Change Process	Manage Strategic Change Process standards are established.	Portfolio				Standardize
5140	Standardize Manage Portfolio Risks Process	Manage Portfolio Risks Process standards are established.	Portfolio				Standardize
5170	Use Common Project Language	The organization uses a common language to describe project activities and deliverables.	Portfolio			Organizational Project Management Techniques	
5180	Educate Executives	The organization educates its executives on the benefits of organizational project management.	Portfolio	Program	Project	Organizational Project Management Policy and Vision	
5190	Facilitate Project Manager Development	The organization ensures project manager development.	Portfolio	Program	Project	Competency Management	
5200	Provide Project Management Training	The organization provides project management training appropriate for all roles within the project hierarchy.	Portfolio	Program	Project	Project Management Training	
5210	Provide Continuous Training	The organization provides continuous training in the use of tools, methodology, and deployment of knowledge.	Portfolio	Program	Project	Project Management Training	

Best Practice ID	Best Practice Name	Best Practice Description	Portfolio Domain	Program Domain	Project Domain	Organizational Enabler	Process Improvement Stage
5220	Provide Competent Organizational Project Management Resources	The organization's project management community provides sufficient competent resources to manage organizational project management.	Portfolio	Program	Project	Resource Allocation	
5240	Establish Internal Project Management Communities	The organization establishes an internal community that supports project management.	Portfolio	Program	Project	Organizational Project Management Communities	
5250	Interact With External Project Management Communities	The organization encourages membership of external communities that support project management expertise. These can include professional associations or initiatives.	Portfolio	Program	Project	Organizational Project Management Communities	
5260	Customize Project Management Methodology	The organization customizes a generally accepted project management methodology to meet organizational requirements.			Project	Organizational Project Management Methodology	
5270	Integrate Project Management Methodology with Organizational Processes	The organization integrates the project management methodology with strategic, operational, and tactical processes.	Portfolio	Program	Project	Organizational Project Management Methodology	
5280	Establish Common Project Management Framework	The organization uses a project management framework for all phases of a project.	Portfolio	Program	Project	Management Systems	
5300	Establish Training and Development Program	The organization establishes a training and development program to improve the skills of project personnel.	Portfolio	Program	Project	Project Management Training	
5320	Certify Quality Management System	Independent bodies certify the quality management system.	Portfolio			Management Systems	

Best Practice ID	Best Practice Name	Best Practice Description	Portfolio Domain	Program Domain	Project Domain	Organizational Enabler	Process Improvement Stage
5340	Establish Executive Support	The executives strongly support the project management process.	Portfolio	Program	Project	Sponsorship	
5490	Recognize Value of Project Management	The organization recognizes the value of project management.	Portfolio	Program	Project	Organizational Project Management Policy and Vision	
5500	Define Project Management Values	The organization defines and applies project management vision and values within the organization.	Portfolio	Program	Project	Organizational Project Management Policy and Vision	
5520	Collaborate on Goals	People in different roles and functions throughout the organization collaborate to define and agree on common goals.			Project	Organizational Project Management Policy and Vision	
5620	Establish Career Path for all Organizational Project Management Roles	The organization has progressive career paths for organizational project management related roles.	Portfolio	Program	Project	Competency Management	
5940	Measure Develop Portfolio Communication Management Plan Process	Develop Portfolio Communication Management Plan Process measures are established, assembled, and analyzed.	Portfolio				Measure
5980	Measure Manage Portfolio Information Process	Manage Portfolio Information Process measures are established, assembled, and analyzed.	Portfolio				Measure
5990	Measure Portfolio Manage Strategic Change Process	Manage Strategic Change Process measures are established, assembled, and analyzed.	Portfolio				Measure

Best Practice ID	Best Practice Name	Best Practice Description	Portfolio Domain	Program Domain	Project Domain	Organizational Enabler	Process Improvement Stage
6050	Measure Manage Portfolio Risks Process	Manage Portfolio Risks Process measures are established, assembled, and analyzed.	Portfolio				Measure
6450	Control Develop Portfolio Communication Management Plan Process	Develop Portfolio Communication Management Plan Process controls are established and executed to control the stability of the process.	Portfolio				Control
6490	Control Manage Portfolio Information Process	Manage Portfolio Information Process controls are established and executed to control the stability of the process.	Portfolio				Control
6500	Control Portfolio Manage Strategic Change Process	Manage Strategic Change Process controls are established and executed to control the stability of the process.	Portfolio				Control
6560	Control Manage Portfolio Risks Process	Manage Portfolio Risks Process controls are established and executed to control the stability of the process.	Portfolio				Control
6840	Improve Develop Portfolio Communication Management Plan Process	Develop Portfolio Communication Management Plan Process problem areas are assessed, root causes are identified, process improvement recommendations are collected, and process improvements are implemented.	Portfolio				Improve
6880	Improve Manage Portfolio Information Process	Manage Portfolio Information Process problem areas are assessed, root causes are identified, process improvement recommendations are collected, and process improvements are implemented.	Portfolio				Improve

Best Practice ID	Best Practice Name	Best Practice Description	Portfolio Domain	Program Domain	Project Domain	Organizational Enabler	Process Improvement Stage
6890	Improve Portfolio Manage Strategic Change Process	Manage Strategic Change Process problem areas are assessed, root causes are identified, process improvement recommendations are collected, and process improvements are implemented.	Portfolio				Improve
6950	Improve Manage Portfolio Risks Process	Manage Portfolio Risks Process problem areas are assessed, root causes are identified, process improvement recommendations are collected, and process improvements are implemented.	Portfolio				Improve
6980	Create an Organizational Maturity Development Program	The organization creates a program to achieve project management maturity.	Portfolio			Organizational Project Management Policy and Vision	
7005	OPM Leadership Program	The organization has a leadership program for their OPM managers.	Portfolio	Program	Project	Organizational Project Management Policy and Vision	
7015	Educate Stakeholders in OPM	The organization educates stakeholders in OPM.	Portfolio	Program	Project	Organizational Project Management Policy and Vision	
7025	Cultural Diversity Awareness	Educate employees on cultural diversity and empower them for working in a multi-cultural environment.	Portfolio	Program	Project	Organizational Project Management Policy and Vision	
7035	Organizational Business Change Management Program	The organization has a business change management program.	Portfolio			Strategic Alignment	
7045	Establish Organizational Project Management Structure	The organization has determined the appropriate organizational structure to support organizational project management.	Portfolio	Program	Project	Organizational Structures	
7055	Adopt Organizational Project Management Structure	Adopt organizational project management structure across the organization.	Portfolio	Program	Project	Organizational Structures	

Best Practice ID	Best Practice Name	Best Practice Description	Portfolio Domain	Program Domain	Project Domain	Organizational Enabler	Process Improvement Stage
7065	Institutionalize Organizational Project Management Structure	Institutionalize the organizational project management structure across the organization.	Portfolio	Program	Project	Organizational Structures	
7075	Provide Organizational Project Management Support Office	The organization has an organizational project management support office structure.	Portfolio	Program		Organizational Structures	
7105	Manage the Holistic View of the Project	The project managers understand stakeholder needs, project impacts to the overall organization environment, organizational structures both formal and informal, politics, and uses emotional intelligence to understand and explain others' action and attitudes.	Portfolio	Program	Project	Competency Management	
7115	Manage the Environment	Project managers effectively manage project environment.	Portfolio	Program	Project	Competency Management	
7125	The Organization Manages Self Development	The organization provides project managers the ability to effectively manage and develop their competencies.		Program	Project	Competency Management	
7135	Demonstrate Competency in Initiating a Project	The organization's project managers demonstrate their competencies in initiating a project.			Project	Competency Management	
7145	Demonstrate Competency in Planning a Project	The organization's project managers demonstrate their competencies in planning a project.			Project	Competency Management	
7155	Demonstrate Competency in Executing a Project	The organization's project managers demonstrate their competencies in executing a project.			Project	Competency Management	

Best Practice ID	Best Practice Name	Best Practice Description	Portfolio Domain	Program Domain	Project Domain	Organizational Enabler	Process Improvement Stage
7165	Demonstrate Competency in Monitoring and Controlling a Project	Project managers are able to demonstrate their competencies in monitoring and controlling a project.			Project	Competency Management	
7175	Demonstrate Competency in Closing a Project	Project managers are able to demonstrate their competencies in closing a project.			Project	Competency Management	
7185	Demonstrate Communicating Competency	Project managers are able to demonstrate their communicating competency.	Portfolio	Program	Project	Competency Management	
7195	Demonstrate Leading Competency	Project managers are able to demonstrate their leading competency.			Project	Competency Management	
7205	Demonstrate Managing Competency	Project managers are able to demonstrate their managing competency.			Project	Competency Management	
7215	Demonstrate Cognitive Ability Competency	Project managers are able to demonstrate their cognitive ability competency.			Project	Competency Management	
7225	Demonstrate Effectiveness Competency	Project managers are able to demonstrate their effectiveness competency.			Project	Competency Management	
7235	Demonstrate Professionalism Competency	Project managers are able to demonstrate their professionalism competency.			Project	Competency Management	
7305	Estimating Template/ Tools Established for Use Across Organization	Standardize estimating so that there is consistency in the percentage applied to similar activities, consistent risk factors applied. This also provides a foundation for similar meaning for metrics collected during and after project execution.		Program	Project	Organizational Project Management Techniques	

Best Practice ID	Best Practice Name	Best Practice Description	Portfolio Domain	Program Domain	Project Domain	Organizational Enabler	Process Improvement Stage
7315	Define OPM Success Metrics	The organization defines how it will measure the success and value of portfolio, program, and project management.	Portfolio			Project Management Metrics	
7325	Collect OPM Success Metrics	The organization uses and maintains a formal performance system to collect OPM success metrics.	Portfolio	Program	Project	Project Management Metrics	
7335	Use OPM Success Metrics	The organization uses the OPM success metrics to improve the performance of portfolio, program, and project management against plans, and improve realization of benefit to the organization.	Portfolio	Program	Project	Project Management Metrics	
7345	Verify OPM Success Metric Accuracy	The organization ensures that OPM and benefit to the organization data is valid and accurate.	Portfolio	Program	Project	Project Management Metrics	
7355	Analyze and Improve OPM Success Metrics	The organization continuously improves its OPM data collection and use processes.	Portfolio	Program	Project	Project Management Metrics	
7365	Project Management Information System	The organization has a mechanism for the storage, retrieval, dissemination, and reporting of organizational project management information.	Portfolio	Program	Project	Knowledge Management and PMIS	
7375	Intellectual Capital Reuse	Intellectual capital is stored and reused.	Portfolio			Knowledge Management and PMIS	
7405	Achieve Strategic Goals and Objectives Through the Use of Organizational Project Management	Organizations adopt organizational project management as the means of achieving organization's goals and objectives.	Portfolio	Program	Project	Strategic Alignment	

Best Practice ID	Best Practice Name	Best Practice Description	Portfolio Domain	Program Domain	Project Domain	Organizational Enabler	Process Improvement Stage
7500	Standardize Project Plan Scope Management Process	Plan Scope Management Process standards are established.			Project		Standardize
7510	Standardize Project Plan Schedule Management Process	Plan Schedule Management Process standards are established.			Project		Standardize
7520	Standardize Project Plan Cost Management Process	Plan Cost Management Process standards are established.			Project		Standardize
7530	Standardize Project Plan Stakeholder Management Process	Plan Stakeholder Management Process standards are established.			Project		Standardize
7540	Standardize Project Control Stakeholder Engagement Process	Control Stakeholder Engagement Process standards are established.			Project		Standardize
7550	Measure Project Plan Scope Management Process	Plan Scope Management Process measures are established, assembled, and analyzed.			Project		Measure
7560	Measure Project Plan Schedule Management Process	Plan Schedule Management Process measures are established, assembled, and analyzed.			Project		Measure
7570	Measure Project Plan Cost Management Process	Plan Cost Management Process measures are established, assembled, and analyzed.			Project		Measure
7580	Measure Project Plan Stakeholder Management Process	Plan Stakeholder Management Process measures are established, assembled, and analyzed.			Project		Measure
7590	Measure Project Control Stakeholder Engagement Process	Control Stakeholder Engagement Process measures are established, assembled, and analyzed.			Project		Measure

Best Practice ID	Best Practice Name	Best Practice Description	Portfolio Domain	Program Domain	Project Domain	Organizational Enabler	Process Improvement Stage
7600	Control Project Plan Scope Management Process	Plan Scope Management Process controls are established and executed to control the stability of the process.			Project		Control
7610	Control Project Plan Schedule Management Process	Plan Schedule Management Process controls are established and executed to control the stability of the process.			Project		Control
7620	Control Project Plan Cost Management Process	Plan Cost Management Process controls are established and executed to control the stability of the process.			Project		Control
7630	Control Project Plan Stakeholder Management Process	Plan Stakeholder Management Process controls are established and executed to control the stability of the process.			Project		Control
7640	Control Project Control Stakeholder Engagement Process	Control Stakeholder Engagement Process controls are established and executed to control the stability of the process.			Project		Control
7650	Improve Project Plan Scope Management Process	Plan Scope Management Process problem areas are assessed, root causes are identified, process improvement recommendations are collected, and process improvements are implemented.			Project		Improve
7660	Improve Project Plan Schedule Management Process	Plan Schedule Management Process problem areas are assessed, root causes are identified, process improvement recommendations are collected, and process improvements are implemented.			Project		Improve

Best Practice ID	Best Practice Name	Best Practice Description	Portfolio Domain	Program Domain	Project Domain	Organizational Enabler	Process Improvement Stage
7670	Improve Project Plan Cost Management Process	Plan Cost Management Process problem areas are assessed, root causes are identified, process improvement recommendations are collected, and process improvements are implemented.			Project		Improve
7680	Improve Project Plan Stakeholder Management Process	Plan Stakeholder Management Process problem areas are assessed, root causes are identified, process improvement recommendations are collected, and process improvements are implemented.			Project		Improve
7690	Improve Project Control Stakeholder Engagement Process	Control Stakeholder Engagement Process problem areas are assessed, root causes are identified, process improvement recommendations are collected, and process improvements are implemented.			Project		Improve
7710	Standardize Program Component Cost Estimation Process	Component Cost Estimation Process standards are established.		Program			Standardize
7720	Standardize Program Financial Closure Process	Program Financial Closure Process standards are established.		Program			Standardize
7780	Standardize Program Quality Assurance Process	Program Quality Assurance Process standards are established.		Program			Standardize
7790	Standardize Program Quality Control Process	Program Quality Control Process standards are established.		Program			Standardize
7800	Standardize Program Resource Planning Process	Resource Planning Process standards are established.		Program			Standardize

Best Practice ID	Best Practice Name	Best Practice Description	Portfolio Domain	Program Domain	Project Domain	Organizational Enabler	Process Improvement Stage
7810	Standardize Program Resource Prioritization Process	Resource Prioritization Process standards are established.		Program			Standardize
7820	Standardize Program Resource Interdependency Management Process	Resource Interdependency Management Process standards are established.		Program			Standardize
7880	Measure Program Component Cost Estimation Process	Component Cost Estimation Process measures are established, assembled, and analyzed.		Program			Measure
7890	Measure Program Financial Closure Process	Program Financial Closure Process measures are established, assembled, and analyzed.		Program			Measure
7950	Measure Program Quality Assurance Process	Program Quality Assurance Process measures are established, assembled, and analyzed.		Program			Measure
7960	Measure Program Quality Control Process	Program Quality Control Process measures are established, assembled, and analyzed.		Program			Measure
7970	Measure Program Resource Planning Process	Resource Planning Process measures are established, assembled, and analyzed.		Program			Measure
7980	Measure Program Resource Prioritization Process	Resource Prioritization Process measures are established, assembled, and analyzed.		Program			Measure
7990	Measure Program Resource Interdependency Management Process	Resource Interdependency Management Process measures are established, assembled, and analyzed.		Program			Measure

Best Practice ID	Best Practice Name	Best Practice Description	Portfolio Domain	Program Domain	Project Domain	Organizational Enabler	Process Improvement Stage
8050	Control Program Component Cost Estimation Process	Component Cost Estimation Process controls are established and executed to control the stability of the process.		Program			Control
8060	Control Program Financial Closure Process	Program Financial Closure Process controls are established and executed to control the stability of the process.		Program			Control
8120	Control Program Quality Assurance Process	Program Quality Assurance Process controls are established and executed to control the stability of the process.		Program			Control
8130	Control Program Quality Control Process	Program Quality Control Process controls are established and executed to control the stability of the process.		Program			Control
8140	Control Program Resource Planning Process	Resource Planning Process controls are established and executed to control the stability of the process.		Program			Control
8150	Control Program Resource Prioritization Process	Resource Prioritization Process controls are established and executed to control the stability of the process.		Program			Control
8160	Control Program Resource Interdependency Management Process	Resource Interdependency Management Process controls are established and executed to control the stability of the process.		Program			Control

Best Practice ID	Best Practice Name	Best Practice Description	Portfolio Domain	Program Domain	Project Domain	Organizational Enabler	Process Improvement Stage
8220	Improve Program Component Cost Estimation Process	Component Cost Estimation Process problem areas are assessed, root causes are identified, process improvement recommendations are collected, and process improvements are implemented.		Program			Improve
8230	Improve Program Financial Closure Process	Program Financial Closure Process problem areas are assessed, root causes are identified, process improvement recommendations are collected, and process improvements are implemented.		Program			Improve
8290	Improve Program Quality Assurance Process	Program Quality Assurance Process problem areas are assessed, root causes are identified, process improvement recommendations are collected, and process improvements are implemented.		Program			Improve
8300	Improve Program Quality Control Process	Program Quality Control Process problem areas are assessed, root causes are identified, process improvement recommendations are collected, and process improvements are implemented.		Program			Improve
8310	Improve Program Resource Planning Process	Resource Planning Process problem areas are assessed, root causes are identified, process improvement recommendations are collected, and process improvements are implemented.		Program			Improve

Best Practice ID	Best Practice Name	Best Practice Description	Portfolio Domain	Program Domain	Project Domain	Organizational Enabler	Process Improvement Stage
8320	Improve Program Resource Prioritization Process	Resource Prioritization Process problem areas are assessed, root causes are identified, process improvement recommendations are collected, and process improvements are implemented.		Program			Improve
8330	Improve Program Resource Interdependency Management Process	Resource Interdependency Management Process problem areas are assessed, root causes are identified, process improvement recommendations are collected, and process improvements are implemented.		Program			Improve
8400	Standardize Develop Portfolio Strategic Plan Process	Develop Portfolio Strategic Plan Process standards are established.	Portfolio				Standardize
8410	Standardize Develop Portfolio Charter Process	Develop Portfolio Charter Process standards are established.	Portfolio				Standardize
8420	Standardize Define Portfolio Roadmap Process	Define Portfolio Roadmap Process standards are established.	Portfolio				Standardize
8460	Standardize Provide Portfolio Oversight Process	Provide Portfolio Oversight Process standards are established.	Portfolio				Standardize
8470	Standardize Develop Portfolio Performance Management Plan Process	Develop Portfolio Performance Management Plan Process standards are established.	Portfolio				Standardize
8480	Standardize Portfolio Manage Supply and Demand Process	Manage Supply and Demand Process standards are established.	Portfolio				Standardize

Best Practice ID	Best Practice Name	Best Practice Description	Portfolio Domain	Program Domain	Project Domain	Organizational Enabler	Process Improvement Stage
8490	Standardize Manage Portfolio Value Process	Manage Portfolio Value Process standards are established.	Portfolio				Standardize
8500	Standardize Develop Portfolio Risk Management Plan Process	Develop Portfolio Risk Management Plan Process standards are established.	Portfolio				Standardize
8510	Measure Develop Portfolio Strategic Plan Process	Develop Portfolio Strategic Plan Process measures are established, assembled, and analyzed.	Portfolio				Measure
8520	Measure Develop Portfolio Charter Process	Develop Portfolio Charter Process measures are established, assembled, and analyzed.	Portfolio				Measure
8530	Measure Define Portfolio Roadmap Process	Define Portfolio Roadmap Process measures are established, assembled, and analyzed.	Portfolio				Measure
8540	Standardize Develop Portfolio Management Plan Process	Develop Portfolio Management Plan Process standards are established.	Portfolio				Standardize
8550	Measure Develop Portfolio Management Plan Process	Develop Portfolio Management Plan Process measures are established, assembled, and analyzed.	Portfolio				Measure
8570	Measure Provide Portfolio Oversight Process	Provide Portfolio Oversight Process measures are established, assembled, and analyzed.	Portfolio				Measure
8580	Measure Develop Portfolio Performance Management Plan Process	Develop Portfolio Performance Management Plan Process measures are established, assembled, and analyzed.	Portfolio				Measure

Best Practice ID	Best Practice Name	Best Practice Description	Portfolio Domain	Program Domain	Project Domain	Organizational Enabler	Process Improvement Stage
8590	Measure Portfolio Manage Supply and Demand Process	Manage Supply and Demand Process measures are established, assembled, and analyzed.	Portfolio				Measure
8600	Measure Manage Portfolio Value Process	Manage Portfolio Value Process measures are established, assembled, and analyzed.	Portfolio				Measure
8610	Measure Develop Portfolio Risk Management Plan Process	Develop Portfolio Risk Management Plan Process measures are established, assembled, and analyzed.	Portfolio				Measure
8620	Control Develop Portfolio Strategic Plan Process	Develop Portfolio Strategic Plan Process controls are established and executed to control the stability of the process.	Portfolio				Control
8630	Control Develop Portfolio Charter Process	Develop Portfolio Charter Process controls are established and executed to control the stability of the process.	Portfolio				Control
8640	Control Define Portfolio Roadmap Process	Define Portfolio Roadmap Process controls are established and executed to control the stability of the process.	Portfolio				Control
8650	Control Develop Portfolio Management Plan Process	Develop Portfolio Management Plan Process controls are established and executed to control the stability of the process.	Portfolio				Control
8680	Control Provide Portfolio Oversight Process	Provide Portfolio Oversight Process controls are established and executed to control the stability of the process.	Portfolio				Control

Best Practice ID	Best Practice Name	Best Practice Description	Portfolio Domain	Program Domain	Project Domain	Organizational Enabler	Process Improvement Stage
8690	Control Develop Portfolio Performance Management Plan Process	Develop Portfolio Performance Management Plan Process controls are established and executed to control the stability of the process.	Portfolio				Control
8700	Control Portfolio Manage Supply and Demand Process	Manage Supply and Demand Process controls are established and executed to control the stability of the process.	Portfolio				Control
8710	Control Manage Portfolio Value Process	Manage Portfolio Value Process controls are established and executed to control the stability of the process.	Portfolio				Control
8720	Control Develop Portfolio Risk Management Plan Process	Develop Portfolio Risk Management Plan Process controls are established and executed to control the stability of the process.	Portfolio				Control
8730	Improve Develop Portfolio Strategic Plan Process	Develop Portfolio Strategic Plan Process problem areas are assessed, root causes are identified, process improvement recommendations are collected, and process improvements are implemented.	Portfolio				Improve
8740	Improve Develop Portfolio Charter Process	Develop Portfolio Charter Process problem areas are assessed, root causes are identified, process improvement recommendations are collected, and process improvements are implemented.	Portfolio				Improve

Best Practice ID	Best Practice Name	Best Practice Description	Portfolio Domain	Program Domain	Project Domain	Organizational Enabler	Process Improvement Stage
8750	Improve Define Portfolio Roadmap Process	Define Portfolio Roadmap Process problem areas are assessed, root causes are identified, process improvement recommendations are collected, and process improvements are implemented.	Portfolio				Improve
8760	Improve Develop Portfolio Management Plan Process	Develop Portfolio Management Plan Process problem areas are assessed, root causes are identified, process improvement recommendations are collected, and process improvements are implemented.	Portfolio				Improve
8790	Improve Provide Portfolio Oversight Process	Provide Portfolio Oversight Process problem areas are assessed, root causes are identified, process improvement recommendations are collected, and process improvements are implemented.	Portfolio				Improve
8800	Improve Develop Portfolio Performance Management Plan Process	Develop Portfolio Performance Management Plan Process problem areas are assessed, root causes are identified, process improvement recommendations are collected, and process improvements are implemented.	Portfolio				Improve

Best Practice ID	Best Practice Name	Best Practice Description	Portfolio Domain	Program Domain	Project Domain	Organizational Enabler	Process Improvement Stage
8810	Improve Portfolio Manage Supply and Demand Process	Manage Supply and Demand Process problem areas are assessed, root causes are identified, process improvement recommendations are collected, and process improvements are implemented.	Portfolio				Improve
8820	Improve Manage Portfolio Value Process	Manage Portfolio Value Process problem areas are assessed, root causes are identified, process improvement recommendations are collected, and process improvements are implemented.	Portfolio				Improve
8830	Improve Develop Portfolio Risk Management Plan Process	Develop Portfolio Risk Management Plan Process problem areas are assessed, root causes are identified, process improvement recommendations are collected, and process improvements are implemented.	Portfolio				Improve
8900	Accommodate organization's approved frameworks and governance structures	Design and adopt flexible project management processes to accommodate and comply with frameworks and governance structures approved by the organization, such as CMMI, ITIL, COBIT.	Portfolio	Program	Project	Organizational Project Management Methodology	
8910	Analyze Value Performance	The organization performs value performance analysis against the performance of its endeavors and refines the strategy appropriately.	Portfolio	Program	Project	Strategic Alignment	

Best Practice ID	Best Practice Name	Best Practice Description	Portfolio Domain	Program Domain	Project Domain	Organizational Enabler	Process Improvement Stage
8920	Assess the Realization of Proposed Benefits	The organization establishes a formal process to assess and account the realization of proposed benefits of their portfolio, programs, and projects.	Portfolio	Program	Project	Strategic Alignment	
8930	Benchmark PMO Practices and Results	The PMO is using benchmark data to compare its achieving and current state to other PMOs.	Portfolio	Program	Project	Benchmarking	
8940	Create a Risk-Aware Culture	The organization has created a risk-aware culture, advocating that the portfolio, programs, and projects are less risky when more risks are being identified.	Portfolio	Program	Project	Organizational Project Management Policy and Vision	
8950	Define Key Leading Indicators	The project team defines key leading indicators critical to the success of the project.			Project	Project Management Metrics	
8960	Developing Project Management Templates	Develop templates for organizations adopted project management Knowledge Areas to standardize project management practices.	Portfolio	Program	Project	Organizational Project Management Methodology	
8970	Document Project Management Case Studies	Organization documents case studies for all projects completed to ensure all successes and challenges are recorded.			Project	Knowledge Management and PMIS	
8980	Encourage Adherence to Project Management Code of Ethics	The organization promotes the adherence to the *Project Management Code of Ethics and Professional Conduct* to improve project quality, deliverables and quality.			Project	Organizational Project Management Practices	

Best Practice ID	Best Practice Name	Best Practice Description	Portfolio Domain	Program Domain	Project Domain	Organizational Enabler	Process Improvement Stage
8990	Establish Competent Project Sponsors	Project sponsors are competent in project sponsorship.			Project	Sponsorship	
9000	Establish Enterprise Risk Management Methodology	The organization captures enterprise risk (market, financial, business and environment) and their impact on strategy and portfolio, programs, and projects.	Portfolio	Program	Project	Strategic Alignment	
9010	Establish Executive Summary Dashboards	Organization has dashboards for executives that summarize project progress with clear indicators of project status.	Portfolio	Program	Project	Knowledge Management and PMIS	
9020	Establish Governance Policies Across the Organization	The organization establishes governance policies across the organization.	Portfolio	Program	Project	Governance	
9030	Establish Organizational Project Management Reporting Standards	Organization has created consistent organizational project management reporting standards to ensure repeatable quality reporting of projects, programs, and portfolios for all stakeholders.	Portfolio	Program	Project	Knowledge Management and PMIS	
9040	Establish Project Delivery Tips and Techniques Special Interest Group	Organization establishes special interest groups for the project management community to share project delivery tips and techniques with respective colleagues. The organization will invite speakers to present relevant topics to the project management community.	Portfolio	Program	Project	Organizational Project Management Communities	

Best Practice ID	Best Practice Name	Best Practice Description	Portfolio Domain	Program Domain	Project Domain	Organizational Enabler	Process Improvement Stage
9050	Establish Project Management Template Tailoring Guidelines	Organization provides tailoring guidelines for the project management templates to allow controlled customization of templates amended based on project approach.			Project	Organizational Project Management Methodology	
9060	Establish Resource Allocation and Optimization Processes	The organization utilizes resources in an optimized manner matching available resources with project and program needs.	Portfolio	Program	Project	Resource Allocation	
9070	Establish Scarce Resource Allocation Criteria	The organization allocates its scarce resources to its highest priority initiatives.	Portfolio			Resource Allocation	
9080	Establish Strategic Alignment Framework	The organization reviews the strategy, current conditions and results and adjusts the portfolio components accordingly.	Portfolio	Program	Project	Strategic Alignment	
9090	Incorporate Performance Benchmarks into Balanced Scorecard System	Augment traditional financial measures with benchmarks for performance in relationship with customers, key internal processes, and learning and growth using balanced scorecard system.	Portfolio	Program	Project	Benchmarking	
9100	Project Management Case Studies Included in Induction Program	Organization includes the project management case studies in the project management induction program to ensure success and key learning's are made available.			Project	Project Management Training	
9110	Project Management Training is Mapped to Career Development Path	Career development of staff needs to be supported by trainings.			Project	Project Management Training	

Best Practice ID	Best Practice Name	Best Practice Description	Portfolio Domain	Program Domain	Project Domain	Organizational Enabler	Process Improvement Stage
9120	Provide Mentoring to Project Managers	Provide continuous mentoring to project managers on organizations project management processes.			Project	Competency Management	
9130	Report OPM Performance to Strategy	The OPM system delivers feedback from the completion of projects and the realization of benefits back to the strategy of the organization.	Portfolio	Program	Project	Strategic Alignment	
9140	Report Project Program Strategic Performance	Review and report strategic benefits of project and program metrics and their importance to portfolio performance.	Portfolio	Program	Project	Strategic Alignment	
9150	Specialists are Shared Between Projects	The organization provides adequate staffing with specialized resources, sharing them between the projects.	Portfolio	Program	Project	Resource Allocation	
9160	Consistent Project Orientation Process	The organization has a standardized project orientation process to help prepare new team members to perform their work according to the project defined process and plan.			Project	Organizational Project Management Practices	
9170	Consistent Project, Program, and Portfolio Governance Across the Enterprise	The organization establishes a governance board over all the portfolio, program, and project processes across the enterprise to optimize business value.	Portfolio	Program	Project	Governance	

Best Practice ID	Best Practice Name	Best Practice Description	Portfolio Domain	Program Domain	Project Domain	Organizational Enabler	Process Improvement Stage
9180	Use Mathematically Sound Methods for Prioritization	The result of this prioritization along with the objectives prioritization produces ratio-scale relative benefit for each project candidate so they can be compared meaningfully.	Portfolio	Program	Project	Organizational Project Management Techniques	
9190	Use an Optimizer to Select the Portfolio	Select the optimal portfolio rather than ranking and choosing until budget runs out.	Portfolio			Organizational Project Management Techniques	
9200	Use Formal Performance Assessment	Formally assess the performance of project(s) or phase(s) in relation to business case used during initiation.	Portfolio	Program	Project	Strategic Alignment	
9210	Manage Program Resources	The program manager allows for the adjustment and reallocation of resources required to meet the needs of the program.		Program		Organizational Project Management Techniques	
9220	Manage Program Issues	The program team identifies, tracks, and closes issues effectively to ensure stakeholder expectations are aligned with program activities and deliverables.		Program		Organizational Project Management Techniques	
9230	Manage Component Interfaces	The program team maintains the adherence of program delivery and its constituent parts and manages relationships between the program components.		Program		Organizational Project Management Techniques	
9240	Plan Program Stakeholder Management	The program manager covers planning how stakeholders will be identified, analyzed, engaged, and managed throughout the life of the program.		Program		Organizational Project Management Techniques	

Best Practice ID	Best Practice Name	Best Practice Description	Portfolio Domain	Program Domain	Project Domain	Organizational Enabler	Process Improvement Stage
9250	Identify Program Stakeholders	The program team addresses the systematic identification and analysis of program stakeholders and creates the stakeholder register.		Program		Organizational Project Management Techniques	
9260	Engage Program Stakeholder	The program team ensures that stakeholders are involved in the program.		Program		Organizational Project Management Techniques	
9270	Manage Program Stakeholder Expectations	The program team manages communications to satisfy the requirements of and resolves issues with program stakeholders.		Program		Organizational Project Management Techniques	
9280	Plan and Establish Program Governance Structure	The program team identifies governance goals and defines the governance structure, roles, and responsibilities.		Program		Governance	
9290	Plan for Audits	The program team prepares for both external and internal audits of program finances, processes and documents and demonstrates compliance with approved organizational program management processes.		Program		Organizational Project Management Techniques	
9300	Provide Governance Oversight	The program team provides governance and audit ability throughout the course of the program.		Program		Governance	
9310	Strategic Alignment of Programs	The organization establishes and maintains the alignment of programs with the organization strategy.		Program		Strategic Alignment	

APPENDIX X1
THIRD EDITION CHANGES

X1.1 General Changes

The purpose of this appendix is to provide explanations of the changes made to the *Organizational Project Management Maturity Model* (*OPM3®*) – Third Edition. The team, as chartered, simplified the messaging with a business focus, harmonized with PMI standards, harmonized with the *Lexicon of Project Management Terms*, addressed deferred comments, and conducted working sessions to understand evolving practices. Major changes not detailed under Section X1.2 on Structural Changes in this appendix include:

X1.1.1 Harmonization with Other Revised PMI Standards

The third edition of *OPM3* maintains and expands on its alignment with the *PMBOK Guide®* – Fifth Edition, and the third editions of *The Standard for Program* Management and *The Standard for Portfolio Management* standards in addition to the *Lexicon* by ensuring that all fundamental concepts, are described in the same manner. The augmented third edition of *OPM3* delivers revised and updated Best Practices, reflecting the changes made to these other PMI standards.

X1.1.2 Update of Self-Assessment Method (SAM)

This edition of *OPM3* contains an update of the *Self-Assessment Method (SAM)* in alignment with *The Standard for Portfolio Management* – Third Edition, *The Standard for Program Management* – Third Edition, the *PMBOK Guide®* – Fifth Edition, and organizational enablers. An evaluation at the Best Practice level while utilizing the SAM requires that the user determine the Capabilities needed to establish the Best Practice. The composition of Best Practices is described in Sections 2 and 3.

X1.1.3 Consolidation and Alignment of Chapters

OPM3 is now structured to better communicate the business value of using the Organizational Project Management Maturity Model, as the standard by which an organization can measure itself against and thus increase project management capability in the appropriate areas to more effectively and efficiently transpose the organization's strategy into business results with the target audience.

X1.2 Structural Changes

The most pronounced restructuring of this edition of *OPM3* is the transition of content to harmonize with the structure of other PMI standards, including inputs, tools and techniques, and outputs. The model is described, constructed from its individual components, and discussed in Section 3 rather than spread among Sections 2 through 6. Sections 4 on Acquire Knowledge, 5 on Perform Assessment, and 6 on Manage Improvement provide greater depth of the *OPM3* Cycle Elements for practical application and training.

Table X1-1 describes and displays a side-by-side comparison of the changes in each section.

Table X1-1. Comparison of Structural Changes

Second Edition	Third Edition
Preface Executive summary view of *OPM3*	**Preface** This section communicates to Executives and Practitioners what is contained in this book
Section 1 Introduction to *OPM3* Chapter 1 Introduction Chapter 2 Foundational Concepts	**Section 1** Introduction **Section 2** Foundational Concepts
Section 2 Understanding the Model Chapter 3 The *OPM3* Cycle Chapter 4 The Organizational Project Management Processes	**Section 3** *The Organizational Project Management Maturity Model (OPM3)*
Section 3 Using the Model Chapter 5 The *OPM3* Construct Chapter 6 The *OPM3* Best Practices	**Section 4** Acquire Knowledge **Section 5** Perform Assessment **Section 6** Manage Improvement
Section 4 Appendices Appendix A Second Edition Changes Appendix B Evolution of the *OPM3* Maturity Model Appendix C Contributors and Reviewers of *OPM3* Second Edition Appendix D Self Assessment Method Appendix E Online Tools Appendix F *OPM3* Case Study Appendix G Implementing the Process Model	**Annex A1** *OPM3* Best Practices List Appendix X1 Third Edition Changes Appendix X2 Development of the Standard Appendix X3 Contributors and Reviewers of *OPM3* Third Edition Appendix X4 The Self-Assessment Method (SAM) Appendix X5 Case Studies and Success Stories Glossary Index

X1.2.1 Changes to Section 1 of Second Edition– Introduction to *OPM3*

Section 1 of the third edition outlines the distinction between *OPM3* and OPM and the relationships among portfolio management, program management, project management, and organizational project management. It also outlines the business value of *OPM3* and the key stakeholders engaged in *OPM3* initiatives.

Section 2 of the third edition outlines OPM foundational concepts while focusing on the business value that *OPM3* conveys by helping organizations translate strategy into business value realization in an efficient and effective manner.

Table X1-2. Changes to Section 1

Second Edition	Third Edition
Chapter 1 Introduction 1.1 *OPM3* Organizational Perspective 1.6 Overcoming the Improvement Dilemma	Section 1 Overview 1.1 Introduction 1.2 Purpose of *OPM3* 1.3 What is *OPM3* 1.4 What is OPM 1.5 Relationship among Portfolio Management, Program Management, Project Management, and Organizational Project Management 1.6 Business Value 1.7 Stakeholders (Roles)
Chapter 2 Foundational Concepts 1.2 Strategy Execution 2.2 Organizational Project Management 2.3 Organizational Project Management Maturity 2.1 *OPM3* Purpose and Scope	Section 2 Foundational Concepts 2.1 Organizational Project Management Described 2.2 Organizational Life Cycles 2.3 Organizational Project Management Maturity Model

X1.2.2 Changes to Section 2 Second Edition—Understanding the Model

All Chapters from Section 2 of the second edition have been relocated in their entirety to Section 3 on The Organizational Project Management Maturity Model with a detailed look at the construct, framework, application, and scoring methods. Some materials from other second edition chapters are also relocated to Section 3 of the third edition creating comprehensive detail on how the model is built and how to apply it. This change brings the structure of the third edition in line with the framework of other PMI standards.

Table X1-3. Changes to Section 2

Second Edition	Third Edition

1.3 *OPM3* Components
1.5 Organizational Improvement Plan
1.4 Maturity Assessment
2.4 *OPM3*
    2.4.1 Domains
    2.4.2 Organizational Enablers
    2.4.3 Multi-Dimensional View of Maturity
Chapter 3 The *OPM3* Cycle
3.1 Knowledge, Assessment, and Improvement
3.2 Introduction to the *OPM3* Improvement Cycle
4.1 Introduction
4.2 Project Management Processes
4.3 Program Management Processes
4.4 Portfolio Management Processes
4.5 Attributes of Portfolio, Program, and Project Management Processes
Chapter 5 The *OPM3* Construct
5.2 SMCI and Organizational Enablers
5.3 Dependencies Among Best Practices and Capabilities
	Chapter 3 The *Organizational Project Management Maturity Model (OPM3)*
	3.1 Introduction
	3.2 The *OPM3* Construct
	3.3 *OPM3* Framework
	3.4 *OPM3* Application
	3.5 *OPM3* Scoring Methods

X1.2.3 Changes to Section 3—Using the Model

Section 3 of the second edition is now replaced by Sections 4, 5 and 6 of the third edition. These sections are structured in the same manner as the Knowledge Areas found in the *PMBOK Guide®* with inputs, tool and techniques, and outputs (ITTO). These changes are a result of the standardization of the PMI standards and are intended to equip the *OPM3* practitioner with a depth of knowledge needed to (a) carry out an assessment covering the key areas of acquiring the knowledge needed to perform the assessment, (b) carry out the assessment itself, and (c) manage relative organizational project management improvements within that particular organization.

Table X1-4. Changes to Section 3

Second Edition	Second Edition
	Chapter 4 Acquire Knowledge 4.1 Understanding OPM 4.2 Understanding Organization 4.3 Assess Change Readiness
	Chapter 5 Perform Assessment 5.1 Establish Plan 5.2 Define Scope 5.3 Conduct Assessment 5.4 Initiate Change
	Chapter 6 Manage Improvement 6.1 Create Recommendations 6.2 Select Initiatives 6.3 Implement Improvement Initiative 6.4 Measure Results 6.5 Manage Change
Chapter 6 *OPM3* Best Practices 5.1 Best Practices	Annex A1 Best Practices List

X1.2.4 Changes to Section 4—Appendices

Changes to the Appendices include:

- Appendix X1 Third Edition Changes
- Appendix X2 Evolution of the Organizational Project Management Maturity Model now includes subsection
- Appendix X3 Contributors and Reviewers of OPM3 third edition
- Appendix X4 The Self-Assessment Method
- Appendix X5 OPM3 Case Study, illustrating a real example of how OPM3 was used in an organization and the outcomes of that process are replaced with case studies
- Glossary
- Index

APPENDIX X2
CONTRIBUTORS AND REVIEWERS OF THE *OPM3*® STANDARD

X2.1 Contributors and Reviewers of the *OPM3*®—Third Edition

X2.1.1 *OPM3*®—Third Edition Core Committee

The following individuals were members of the project Core Committee responsible for drafting the revision of the standard, including review and adjudication of reviewer recommendations.

Timothy A. MacFadyen, MBA, PMP, Committee Chair
David Christopher Miles, CEng, OPM3 Certified Professional, Committee Vice Chair
Nada Abandah, PgMP, OPM3 Certified Professional
Claudia M. Baca PMP, OPM3 Certified Professional
Folake Dosunmu, PgMP, OPM3 Certified Professional
Stephan Ernst, Dipl-Ing oec, PMP
Ivo Gerber, PMI-SP, OPM3 Certified Professional
Greg Hart
Kenji Hiraishi, PMP
Felicia E. Hong, MBA, PMP
Burkhard Meier, MBA, PMP
Lambert Ofoegbu, MSc, OPM3 Certified Professional
Valerie van der Klis, PMP, OPM3 Certified Professional
Karl Best, CAPM, CStd, Standards Project Specialist

X2.1.2 *OPM3*®—Third Edition Best Practices Review Team

The following individuals were members of the Best Practices Review team responsible for review and further development of the Annex A1 Best Practices list.

Claudia M. Baca, PMP, OPM3 Certified Professional, Review Team Chair
Imad Alsadeq, MSP, OPM3 Certified Professional
Shrikant Arya, ME, PMP
Mardav Bakshi
Shanmugaraj Balasubramanian, PMP, PMI-ACP
Randy Bennett
Jane Betterton, PMP, OPM3 Certified Professional

Martin Bittner, PMP

Susan S. Bivins, MSPM, PMP

Ravi Shanker Rao Bodkai, BTech, PMP

Peggy J. Brady

Giovanni Chin-A-Sen

Jorge Cogno, PhD, PMP

Sanjay Kumar Das, PMP, ITIL

Hao Deng, MPM, OPM3 Certified Professional

John F. Filicetti, PMP, MBA

Anil Garg

Carl M. Gilbert, PMP, OPM3 Certified Professional

Sanjeev Gupta

Suhail Iqbal, PgMP, PMP

Ashok Jain, PMP, ITIL

Chandrashekhar S. Joshi, PMP, Chartered Engineer

Paulo F. W. Keglevich de Buzin, MSc, PMP

Gabriel Kam-sun Lau, PMP, PMI-RMP

Anand Lokhande, PMP

Charles A. McLaughlin, MSPM, PMP

Vladimir Antonio Mininel, PMP

M. Aslam Mirza, MBA, PMP

Kannan Sami Nadar, PMP

Ony Nwankpa

Krupakar Reddy, PMP, PRINCE2 Practitioner

Fabio Salazar, PE, PMP

Paul Szwed

Gerhard Tekes, PMP, OPM3 Certified Professional

Chitra Venkatramani, MBA, PMP

Matthew J. Weaver, PMP

X2.1.3 *OPM3*®—Third Edition Subject Matter Expert Reviewers

The following individuals were invited subject matter experts who reviewed the draft and provided recommendations through the SME Review.

Farhad Abdollahyan, MSc, OPM3 Certified Professional

Hamidreza Afshari, PMP, OPM3 Certified Professional

Rania Al-Maghraby, PMP, OPM3 Certified Professional

Susan S. Bivins, MSPM, PMP

Larry Bull

Giovanni Chin-A-Sen

Jorge Cogno, PhD, PMP

Carlos Colon, PMP, OPM3 Certified Professional

Brenda L. Comfort, MSc, PMP

Hao Deng, MPM, OPM3 Certified Professional

Maggie S.Y. Hsu, OPM3 Certified Instructor, PMI-ACP

Suhail Iqbal, PgMP, PMP

Ashok Jain, PMP, CSM

Chandrashekhar S. Joshi, PMP, Chartered Engineer

Paulo F. W. Keglevich de Buzin, MSc, PMP

Tom Keuten, PMP, OPM3 Certified Professional

Giovani Lage de Castro, OPM3 Certified Professional, PgMP

Vladimir Antonio Mininel, PMP

M. Aslam Mirza, MBA, PMP

Sara Núñez, PMP, OPM3 Certified Professional

Onyinye Nwankpa, MBA

Fabio Salazar, PE, PMP

X2.1.4 *OPM3®*—Third Edition Public Exposure Draft Reviewers

The following individuals were volunteers who reviewed the draft and provided recommendations through the Public Exposure Draft Review.

Farhad Abdollahyan, PMI-RMP, OPM3
    Certified Professional

Yaser T. A. Afaneh, PMP

José Rafael Alcalá Gómez, MBA, PMP

Bill Allbee, MPM, PMP

Rania Al-Maghraby, PMP, OPM3 Certified
    Professional

Haluk Altunel, PhD, PMP

Tony Appleby, PMP, OPM3 Certified Professional

Zaher Asfari, MBA, PMI-ACP

Bakul Banerjee, PhD, PMP

Manuel F. Baquero V., MSc, PMP

Eduardo Bazo

Wayne F. Best

Pieter Botman

Rodolphe Boudet, PMP

Farid F. Bouges, MSc, PMP

Lynda Bourne DPM, PMP

Yuri Braz, PMP, CCNA

Joseph Calinski

Giovani Castro

Brenda Comfort

Sergio Concha, MTIG, PMP

Mike Cooley, PMP

Kevin L. Cooper, MBA, PMP

William J. Cottun, PMP

Ana Cronin

P. H. Manjula Deepal De Silva, BSc, PMP

Marc DeBord, MS-MOT, PMP

George Diakonikolaou

Victor Espinosa, MBA, PMP
Fam Woon Fong, PMP, PMI-RMP
Anna Maria Felici, PMP
Ali Forouzesh, PMP, OPM3 Certified Professional
Gerardo A. Garavito F., PMP, PMI-ACP
Ahmad Khairiri Abdul Ghani
Carl M. Gilbert, PMP, OPM3 Certified Professional
Theofanis C. Giotis, PMP, PMI-ACP
Greg Githens, PMP
Mustafa Hafizoglu, PMP
Akram Hassan, PhD, OPM3 Certified Professional
Timothy Hix, CAPM, CSCP
Knut Vidar Hoholm
Keith D. Hornbacher, MBA
Gheorghe Hriscu, PMP, CGEIT
Shuichi Ikeda, PMP
Takafumi Isogawa, PMP
Rajesh Jadhav, PgMP, PMI-RMP
Ashok Jain, PMP, CSM
Etiénne Joubert, MDipTech, PMP
Shinobu Komai
Abhilash Kuzhikat, PMP, CISA
Arun Lal, PMP
David Lavery
Craig Letavec, PMP, PgMP
Ginger Levin, PMP, PgMP
Arden C. Lockwood, MBA, MCS
Konstantinos Maliakas, MSc, PMP
Anuj Malik, GMITE
Anthony Mampilly, MS, PMP
Sangu Maharajan Mangkuppa, IFRS, MSME
Ammar W. Mango, CSSBB, PgMP
Orlando Marone, PMP
Thomas F. McCabe, PMP, CSSMBB
Yan Bello Méndez, PMP

Werner Meyer, MSc, OPM3 Certified Professional
Arash Momeni, MBA, PMP
Alaa Mostafa, PMP, PgMP
Nathan M. Mourfield, MHA, PMP
Adriano José da Silva Neves, MSc, PMP
Darci Oltman, PMP
Michelle Pallas, PMP, CIRM
Jason Papadopoulos, MBCS, CITP
Scott Patton, PMP, OPM3 Certified Professional
Jose Angelo Pinto, PMP, OPM3 Certified Trainer
Raju N. Rao, SCPM, OPM3 Certified Professional
Michael Reed, PMP
Jorge F. Rojas-Meluk, MIS, PMP
Rafael Fernando Ronces Rosas, PMP, ITIL
Koroush Sanaeimovahed
Luis Sanchez
John Schlichter, MBA, OPM3 Certified Professional
G. Lakshmi Sekhar, BE, PMP
Sandra Shadchehr PMP, LEED Green Associate
Korinna Shaw, MBA, PMP
Jen L. Skrabak, PMP, MBA
Joseph A. Sopko, PMP, OPM3 Certified Professional
Thierry Soulard, PMP, OPM3 Certified Professional
Chuck Stakston, MBA, PE
Shoji Tajima, PMP, ITC
Gerhard Tekes, PMP, OPM3 Certified Professional
Suzanne M. Testerman, MBA, PMP
Edward John Thomas, MPM, PMP
Mangi Vishnoi, MAIPM, PMP
Poonam Vishnoi, PMGTI, ProgGTI
Kevin R. Wegryn, MA, PMP
Moataz Yousif, MEng, OPM3 Certified Professional
Bin Zhang, PhD, OPM3 Certified Professional
Kelly A. Zrubek, PMP
Alan Zucker, PMP

X2.1.5 PMI Standards Member Advisory Group (MAG)

The following individuals are members of the PMI Standards Member Advisory Group, who provided direction to and final approval for the *OPM3®*—Third Edition draft.

Monique Aubry, PhD, MPM
Margareth Fabiola dos Santos Carneiro, MSc, PMP
Larry Goldsmith, MBA, PMP
Cynthia Snyder, MBA, PMP
Chris Stevens, PhD
Dave Violette, MPM, PMP

X2.1.6 PMI Consensus Body

The following individuals are members of the PMI Standards Consensus Body, who gave final approval for the *OPM3®* – Third Edition draft.

Monique Aubry, PhD, MPM
Robert E. Baker, PMP
Nigel Blampied, PE, PMP
Nathalie A. Bohbot, PMP
Dennis L. Bolles, PMP
Peggy J. Brady
Chris Cartwright, MPM, PMP
Terry Cooke-Davies, PhD
Sergio Coronada, PhD
Andrea G. Demaria, PMP
John Dettbarn, DSc, PE
Charles T. Follin, PMP
Larry Goldsmith, MBA, PMP
Dana J. Goulston, PMP
Dorothy Kangas, PMP
Thomas M. Kurihara
Mike Musial, PMP, CBM
Eric S. Norman, PMP, PgMP
Debbie O'Bray, CIM (Hons)
Nanette Patton, MSBA, PMP

Crispin ("Kik") Piney, BSc, PgMP
Michael Reed, PMP
Chris Richards, PMP
David W. Ross, PgMP, PMP
Paul Shaltry, PMP
Jen L. Skrabak, MBA, PMP
Carol Steuer, PMP
Geree Streun, PMP, PMI-ACP
Matthew Tomlinson, PgMP, PMP
Dave Violette, MPM, PMP
Quynh Woodward, MBA, PMP
John Zlockie, MBA, PMP

X2.1.7 PMI Standards Harmonization Team

The following individuals are members of the PMI Standards Harmonization Team, who reviewed and provided direction on the harmonization of content between the *PMBOK® Guide – Firth Edition, The Standard for Program Management – Third Edition, The Standard for Portfolio Management – Third Edition,* and the *OPM3® — Third Edition.*

Karl F. Best, CAPM, CStd
Steve Butler, MBA, PMP
Folake Dosunmu, PgMP, OPM3
Randy Holt, MBS, PMP, Chair
Dorothy L. Kangas, PMP
Joseph W. Kestel, PMP
M. Elaine Lazar, AStd, MA
Timothy MacFadyen
Vanina Mangano
David Christopher Miles CEng, OPM3-CC
Eric S. Norman, PgMP, PMP
Michael Reed, PMP
Chris Richards, PMP
Jen L. Skrabak, MBA, PMP
Carol Steuer, PMP
Bobbye S. Underwood, PMP, PMI-ACP
Dave Violette, MPM, PMP
Kristin Vitello, CAPM
Quynh Woodward, MBA, PMP
John Zlockie, MBA, PMP

X2.1.8 PMI Production Staff

Donn Greenberg, Manager, Publications
Roberta Storer, Product Editor
Barbara Walsh, Publications Production Supervisor

X2.2 Contributors and Reviewers of the *OPM3*® — Second Edition

X2.2.1 *OPM3*® Second Edition Core Team Members

Karl Andy Anderson, *OPM3*-CC, PMP, Research Team Lead
Claudia M. Baca, PMP, *OPM3*-CC, Development Team Lead
Bernard Hill, PhD, PMP, Knowledge Foundation Development Team Lead
Rashed Iqbal, PMP, PhD, Marketing Team Lead
Timothy A. MacFadyen, MBA, *OPM3* – CC, Project Manager
J. Alan Northrup, PMP, Self-Assessment Development Method Team Lead
Auristela Oxman, Filter Team Lead
Raju N. Rao, PMP, SCPM, Baseline Network Development Team Lead
Jim Sloane, *OPM3*-CC, PMP, Harmonization Team Lead, Deputy Project Manager
Dennis E. Stevens, Deputy Project Manager
Earnest C. Valle, MBA, PMP, Architecture Team Lead
Valerie van der Klis, PMP, Benchmarking Team Lead, Support Team Lead, Quality Team Lead
Nancy E. Wilkinson, MBA, PMP, Standards Project Specialist

X2.2.2 Other Contributors

Farhad Abdollahyan, MSc, PMP
Raul M. Abril, PhD, PMP
Suresh Adina, PMP
Yasser Afaneh, PMP
Maria Affan
Pankaj Agrawal, PMP, OPM3-CC
Sheikh Nisar Ahmed (MSc)
Zubair Ahmed, PMP
Ali Akl, CISM, CISSP
Hussain Ali Al-Ansari,
    Eur Ing, CEng
Fernando Albuquerque, MBA

Mohammed Mansoor Ali, PMP
Selim Alkaner, PhD, PMP
Mohammed Abdulla Al-Kuwari,
    Eur Ing, PMP
Imad Muhammad al-Sadeq,
    PMP, PMOC
Alexandre Alves
Michael Andersen
Rajeev Andharia, PMP, ITIL
    Manager
Marc C. Andiel, PMP, MBA
Jagathnarayanan Angyan, FIE, CE

Kapil Shripad Apshankar, PMP
Rahayu Setyawati Arifin
Parag Y. Arjunwadkar, MBA, PMP
Julie Arnold, PMP
Shrikant Arya, PMP
David V. Auman
Naing Moe Aung, PMP
Darwyn Azzinaro, PMP
Subrata Baguli, PMP
Sivakumar Balasubramaniam,
    PMP
Michael Balay, PMP

Krishnaprasad Bhat
  Bannanje, PMP
David Barcklow, PMP
A. Lee Barco, PE, PMP
Vikas Basantani, PMP
Sujoy K. Basu, PMP, MBA
Mohammed Safi Batley, MIM
Gregory M. Becker, PMP
Julia M. Bednar, PMP
Jeanne Belin, PMP
Vincent L. BenAvram, PMP
Gary Ben-Israel, PMP
Randy Bennett, PMP
P. Ionut Bibac
Christie Biehl, PhD, PMP
David Bissessar, PMP
Karen Board, MBA, PMP
Theodore R. Boccuzzi, PMP
Ravi Shanker Rao Bodkai, PMP
Stephen F. Bonk, PE, PMP
Lynda Bourne DPM, PMP
Mila Bozic, MScEE, PMP
Christie D. Bradley, PMP
Christophe N. Bredillet, PhD,
  DSc, MBA
Greg Brown, PMP
Iris S. Burrell, PMP
Sergio de Oliveira Caballero
Andrea Caccamese, PMP,
  PRINCE2
Charles L. Campbell, PMP
Esteban Villeda Carmona, PMP
Chris Cartwright, MPM, PMP
Stephan J. Cassidy, MBA, PMP
Marzon Castilho, PMP
Sherry Ceallaigh, MPM, PMP
Akkaraju Sailesh Chandra
Subramanian Chandramouli
BhanuSmitha Chanduri

Porfirio Chen Chang, PMP
Chan Cheah, PhD, MsBS
Xiao Cheng, PMP
Giovanni Chin-A-Sen
Darrel S. F. Chong
Christos A. Christou, MBA, PMP
Kevin Chui, MBA, PMP
Sebastian Chung, PMP
Rachel Ciliberti, PMP
Manuel Cisneros, MBA, PMP
Douglas Clark
Robert D. Clark, MBA, PMP
Barbara J. Clark, MSM
Steven Bradley Clark, PMP
Sergio Concha, PMP, MTIG
Terry Cooke-Davies, PhD, FCMI
Aline L. Costa, PMP
Jorge S. Miranda Cruz
Wanda Curlee, PgMP, DM
Steve Dale, PMP
Damyan Damyanov
Thomas Daniel
Sanjay Kumar Das, PMP
Dipanker Das, PMP, MTech
Rafat Dasan, PMP
Trilochan Dave, PMP
Johnnie Davis, PE, PMP
Paulo Keglevich de Buzin,
  MSc, PMP
Nicolas De Dobbeleer, MSc, PMP
Paulo R. C. de Espindola, PMP
Carmen De Leon, PMP
Sudipta De, PMP
Muhammad Din, PMP
Vivek Dixit
Qingyun (Peter) Dou, PMP, CLO
Alan B. Downs, PMP
Zhen Du, PMP
Giancarlo Duranti, PMP

Usman Khan Durrani, PMP
Kiran Kumar Dusi, BTech, PMP
Anoop Dwivedi, PMP
Valecia Dyett, PMP
Thomas Eberhard, PMP
Scott Eddy, PMP
Marcel Ekkel, Ing, PMP
Hesham El Bialy El Sayed,
  MSc, PMP
Mohamed Mahmoud
  Elgamal, PMP
Bill Engel, PMP
Defne Erogul
Steven L. Fahrenkrog, PMP
Anna Maria Felici, PMP, CMC
Katherine Felix
Jose Guilherme Filho, PMP
John Filicetti, MBA, PMP
Augusto Jaramillo Forcada
Charles S. Fraley, PMP
Melinda Francis, PMP
Larry Franklin, PMP
Kristina Frazier-Henry, PMP
Amanda Freitick
Ralf Friedrich, PMP, ACC
Chandrasekhar Ganduri, PMP
Anil Garg, PMP
Stanisław Gasik
Santosh Lawoo Gawande
Peggy Gemert, PMP
Alexandre Sörensen Ghisolfi
  MBA PMP
Theofanis C. Giotis, MSc, PMP
Leo A. Giulianetti, PMP
Dan Goldfischer
Balasubramaniam Hari Gopal,
  FCA, PMP
Larry Gordon, PMP, ITSM
  Manager

Radha Goverdhan, PMP

Donn Greenberg

Brenda L. Grime, PMP

Stephen Gristock, PMP

Tom Grzesiak, PMP

Ruth Anne Guerrero, MBA, PMP

Sumit Gupta, CSQA

Yuli Gutmanas, PMP

William Haeck, PMP

Chris Hagenbuch, PMP

Frank L. Harper, Jr., PhD, PMP

Sheriff Hashem, PhD, PMP

Charles Hawk, PMP

T. Heather, MBA

Carlos Heble, MPA

Mohamed S. Hefny, MSc, PMP

Michael Heiberg, PMP

John Hermarij, PMP

Bernard Hill, PhD, PMP

Kenji Hiraishi, MS, PMP

M. S. Hiremath. PMP, FIE

Tsan Fai Ho, PMP

Gregory Hoffnagle, MSTM, PMP

Kathryn Hoke, PMP

Carol Holliday, MA, PMP

Randall Holt, PMP

Felicia E. Hong, PMP, MBA

Tim Hornett, PMP, MIET

Tampi Houman, MBA, BSc

Zulfiqar Hussain, PE, PMP

Isao Indo PMP, PE, JP

Suhail Iqbal, PMP, PE

Brian Irwin, MSM, PMP

Ayodeji Ishmael, PMP

Lisa Marie Jacobsen, CAPM

Patti Jansen, PMP

Christie Jean-Baptiste, PMP

Remington Ji, PMP

Tony Johnson, PMP, PgMP

Yannick Jolliet, PMP

Michele J. Jones, PMP

Pramoth Kumar Joseph, PMP

Thomas R. Joseph, PMP

George Thomas Kalacherry

Dongsu Kang, PMP

Govindaswamy Kannappan, PMP

Satya Sai Ram Kantheti,
MBA-Fin, PMP

Bharat Kapoor, PMP

Waffa Karkukly, PMP, MIT

Satish Karnam, PMP

Ramakrishna Kavirayani, PMP

David J. Kell

Harold Kerzner, PhD

Rameshchandra B Ketharaju,
CSQA

Thomas C. Keuten, PMP,
OPM3-CC

Atique Khan, PMP

Dhananjay P. Khanzode, PMP, PE

Julie Kihneman-Wooten,
MPM, PMP

Sun Kim, MBA, PMP

Marcia Klingensmith, MBA, PMP

Edmund Kosenski, PMP

Purathatil Krishnan, PMP

Elena B. Krumova, MBA

Deepak Kulkarni, PMP

Ajith Kumar P. N., PMP

Prasanth Kumar, PMP

Deepak Kumar, PMP

Amitava Kundu, PMP

Phelia M. L. Kung, MScIT

Thomas M. Kurihara

William T. W. Kwan, PMP, CSQA

Rogerio T. O. Lacerda, PMP

Luc R. Lang, PMP

Pascal Le Deley, PMP

Mike Lemmon, PMP

Ade Lewandowski

John D. Lewis, PMP

Grace Li, MA, PMP

Farhan Liaquat, MBA

Chin Yen Lim, PMP

Maria Lindell, PMP

Jose G. Linhares, Jr., PMP

Herb Lloyd, PMP

Anand Lokhande, PMP

Igor Luhan, PMP

Michael Lyzaniwski, PMP

Prakasha MS, PMP

Fengmin Ma, PMP

Andy Macklin, PMP

Saji Madapat, PMP, CSSMBB

Sandhya Mahadevan

Himanshu S. Mahanta, PMP

Vinuttha Mallikarjunaiah, PMP

George Manya, PMP

Marisol Marion-Landais, PMP

Chris Markopoulos, MPM

Donald F. Martin, PE, PMP

Greg Martin, PhD, PMP

Jojy Mathew, PE

Patrick McGonigle, PMP

Graham McHardy

Jasmijn Medina, PMP

Aamir Mehmood, PMP

Frank Meier, PMP, CSSBB

Yan Bello Méndez, PMP

Concepcion Merino

Diane D. Miller, PMP

Ted Mills, PMP

Vladimir Antonio Mininel, PMP

Barbara J. Minions, PMP

M. Aslam Mirza, MBA, PMP

Vivienne Mitchell, PMP

Alf Mittelstaedt, PMP

Prasanjit Mohapatra, PMP
Tebogo Molefe
Amrit R. Moola, PMP
Carlos Morais, PMP
Aziz Moujib, PMP
Valdery F. Moura, Jr., PMP
Balaram Muddapu, PMP, MBB
Sandip Mukhopadhyay,
    MBA, PMP
Luis G. Ortiz Muller, PMP,
    OPM3-CC
Angelo Muscaridola, MBA, PMP
Kannan Sami Nadar, PMP, COP
Jayarajan Nanoo PhD, PMP
Krish Narayan, MS, PMP
Latha Narayan, PMP
Kumar Narayanan, PMP
Kalyanraman
    Narayanswamy, PMP
Muthukumar Natesan, BE, MBA
Paulo Farah Navajas, MsC
Ifakat Nayki, PMP
Fozia Naz
Renee J. Nelson, PMP
Karen Jane Nimmons, PMP
Tom Nodar, PMP
Lori Ann Nollet, PMP
Sara Nunez, PMP, OPM3 – CA
Onyinye Nwankpa
Deborah O'Bray, CIM (Hons)
Amruta Oak, PMP
Solomon Oluwaseyi,
    MArch, MSc
Rodger Oren, MBA, PMP
Juan Alberto Otero, PMP
Ramesh (Jude) Pachamuthu,
    MSc, PMP
Frank R. Parth, MBA, PMP
George Pasieka, PMP, OPM3 – CA

Deepika Patni-Hopf, PMP, CISA
Steven Paul, PMP
Martin Pazderka, PMP
Marcela J. Peñaloza-Baez, PMP
Livio G. Perla
Greg Philliban, PMP
Fabiano Ciglio Pinto, PMP
Søren Porskrog, PMP, OPM3 – CC
Fernando Portes, MBA, PMP
Veronika Pribusz, PMP
Mitchell Provost, PE, PMP
Abrachan Pudusserry, PMP, CSM
Ajay Purohit, PMP
M. George Puziak, PMP
Moisés Quezada, PMP
Vladimir Quiñones, PMP
Nathaniel J. Quintana, PMP,
    OPM3 – CC
Omer Qureshi, PMP
Sueli dos Santos Rabaca, PMP
Alison T. Rabelo, PMP
Yves Racine, PMP
Chandramukhi Radhakrishnan,
    PMP
Anil R. Rahate, MTech
Waseem Raja, PMP
Manjula Rajaram, MBA, PMP
Uma Ramakrishnan, PMP
S. Ramani, PMP, PgMP
Krishnan Ramaskrishnan, PMP
E. A. Ramirez, PMP
Claudia Elisa Ramírez, PMP
Ashok Ranade, PMP
Pranay Ranajn, PMP
Prem Ranganath, PMP
Geoffrey J. Rankins,
    MApplSci, MPD
Ed Rao, PE, PMP
Sadhu Srinivas Rao, PMP

Yoshit Rastogi, MBA, PMP
Carol Rauh, PhD, PMP
Krupakar Reddy, PMP, PRINCE2
Juliano Reis, MBA, PMP
Michael Ribeiro, MBA, PMP
Arthur Richard, CEng, PMP
Cara Richardson, PMP
Carlos Colón Riollano, PMP,
    OPM3-CC
Brenda Roberts, PMP
Andy Robinson MBA, PMP
Charles C. Roder, Jr., PMP
Ted Rohm, PMP
Asbjørn Rolstadås, PhD, Ing
David W. Ross, PMP, PgMP
Scott T. Rowe, MS, PMP
Milind S. Rumade, PMP
Diana Russo, PMP
Lotfy Sabry, OPM3-CC, PMP
John F. Sage, PMP
Alcides Santopietro Jr., PMP
Richard Sargeant, PMP
Kulasekaran C. Satagopan,
    PMP, CQM
Vinaya Sathyanarayana, PMP
John Schlichter, MBA, OPM3-CC
Andrew Schuster, PMP, FIBC
Mark N. Scott
Edmund Seddon, PMP
Paul W. Seljeseth, PMP
Gurkan Aydin Sen, Sr., PMP
Vaddy Venkata Naga
    Seshu, PMP
Hatem Hamed Shabaan,
    Eng, PMP
Viresh C. Shah, PhD, PMP
Paul E. Shaltry, PMP
Archana Sharma, MS, BE, PMP
Vijaysarathi Sharma, PMP

Ian D. Shaw, PMP

Sayeed Ahmed Sheikh, PMP

Anuya Sheorey, PMP

Mei-Jing Subrina Shih,
    PMP, CPIM

Kazuo Shimizu, PMP

Don Shively, PMP

Veeresh Shringari, PMP

Alexandre A. Silva

Kalpana Singh

Mayank Singh, MBA, PMP

Shiv Pratap Singh, PMP

Selva Sivahami, PMP

Raji Sivaraman, MS, PMP

Tina Slankus, PMP

Jim Sloane, PMP, OPM3-CC

Susan Y. Snider, MBA, PMP

Joseph A. Sopko, PMP, OPM3 – CC

Mauro Sotille, PMP

Thierry Soulard, PMP, OPM3-CC

Nammi Sriharan

Cynthia (Snyder) Stackpole,
    MBA, PMP

Joyce Statz, PhD, PMP

Marie Sterling, PMP

Curtis D. Stevenson, PMP

Ian Stewart

John Stinnett

Roberta Storer

Aneita Strauss, PMP

Nico Stroebel, PMP

Jürgen Sturany, PMP

G. V. B. Subrahmanyam, PhD, PMP

Raymond Sun, PMP

Shyam Sundhararajan, PMP

Venkat Mangudi
    Swaminathan, PMP

Sarah Swinglehurst

Habeeb I. Syed, MBA, PMP

Adam Sykes, PMP

Masanori Takahashi, MA, PMP

Martin D. Talbott, PMP, CSSBB

Gerhard Tekes, PMP

Thomas. P. Thomas, MBA, PMP

Jamal Tiari, MSc

Donghui Oliver Tong, PMP

Massimo Torre, PhD, PMP

Luciano Cerqueira Torres, PMP

Richard N. Tretheway, PMP, PE

Ricardo Triana, PMP

Sandra Dunny Troutman,
    EdM, PMP

Srinkath U. S.

Muhammad Usman, PMP

Vijai Vadlamuri, PMP

Nageswaran Vaidyanathan,
    MBA, PMP

Sharon M. Valencia, PMP

Carmen M. Valle, PMP, CBCP

Dennis K. Van Gemert, MS, PMP

Fred van Staden, PMP

Laxman Vasan

Robert Victor

Alika L. Victor, PMP, Prince2

Jaywanth Vijayapuri, PMP

David Violette, MPM, PMP

Kristin L. Vitello

Abhijeet Wadkar

Barbara Walsh, CAPM

Min Wang, PhD

Brian Watson, PMP

Patrick Weaver, PMP

Kevin R. Wegryn, PMP, CPM

Simone Weilacher

Rajendra Welankar, PMP

Ken Whiting, PMP

James Wilson, PMP

Simmone Wishart

Lawrence R. Witham MBA, PMP

Hannah J. Wolf, PMP

Nan Wolfslayer, AStd

James M. Wood, PhD, PMP

Walter J. Wright, PMP

Yan Xiaojing, PMP

Anna Yarashus, PMP

Naumann Yousef, PMP

Syed Arslan Sabah Zaidi, PMP

Karla Zanker, PMP

Wei Zhan, PhD

John Zlockie, PMP

X2.3 Contributors and Reviewers of the *OPM3®*—First Edition

X2.3.1 *OPM3®* First Edition Core Team Members

Ralf Friedrich, MSc, PMP, OPM3 Program Manager
William Haeck, MBA, PMP, OPM3 Deputy Program Manager
Fred Abrams, PMP, CPL
Claudia M. Baca, PMP
Mila Bozic, PMP
Peggy Brady, PMP
Glenn Carleton, PMP
Ajit Ghai, MSc, PMP
Santosh Guha, MBA, PMP
Craig Hardy, PMP
Thomas Keuten, PMP, CMC
Lisa Marie Kruszewski
Ade Lewandowski,
Rabbani Lutfur, MBA, PMP
Narasimha "Naru" Nayak, PMP, PGDIE
Jim Sloane, PMP, CM
Martin Talbott, PMP
Micheal Tipman, PEng, PMP
Clarese Walker, PMP
David Whelbourn, MBA

X2.3.2 Other Contributors

John J. Abbott, PhD
Farhad Abdollahyan, MBA, PMP
Bernard E. Abey, PE, PMP
Matthew Abraham
Fred Abrams, PMP, CPL
Rajendra Achanta
Ravi Advani, MBA
Areeb Afsah, PMP
Kevin J. Aguanno, MAPM, PMP
Sheikh Nisar Ahmed, MS, MCSP
Emine Aydin Akkaya, BSA
Randall Alberts, CPM, PMP
Italo Albidone

Jon K. Aldridge, PMP
Petya Alexandrova, PMP
Madinah S. Ali
Tobías Aliaga, MBA, PMP
Sheila Alvey
Andrew A. Anderson
Harmon Anderson
Karl "Andy" Anderson, PMP
Terry R. Anderson, PMP
Jose Aniceto
Deborah L. Anthony
Victor E. Anyosa, PMP
Joan Allen B. Arch, PMP

Alexey Arefiev
O. Arivazhagan
Scott E. Artmann
Lisset Avery, MEd
Assolari Mohammad Aziz
James Ballew, DM, MBA
Michael Barr
Jorge Barros
Mike Bartmanovich, PMP
Richard Barton
Stacy Baskin
Pierre H. Batheret, PMP
Leslie Bayer

Michel Bazinet, PMP

Norm Beal

Roger D. Beatty, PhD, PMP

Chris Beautement, PMP

Patrick Beauvillard

Nabil E. Bedewi, DSc, PMP

Arley R. Bedillion

Julia M. Bednar, PMP

Jeff Begeman, MSPM, PMP

Jim Beierschmitt

George C. Belev, CPM, CPCM

Michael J. Bennett

Randy Bennett, MS, PMP

Deo Karan Bhalotia, MS, PMP

Sapna Bhargava Atulkumar N.
    Bhatt, MBA, PMP

Mark Bierbaum

Marty Biggs

Richard M. Bingman Jr., PMP

G. Bittencourt, BSc, MBA

Susan S. Bivins, PMP

John A. Blakely, MS, PMP

Nigel Blampied, PE, PMP

Jim Blaylock

Victoria Bondy, BSc, PMP

Stephen F. Bonk, PE, PMP

Herbert Borchardt

Eugene O. Borden, MBA, PMP

Robert J. Borotkanics

David A. Boss, PMP

Rejean Boucher, CD, PMP

Eugene C. Bounds, PMP

Lynda Bourne, PMP

Stewart Bowman J.

Chris Boyd, PMP

Savo Bozic, BSc

David Bradford, PMP

Michael Branch

Christophe N. Bredillet, DSc

Brenda L. Breslin, PMP

Steve Briggs, MBA, PMP

John A. Briggs, PMP

Damien Brignell

Will Brimberry

Timothy J. Briscoe, PMP,
    PMO CAQ

Alberto S. Brito

Timothy S. Brown

Valerie Brown

Robert I. R. Brown, APMP, ACIB

Connie Brown, PMP

Donald Bruck

Vicki Bryant-Cano

Kim Buchalski

Nina M. Burgess, CCM, PMP

John Buziak, PE, PMP

Trony "Yi" Cai, MBA, PMP

Laura Caldwell, PMP

Eoin J. P. Callan, MBA, PMP

Linda Campbell-Brooks

Kim Caputo

Norman H. Carter, MBA

Bruce C. Chadbourne, PMP

J. Brett Champlin, MBA,
    CSP/CCP

Pradeep Chandra, PMP

Ramesh Chandrasekaran,
    MBA, PMP

Carolyn Chapman

Catherine Joy Chapman

Trevor Chappell, EurIng, PMP

Hemchander Chari

Gordon Chastain

Monica Chauhan

Guadalupe M. Chavez

David C. Chen

Clala Xiao Cheng, MBA, PMP

Gary L. Chin, PMP

Patrick Chouteau, MBA, PMP

Ana Christina P.

Joe Ciccione

Curtis W. Clark, MBA, PMP

Juana F. Clark, PMP

Alan Coates, PMP

Mary Pat Collins, MS, PMP

Ronald E. Collins, PMP

Edna Colon, MBA, MSIS

Carlos Colon, MBA, PMP

Marge Combe

David L. Conrad, MBA

Helen S. Cooke, PMP

Laurie Cooke, RPh

Terence J. Cooke-Davies,
    PhD, BA

Nancy A. Corbett, PMP

John E. Cormier

Patti Corrigan, CPCU, PMP

Daniel E. Crabtree

Charles B. Craytor

Douglas J. Cretsinger, MBA, PMP

Colin H. Cropley, BE (Chem), PMP

Jack Crowley

Margery Cruise

Patricia Louise Cunnington

Wanda Curlee, DM, PMP

Darren Dalcher, PhD, MAPM

Mario Damiani, PMP

David L. Davis

David Davitian

Fabricio P. de Farias, PMP

Aline Lucas de Moura Costa, PMP

Marcos Paulo de Oliveira

Valadares de Oliveira

Brian K. Dean, MBA, PMP

Wendy Decker, PMP

Zamir Deen

Pasquale DeFilippis

Jim Delrie, PE, PMP

Berry C. Densman, PMP

Meena Desai

Ranjana Deshmukh

John L. Dettbarn Jr., DSc, PE

Chuck Detwiler

Sheila L. Diduck, MBA, PMP

Syed Ali Dilawer

Jerry Dimos, PMP

Peter Dimov, CBM, PMP

Paul Dinsmore

Julie Ditmore

Peter H. Dittmar, MBA

Vivek Dixit, CQA

Miles Dixon, MA

Serif Haluk Dogancay, MBA

Dan Dorion, PMP

Luis Augusto dos Santos

Thomas James Douglas

Magnus K. Drengwitz, PMP

Philippe Dubernard

Judith L. Dunlop

Gloria J. Durham, MPM

Stefano Durighello, PMP

Mark Dushanko

Mukesh Dutta, MBA, PMP

Robert P. Eagan, MBA, PMP

Jason Eddinger

Nancy Edgar

Tim Egan, PMP

Marlies Egberding, PMP

Ruth Eisenhauer

Karen Ekrem

John M. Elash, PMP

Gary S. Elliott, MS

Lenita Elon

Patrick J. Engesser

Tibor Eperjesi

Patricia A. Erickson

Michael P. Ervick, MBA, PMP

Guy Euget, PhD, PMP

David C. Evenson, PMP

Steve Fahrenkrog, PMP

Pamela Farmer, PMP

Dax Faulstich

Chris Fawcett

Linda Fernandez, MBA

Madhu Fernando, MEng

Jack P. Ferraro, PMP

John F. Filicetti, MBA, PMP

Michael Fisher

Daniel Forgues, MSc, PMP

Robert J. Fortin

Paul Fosland

John M. Foster, MBA, PMP

Kitty Francen, PMP

Fran Stoss Frank, MSPM, PMP

Ann Franklin

William L. Franklin, PE, PMP

Stephen L. Fritts, MBA, CMC

Kenneth Fung, MBA, PMP

Michael J. Funke

Herman N. Gaines Jr., PMP

Rajeev Garg, PMP

Gail E. Garland, MSOD, PMP

Peggy Gartner, Dipl-Inf Wiss, PMP

Daniel J. Garvin

T. K. (Ted) Gaughan

Bruce A. Geanaros

Robert M. Gerbrandt

Vivian Gericke, MScEng, PMP

Philip J. Gerson

David W. Gibson

Timothy A. Gikas

Jeff Gold, MBA, CMC

Peter B. Goldsbury, BE, DMS

Herman Gonzalez, PMP

Michael J. Goodman, PMP, MSEE

Kimberly Gordon

Joe Gorman

Jackie Goss, PMP

Alan E. Gould, PMP

Robert Graham

Mar Freire Grande

Jackie Gray, PMP

Don J. Green

Leon S. Green, MSc, PMP

Lianne Griffin, PMP

David G. Grimmer, PMP

Angie Groves, PMP

Michael J. Guffey

Karthika Rao Gupta, PMP

Bulent E. Guzel

Jacqueline Haddad

Nathalie Haddad

Warren J. Hall, BE, NZCE

Aaron S. Hall, PMP

Donna Hall, PMP

Jody Hampshire

Frederick S. Hansen

Jeffrey R. Hansen

Frank L. Harper Jr., PhD(c), PMP

Peter Harpum

Polly Harringon

Sue Hasso, PMP

Saket R. Havaldar

Harlton G. Hawk, CISSP, PMP

Michael R. Heiberg, JD, PMP

Deborah H. Heintz, MBA, PMP

Penny Hendrix

Rosemary E. Henley, PMP

Cynthia Hennig

Bonnie J. Hereford, PMP

James (Jim) A. Hessel, BEng, PMP

Claire Hevey, PMP	Aadham Junaidallah, CISSP, CQA	Guilherme Ponce de Leon
Jason Highberger	Deepak Kadam	Lago, PMP
Jay R. Hilton, MBA, PMP	Nikitas J. Kalantjakos, PMP	Winnie Lam, PMP
Cindy Hochart	Katsayuki Kanaji	Bruce Lambly
Lisa R. Hodges, MCSM, PMP	Russ Kane, PMP	J.C. Lamkin, CNA, PMP
Jeffrey Hoffman	Deborah Katz	Scott Langton
Robert Hogzett	Omar Kayed, MBA	David J. Lanners, MBA, PMP
Carol A. Holliday, PMP	Michel Kabanga Kayembe	Rodney D. Larson, PMP
Valerie Hood-Moore	Karl Kaylor	Mário Lavado
Jacquelyn Hope	Kathy Keele	Fernando Ledesma, MBA
Richard Horne	Michael Kehoe, PMP	Gregory Lehn
April E. Horne, MBA, PMP	Eleanor B. Kellett	Richard Leight
Tim Hornett, PMP	John C. Kelly	Ronald A. Lester
Andy Horsfall, PMP	John Kennedy	Craig J. Letavec, MSPM, PMP
George M. Horsham	Brian P. Kennemer	Ralph J. Levene, PhD, FAPM
John Howe, PMP	Larry S. Kilmer	Ginger Levin
Darrel G. Hubbard, PE	David Kim	Andrew Levy
Edmund N. Hudon, PMP	Wendy J. King, PMP	Ade Lewandowski
Rose-Helene Humeau, PMP	Naresh Kirpalani	Robin Liang
Chuck Hunt	Ranko Klacar, HBSc	Beth Lillie
Harold S. Hunt, PMP, IT Project+	William T. Knudsen, MBA, PMP	Lori B. Lindbergh, MBA, PMP
Drew R. Hunter	Joan Knutson	Tony Lindeman, PMP
John Hunter	Kenneth Kock	Gábor Lipi, PMP
Joan L. Hyland, CSQE, PMP	Theodore Koike, CPIM, PMP	Jack Lippy
Christine Hynes	Erin J. Kolias, CGA, PMP	Brett M. Locke, CQM, PMP
Subrahmanyam Ivatury	Derek Konrad	Neil Love
Mitchell J. Iverson, PMP	Mitja Kozman	Ann L. Lovejoy, MBA
Stasia Iwanicki, PMP	George E. Kramer, PMP	Maureen Lovell
Angyan P. Jagathnarayanan,	Walther Krause, PMP	Brenda Lown
FIE, CE	John Krigbaum	Bill Lowthian MEng, PEng
Michael K. Jakoby, CFP, PMP	Karel Krikke, MA, PMF	Shay Lubianiker
Cornelius Jansen	Robert V. Kulin, BSc, PMP	Padhraic Ludden, PMP
Rob Jeges, MBA, PMP	Prasanna Kumar	Faye A. Lumsden, MBA, PMP
William D. Jenison	K. Bob Kunhardt	Edwin C. Lutz
Mike Jenkinson MSc, CEng	Thomas Kurihara	Mike MacGregor
Pamela D. Johnson	Donna Kurtz	Lawrence Mack
Robert Johnson	Janet Kuster, MBA, PMP	Karen L. MacNeil
Scott A. Johnson	Mark E. Kwandrans, MBA, PMP	Sajith Madapat, CPIM, PMP
Chandrashekar P. Jois, PhD, CQA	Shelli Lackey	David W. Malas, PMP

Larry A. Malcolm, PMP

Jerry Manas, PMP

Jim Mandas

Venkat Mangudi

Tony Maramara, BSME

Andrew Marecek

Joseph A. Marotta

Jackie Marshall

Ronald J. Martin

Michael G. Martin, MBA, PMP

Donald F. Martin, PE, PMP

Richard Mathews

Barbara J. Mauro

Tim Mawhinney

David A. Maynard

John S. Mays

Mike McAndrew, CQE, PMP

Meg McCarthy

Jeremy McClain

John K. McCreery, PhD, PMP

Russ McDowell, MEng, PMP

Jeanine McGuire

Jody McIlrath

Bruce K. McLean, PMP

Paul McMahon

Richard McNeill, PMP

Michael McPherson

Ed Mechler, CCP, PMP

Terri Melchior, PMP

Luis D. Mendieta, BS

Greg Miller

Tina Miller

Tony Miller

Berne C. Miller, CPL, PMP

Robert T. Milner

R. Thomas Milner, PMP

Wayne B. Miner

Vladimir A. Mininel

M. Aslam Mirza, MBA, CE

Anil Kumar Mishra

Nidhi Misra

Megan Mitchell

Subhash G. Modasia

Robert Moeller

Kerri F. Momorella, MBA, PMP

Michael S. Monroe

R. Lynn Montague, MBA, PMP

Danielle Moore

Donald J. Moore

Karla M. Moore

Suzzette Moore

Bruce Morey, MSE(ME), PMP

Barbara K. Most, PMP

Carol A. Mould, BCom(Hons), PMP

Douglas Muir

Bruce R. Mulholland, PEng, MScCE

Ralf Müller, PMP

Electa W. Mulvanity, MBA, PMP

Somasundaram Muralidharan

Robert Murray

Heather A. Murrell, MBA

Rajan Krishna Murthy

Robert J. Myers

Judith M. Myerson

Ravindra Nadkarni, PMP

Subbaraya Mandaya Nagappa, BE

Rohini C. Nagaraj

Madhusudhan Nagarajan,
    MBA, PMP

George Namour

Jay Namputhiripad, MBA, PMP

Anthony J. Naples

Rajesh K. Narayanan, MBA, PMP

Ifakat Nayki

Mohammad Naziruddin

Stephen R. Neuendorf, Esq

Duy Nguyen, MPM, PEng

Jose Ignacio Noguera, MBA, PMP

Jamie A. Northrup

Kimberly D. Norwood

Robert Noteboom

Katharina Nowotny-Boles, PMP

Jose Adir Soibelman Nunes

John Oberdiek, PMP

Lawrence Oliva, MBA, PMP

Linda Oman

Perihan Ongeoglu

Neil Osborne

Else-Marie Östling

Loras (Bob) Osweiler

James G. Owens

Ayo Oyewore

Louis R. Pack Jr.

Gregory C. Packard, PMP

Stephen J. Page

Lorna J. Palmer, PEng, PMP

Arun K. Pandeya, MBA, PMP

Ajay Parasrampuria

David Parker

William P. Parker

Celia Parks

Frank Parth

Sharon L. Paugh

Marcos Paulo

Seenivasan Pavanasam

Adam Pearson

David A. Peck

Pasi Penttilä

Manuel Chaves Pereira, MSc, PMP

Ashley A. Pereira, PEng, MBA

Francisco Perez-Polo, PMP

John Perotti

Allison Perry

Helen Peters, PMP

Norbert Peterson

Vasilj Petrovic, PEng, PMP

Barbara C. Phillips, PMP

Crispin "Kik" Piney, BSc, PMP

Donald Poitras

Joyce Poole, BS, PMP

Gretchen Porkert

Kevin E. Porter

Dan Prather

Gloria Presa

Richard Prosser

Robin Prosser

Saurel Quettan, MBA, PMP

Gloria Quintanilla-Osorio

Srinivas Raghavan, PMP

Sandra L. Rago, PMP

Monwar Rahman, MBA, MSS

Meera Ramachandran, FLMI, PMP

S. K. Raman, CISA, PMP

Linda W. Ramey, PMP

Anneke Randall

Suzanne Rankins

Raju Narsing Rao, PMP

Brett Rawlins, BE

Mary-Lou Raybould, PMP, MBA

Doug Redden

Ravi Narayana Reddy

Chandra Sekhar Reddy,
    BTech, PMP

Tiffany Reilly

Dax Reis

Steve Resnick

Wynn Gerald Richards III

John V. Rickards, FCAM, PMP

Stan Rifkin

Tim Riley

Donald G. Ritchie

Andrew Robertson, PMP

James R. Robinson, PMP

Mark E. Robson, MPM, PMP

Peter J. Rock

Alexandre G. Rodrigues, PhD

Everett Rodriguez

Fabio Zaffalon Rodriguez

Manual A. Rodriguez

Andy Rodriguez, PMP

Fernan Rodriguez, PMP

John Roecker, PhD

Peter W. Rogers, MMA, MS

Asbjørn Rolstadås

Dennis M. Rose

Diana Russo

Gunes Sahillioglu, MSc, MAPM

Nirbhay S. Salar, PMP

Venkat Sankaran

Vinaya Sathyanarayana,
    BTech, PMP

Antony Satyadas

Wayne Richard Sauer, PMP

David Wayne Sauls

Joyce Scales

Anne Marie Schanz

Roberto Schiliro

John Schlichter, MBA

Claudia Schmid

John Schmitt, PMP

William Schneider

Richard Schwartz

Mark N. Scott

Richard A. Scott, MSSM, PMP

Pavanasam Seenivasan,
    MBA, PMP

Paul W. Seljeseth, PMP

Dhruba P. Sen, CSQA, PMP

Amitava Sengupta

Rafael Serrano Jr., PMP

Azeem K. Shah, MBA, PMP

Ajay Sharma

Chetan Sharma

Monica Sharma

Colin A. Sharp

Carol A. Sheehan

Shoukat M. Sheikh, MBA, PMP

Daniel M. Shellhammer, MSc, PMP

Mohammed Sherif, MA, MBA

W. J. Shiflett

Larry Sieck

Anji Siegel

Mike Silhan, PMP

Mike R. Simmons, PMP

Jagannath Sivaramalingam

Gregory Skulmoski

Tina Slankas, PMP

Ken Smith

Tim L. Smith

Paul Smith, CPA, PMP

Sushmita K. Smith, PMP

William Snyder

Joseph A. Sopko, PMP

Thierry M. Soulard, PMP

Randall S. Spires

Kristopher G. Sprague,
    MBA, PMP

Meg Sprangler

Michael E. Spruch, PMP

G. H. Sridhar

Srini B. Srinivasan, CISA, PMP

Julie St. George

Tim R. Stahl

Edward A. Starr

Malcolm Stayner, PMP

Jeffery Stempien, PMP

Dennis G. Stephenson, PMP

Marie Sterling, BSc

Chris Stevens, BSc(Hon), PhD

Sharon B. Stewart

Michael Stockwell, PMP

Paulette Strain

Lee A. Stubbert

Thangavel Subbu, MBA, PMP

Finn Svenning
Brett R. Swartz, PMP
Leon D. Swartz, PMP
Edward P. Swirbalus, PMP
Adam D. Sykes, MS, PMP
Kelly M. Talsma, PMP
Bond R. Tarr, PMP
Christine E. Tauhert, PMP
David E. Taylor, PMP
Harrell Thomas, RCDD
Tracie H. Thompson
John M. Thorsen
Sean P. Tillman
Tobi Timko
B. Ray Tinkler Jr.
Sandra Titus
Roberto Torres, PhD, PMP
Lee A. Towe, MBA, PMP
Joseph P. Townsend, MBA, PMP
Robert C. Trafton, PMP
Yves Trehin, PMP
Theresa Trent
Mario Trevino
Lynne Tribble
Leena V. Tripathi, PMP
Zachary D. Tudor, CISSP, CCP
Ian Turnbull
Rufus A. Turpin, CSQE, CQA
Bobbeye Underwood, PMP
Akhil Uniyal, MBA
Theodore J. Urbanowicz, PMP
Attaback Vahid, PMP

Robert van der Veur
Noah van Loen, PMP
Paul van Tongeren, BSc, PMP
William D. (Bill) Varanese,
    CBCP, PMP
Ricardo Viana Vargas, MSc, PMP
Satish Varma
Jan G. M. Veltman
Deb Verlo
Karen S. Vernon, PMP
Roberto Viale, PMP
Walter A. Viali, CSQA, PMP
Marconi Fábio Vieira, MBA, PMP
Edward M. Vigen, PMP
Tobias Aliaga Vilchez
Dave Violette, MPM, PMP
Viola Visnjevac, PMP
Cornelis (Kees) Vonk, PMP
Ronald P. C. Waller, PMP,
    PMI Fellow
Charlene "Chuck" Walrad
Jennifer Walter, PMP
Qiyu Wang, MBA, PMP
Melissa A. Warchol
Jonathan Ward
Nick Warrillow, APMP, LLB
Melissa Washington
Richard A. Watts
Linda Watts, PMP, CBA-IPI Lead
    Assessor
Mohammad Waziruddi
Dalton Weekley

Joseph E. Weider
David E. Weil
Cynthia T. Weinmann
Paul Wesman, MA
Randy West
John Wetter, PMP, MBA
Michael J. Weymier, PMP
Rosanne M. Wiesen
Jean M. Wilhelm, MSHA, PMP
Sherryl G. Wilkins, MBA, PMP
David Williamson, MBA, PMP
Marcy M. Wilson
Patrick Wilson
Lance E. Wilson, PMP
Gregory Wilt
Doug Winters, SSBB, PMP
Kenneth C. Wiswall
Jacek Wojcieszynski
Peter W. A. Wood
James Woods, PMO-CAQ, PMP
David E. Worrell
William R. Wright
Robert K. Wysocki
Lu Xiao, PMP
Brian R. York, MBA, PMP
Ralph Young
Alan E. Yue, MCNE, PMP
Brenda Zech
Sameh Said Zeid
Marc A. Zocher
Marc Zubrzycki
Ofer Zwikael

APPENDIX X3
OPM3 SELF-ASSESSMENT METHOD (SAM) QUESTIONS

X3.1 OPM3 Self-Assessment Method

The *OPM3* Self-Assessment Method (SAM) is for use by an organization when looking to gain experience with model application at a high level. This does not replace a rigorous assessment performed by an OPM3 Certified Practitioner, but can help acquaint the organization with the model in general. The OPM3 SAM permits organizations to assess their current state of maturity in organizational project management in relation to the set of Best Practices that comprise the *OPM3* standard. The results of the self-assessment indicate where the organization stands on a general continuum of organizational project management maturity, viewed overall in terms of maturity within the domains and process improvement stages. The results identify the list of Best Practices the organization currently demonstrates and a list of Best Practices the organization does not demonstrate, according to the responses given to the survey.

This appendix includes a significant list of self-assessment questions. The SMCI SAM questions appear first, followed by the OE SAM questions.

Best Practice ID	SAM Question	Yes	No	Portfolio Domain	Program Domain	Project Domain	Process Improvement Stage
8400	Does your organization Standardize the "Develop Portfolio Strategic Plan" process?			Portfolio			Standardize
8510	Does your organization Measure the "Develop Portfolio Strategic Plan" process?			Portfolio			Measure
8620	Does your organization Control the "Develop Portfolio Strategic Plan" process?			Portfolio			Control
8730	Does your organization Improve the "Develop Portfolio Strategic Plan" process?			Portfolio			Improve
8410	Does your organization Standardize the "Develop Portfolio Charter" process?			Portfolio			Standardize
8520	Does your organization Measure the "Develop Portfolio Charter" process?			Portfolio			Measure
8630	Does your organization Control the "Develop Portfolio Charter" process?			Portfolio			Control
8740	Does your organization Improve the "Develop Portfolio Charter" process?			Portfolio			Improve
8420	Does your organization Standardize the "Define Portfolio Roadmap" process?			Portfolio			Standardize
8530	Does your organization Measure the "Define Portfolio Roadmap" process?			Portfolio			Measure

Best Practice ID	SAM Question	Yes	No	Portfolio Domain	Program Domain	Project Domain	Process Improvement Stage
8640	Does your organization Control the "Define Portfolio Roadmap" process?			Portfolio			Control
8750	Does your organization Improve the "Define Portfolio Roadmap" process?			Portfolio			Improve
5080	Does your organization Standardize the "Manage Strategic Change" process?			Portfolio			Standardize
5990	Does your organization Measure the "Manage Strategic Change" process?			Portfolio			Measure
6500	Does your organization Control the "Manage Strategic Change" process?			Portfolio			Control
6890	Does your organization Improve the "Manage Strategic Change" process?			Portfolio			Improve
8540	Does your organization Standardize the "Develop Portfolio Management Plan" process?			Portfolio			Standardize
8550	Does your organization Measure the "Develop Portfolio Management Plan" process?			Portfolio			Measure
8650	Does your organization Control the "Develop Portfolio Management Plan" process?			Portfolio			Control
8760	Does your organization Improve the "Develop Portfolio Management Plan" process?			Portfolio			Improve
4945	Does your organization Standardize the "Define Portfolio" process?			Portfolio			Standardize
4955	Does your organization Measure the "Define Portfolio" process?			Portfolio			Measure
4965	Does your organization Control the "Define Portfolio" process?			Portfolio			Control
4975	Does your organization Improve the "Define Portfolio" process?			Portfolio			Improve
4985	Does your organization Standardize the "Optimize Portfolio" process?			Portfolio			Standardize
4995	Does your organization Measure the "Optimize Portfolio" process?			Portfolio			Measure
5005	Does your organization Control the "Optimize Portfolio" process?			Portfolio			Control
5015	Does your organization Improve the "Optimize Portfolio" process?			Portfolio			Improve
5025	Does your organization Standardize the "Authorize Portfolio" process?			Portfolio			Standardize
5035	Does your organization Measure the "Authorize Portfolio" process?			Portfolio			Measure
5045	Does your organization Control the "Authorize Portfolio" process?			Portfolio			Control
5055	Does your organization Improve the "Authorize Portfolio" process?			Portfolio			Improve

Best Practice ID	SAM Question	Yes	No	Portfolio Domain	Program Domain	Project Domain	Process Improvement Stage
8460	Does your organization Standardize the "Provide Portfolio Oversight" process?			Portfolio			Standardize
8570	Does your organization Measure the "Provide Portfolio Oversight" process?			Portfolio			Measure
8680	Does your organization Control the "Provide Portfolio Oversight" process?			Portfolio			Control
8790	Does your organization Improve the "Provide Portfolio Oversight" process?			Portfolio			Improve
8470	Does your organization Standardize the "Develop Portfolio Performance Management Plan" process?			Portfolio			Standardize
8580	Does your organization Measure the "Develop Portfolio Performance Management Plan" process?			Portfolio			Measure
8690	Does your organization Control the "Develop Portfolio Performance Management Plan" process?			Portfolio			Control
8800	Does your organization Improve the "Develop Portfolio Performance Management Plan" process?			Portfolio			Improve
8480	Does your organization Standardize the "Manage Supply and Demand" process?			Portfolio			Standardize
8590	Does your organization Measure the "Manage Supply and Demand" process?			Portfolio			Measure
8700	Does your organization Control the "Manage Supply and Demand" process?			Portfolio			Control
8810	Does your organization Improve the "Manage Supply and Demand" process?			Portfolio			Improve
8490	Does your organization Standardize the "Manage Portfolio Value" process?			Portfolio			Standardize
8600	Does your organization Measure the "Manage Portfolio Value" process?			Portfolio			Measure
8710	Does your organization Control the "Manage Portfolio Value" process?			Portfolio			Control
8820	Does your organization Improve the "Manage Portfolio Value" process?			Portfolio			Improve
5030	Does your organization Standardize the "Develop Portfolio Communication Management Plan" process?			Portfolio			Standardize
5940	Does your organization Measure the "Develop Portfolio Communication Management Plan" process?			Portfolio			Measure
6450	Does your organization Control the "Develop Portfolio Communication Management Plan" process?			Portfolio			Control
6840	Does your organization Improve the "Develop Portfolio Communication Management Plan" process?			Portfolio			Improve
5070	Does your organization Standardize the "Manage Portfolio Information" process?			Portfolio			Standardize

Best Practice ID	SAM Question	Yes	No	Portfolio Domain	Program Domain	Project Domain	Process Improvement Stage
5980	Does your organization Measure the "Manage Portfolio Information" process?			Portfolio			Measure
6490	Does your organization Control the "Manage Portfolio Information" process?			Portfolio			Control
6880	Does your organization Improve the "Manage Portfolio Information" process?			Portfolio			Improve
8500	Does your organization Standardize the "Develop Portfolio Risk Management Plan" process?			Portfolio			Standardize
8610	Does your organization Measure the "Develop Portfolio Risk Management Plan" process?			Portfolio			Measure
8720	Does your organization Control the "Develop Portfolio Risk Management Plan" process?			Portfolio			Control
8830	Does your organization Improve the "Develop Portfolio Risk Management Plan" process?			Portfolio			Improve
5140	Does your organization Standardize the "Manage Portfolio Risks" process?			Portfolio			Standardize
6050	Does your organization Measure the "Manage Portfolio Risks" process?			Portfolio			Measure
6560	Does your organization Control the "Manage Portfolio Risks" process?			Portfolio			Control
6950	Does your organization Improve the "Manage Portfolio Risks" process?			Portfolio			Improve
3270	Does your organization Standardize the "Communications Planning" process?				Program		Standardize
3740	Does your organization Measure the "Communications Planning" process?				Program		Measure
4150	Does your organization Control the "Communications Planning" process?				Program		Control
4540	Does your organization Improve the "Communications Planning" process?				Program		Improve
3370	Does your organization Standardize the "Information Distribution" process?				Program		Standardize
3840	Does your organization Measure the "Information Distribution" process?				Program		Measure
4250	Does your organization Control the "Information Distribution" process?				Program		Control
4640	Does your organization Improve the "Information Distribution" process?				Program		Improve
3410	Does your organization Standardize the "Program Performance Reporting" process?				Program		Standardize
3880	Does your organization Measure the "Program Performance Reporting" process?				Program		Measure
4290	Does your organization Control the "Program Performance Reporting" process?				Program		Control

Best Practice ID	SAM Question	Yes	No	Portfolio Domain	Program Domain	Project Domain	Process Improvement Stage
4680	Does your organization Improve the "Program Performance Reporting" process?				Program		Improve
3210	Does your organization Standardize the "Program Cost Estimation" process?				Program		Standardize
3680	Does your organization Measure the "Program Cost Estimation" process?				Program		Measure
4090	Does your organization Control the "Program Cost Estimation" process?				Program		Control
4480	Does your organization Improve the "Program Cost Estimation" process?				Program		Improve
3715	Does your organization Measure the "Program Financial Framework Establishment" process?				Program		Measure
3725	Does your organization Control the "Program Financial Framework Establishment" process?				Program		Control
3735	Does your organization Improve the "Program Financial Framework Establishment" process?				Program		Improve
3705	Does your organization Standardize the "Program Financial Framework Establishment" process?				Program		Standardize
3755	Does your organization Measure the "Program Financial Management Plan Development" process?				Program		Measure
3765	Does your organization Control the "Program Financial Management Plan Development" process?				Program		Control
3775	Does your organization Improve the "Program Financial Management Plan Development" process?				Program		Improve
3745	Does your organization Standardize the "Program Financial Management Plan Development" process?				Program		Standardize
7710	Does your organization Standardize the "Component Cost Estimation" process?				Program		Standardize
7880	Does your organization Measure the "Component Cost Estimation" process?				Program		Measure
8050	Does your organization Control the "Component Cost Estimation" process?				Program		Control
8220	Does your organization Improve the "Component Cost Estimation" process?				Program		Improve
3220	Does your organization Standardize the "Program Cost Budgeting" process?				Program		Standardize
3690	Does your organization Measure the "Program Cost Budgeting" process?				Program		Measure
4100	Does your organization Control the "Program Cost Budgeting" process?				Program		Control
4490	Does your organization Improve the "Program Cost Budgeting" process?				Program		Improve
3825	Does your organization Control the "Program Financial Monitoring and Control" process?				Program		Control

Best Practice ID	SAM Question	Yes	No	Portfolio Domain	Program Domain	Project Domain	Process Improvement Stage
3835	Does your organization Improve the "Program Financial Monitoring and Control" process?				Program		Improve
3805	Does your organization Standardize the "Program Financial Monitoring and Control" process?				Program		Standardize
3815	Does your organization Measure the "Program Financial Monitoring and Control" process?				Program		Measure
7720	Does your organization Standardize the "Program Financial Closure" process?				Program		Standardize
7890	Does your organization Measure the "Program Financial Closure" process?				Program		Measure
8060	Does your organization Control the "Program Financial Closure" process?				Program		Control
8230	Does your organization Improve the "Program Financial Closure" process?				Program		Improve
3120	Does your organization Standardize the "Program Initiation" process?				Program		Standardize
3590	Does your organization Measure the "Program Initiation" process?				Program		Measure
4000	Does your organization Control the "Program Initiation" process?				Program		Control
4390	Does your organization Improve the "Program Initiation" process?				Program		Improve
3130	Does your organization Standardize the "Program Management Plan Development" process?				Program		Standardize
3600	Does your organization Measure the "Program Management Plan Development" process?				Program		Measure
4010	Does your organization Control the "Program Management Plan Development" process?				Program		Control
4405	Does your organization Improve the "Program Management Plan Development" process?				Program		Improve
3155	Does your organization Standardize the "Program Infrastructure Development" process?				Program		Standardize
3165	Does your organization Measure the "Program Infrastructure Development" process?				Program		Measure
3175	Does your organization Control the "Program Infrastructure Development" process?				Program		Control
3185	Does your organization Improve the "Program Infrastructure Development" process?				Program		Improve
3340	Does your organization Standardize the "Program Execution Management" process?				Program		Standardize
3810	Does your organization Measure the "Program Execution Management" process?				Program		Measure
4220	Does your organization Control the "Program Execution Management" process?				Program		Control

Best Practice ID	SAM Question	Yes	No	Portfolio Domain	Program Domain	Project Domain	Process Improvement Stage
4610	Does your organization Improve the "Program Execution Management" process?				Program		Improve
3215	Does your organization Standardize the "Program Performance Monitoring and Control" process?				Program		Standardize
3225	Does your organization Measure the "Program Performance Monitoring and Control" process?				Program		Measure
3235	Does your organization Control the "Program Performance Monitoring and Control" process?				Program		Control
3245	Does your organization Improve the "Program Performance Monitoring and Control" process?				Program		Improve
4385	Does your organization Improve the "Program Transition and Benefits Sustainment" process?				Program		Improve
4355	Does your organization Standardize the "Program Transition and Benefits Sustainment" process?				Program		Standardize
4365	Does your organization Measure the "Program Transition and Benefits Sustainment" process?				Program		Measure
4375	Does your organization Control the "Program Transition and Benefits Sustainment" process?				Program		Control
3500	Does your organization Standardize the "Program Closure" process?				Program		Standardize
3970	Does your organization Measure the "Program Closure" process?				Program		Measure
4380	Does your organization Control the "Program Closure" process?				Program		Control
4770	Does your organization Improve the "Program Closure" process?				Program		Improve
3320	Does your organization Standardize the "Program Procurement Planning" process?				Program		Standardize
3790	Does your organization Measure the "Program Procurement Planning" process?				Program		Measure
4200	Does your organization Control the "Program Procurement Planning" process?				Program		Control
4590	Does your organization Improve the "Program Procurement Planning" process?				Program		Improve
3665	Does your organization Measure the "Program Procurement" process?				Program		Measure
3675	Does your organization Control the "Program Procurement" process?				Program		Control
3685	Does your organization Improve the "Program Procurement" process?				Program		Improve
3655	Does your organization Standardize the "Program Procurement" process?				Program		Standardize
3400	Does your organization Standardize the "Program Procurement Administration" process?				Program		Standardize

Best Practice ID	SAM Question	Yes	No	Portfolio Domain	Program Domain	Project Domain	Process Improvement Stage
3870	Does your organization Measure the "Program Procurement Administration" process?				Program		Measure
4280	Does your organization Control the "Program Procurement Administration" process?				Program		Control
4670	Does your organization Improve the "Program Procurement Administration" process?				Program		Improve
3490	Does your organization Standardize the "Program Procurement Closure" process?				Program		Standardize
3960	Does your organization Measure the "Program Procurement Closure" process?				Program		Measure
4370	Does your organization Control the "Program Procurement Closure" process?				Program		Control
4760	Does your organization Improve the "Program Procurement Closure" process?				Program		Improve
3240	Does your organization Standardize the "Program Quality Planning" process?				Program		Standardize
3710	Does your organization Measure the "Program Quality Planning" process?				Program		Measure
4120	Does your organization Control the "Program Quality Planning" process?				Program		Control
4510	Does your organization Improve the "Program Quality Planning" process?				Program		Improve
7780	Does your organization Standardize the "Program Quality Assurance" process?				Program		Standardize
7950	Does your organization Measure the "Program Quality Assurance" process?				Program		Measure
8120	Does your organization Control the "Program Quality Assurance" process?				Program		Control
8290	Does your organization Improve the "Program Quality Assurance" process?				Program		Improve
7790	Does your organization Standardize the "Program Quality Control" process?				Program		Standardize
7960	Does your organization Measure the "Program Quality Control" process?				Program		Measure
8130	Does your organization Control the "Program Quality Control" process?				Program		Control
8300	Does your organization Improve the "Program Quality Control" process?				Program		Improve
7800	Does your organization Standardize the "Resource Planning" process?				Program		Standardize
7970	Does your organization Measure the "Resource Planning" process?				Program		Measure
8140	Does your organization Control the "Resource Planning" process?				Program		Control

Best Practice ID	SAM Question	Yes	No	Portfolio Domain	Program Domain	Project Domain	Process Improvement Stage
8310	Does your organization Improve the "Resource Planning" process?				Program		Improve
7810	Does your organization Standardize the "Resource Prioritization" process?				Program		Standardize
7980	Does your organization Measure the "Resource Prioritization" process?				Program		Measure
8150	Does your organization Control the "Resource Prioritization" process?				Program		Control
8320	Does your organization Improve the "Resource Prioritization" process?				Program		Improve
7820	Does your organization Standardize the "Resource Interdependency Management" process?				Program		Standardize
7990	Does your organization Measure the "Resource Interdependency Management" process?				Program		Measure
8160	Does your organization Control the "Resource Interdependency Management" process?				Program		Control
8330	Does your organization Improve the "Resource Interdependency Management" process?				Program		Improve
3230	Does your organization Standardize the "Program Risk Management Planning" process?				Program		Standardize
3700	Does your organization Measure the "Program Risk Management Planning" process?				Program		Measure
4110	Does your organization Control the "Program Risk Management Planning" process?				Program		Control
4500	Does your organization Improve the "Program Risk Management Planning" process?				Program		Improve
3280	Does your organization Standardize the "Program Risk Identification" process?				Program		Standardize
3750	Does your organization Measure the "Program Risk Identification" process?				Program		Measure
4160	Does your organization Control the "Program Risk Identification" process?				Program		Control
4550	Does your organization Improve the "Program Risk Identification" process?				Program		Improve
3615	Does your organization Measure the "Program Risk Analysis" process?				Program		Measure
3625	Does your organization Control the "Program Risk Analysis" process?				Program		Control
3635	Does your organization Improve the "Program Risk Analysis" process?				Program		Improve
3605	Does your organization Standardize the "Program Risk Analysis" process?				Program		Standardize
3310	Does your organization Standardize the "Program Risk Response Planning" process?				Program		Standardize

Best Practice ID	SAM Question	Yes	No	Portfolio Domain	Program Domain	Project Domain	Process Improvement Stage
3780	Does your organization Measure the "Program Risk Response Planning" process?				Program		Measure
4190	Does your organization Control the "Program Risk Response Planning" process?				Program		Control
4580	Does your organization Improve the "Program Risk Response Planning" process?				Program		Improve
3480	Does your organization Standardize the "Program Risk Monitoring and Control" process?				Program		Standardize
3950	Does your organization Measure the "Program Risk Monitoring and Control" process?				Program		Measure
4360	Does your organization Control the "Program Risk Monitoring and Control" process?				Program		Control
4750	Does your organization Improve the "Program Risk Monitoring and Control" process?				Program		Improve
3190	Does your organization Standardize the "Program Schedule Planning" process?				Program		Standardize
3660	Does your organization Measure the "Program Schedule Planning" process?				Program		Measure
4070	Does your organization Control the "Program Schedule Planning" process?				Program		Control
4460	Does your organization Improve the "Program Schedule Planning" process?				Program		Improve
3450	Does your organization Standardize the "Program Schedule Control" process?				Program		Standardize
3920	Does your organization Measure the "Program Schedule Control" process?				Program		Measure
4330	Does your organization Control the "Program Schedule Control" process?				Program		Control
4720	Does your organization Improve the "Program Schedule Control" process?				Program		Improve
3140	Does your organization Standardize the "Program Scope Planning" process?				Program		Standardize
3610	Does your organization Measure the "Program Scope Planning" process?				Program		Measure
4020	Does your organization Control the "Program Scope Planning" process?				Program		Control
4410	Does your organization Improve the "Program Scope Planning" process?				Program		Improve
3440	Does your organization Standardize the "Program Scope Control" process?				Program		Standardize
3910	Does your organization Measure the "Program Scope Control" process?				Program		Measure
4320	Does your organization Control the "Program Scope Control" process?				Program		Control

Best Practice ID	SAM Question	Yes	No	Portfolio Domain	Program Domain	Project Domain	Process Improvement Stage
4710	Does your organization Improve the "Program Scope Control" process?				Program		Improve
1005	Does your organization Standardize the "Develop Project Charter" process?					Project	Standardize
1700	Does your organization Measure the "Develop Project Charter" process?					Project	Measure
2240	Does your organization Control the "Develop Project Charter" process?					Project	Control
2630	Does your organization Improve the "Develop Project Charter" process?					Project	Improve
1020	Does your organization Standardize the "Develop Project Management Plan" process?					Project	Standardize
1710	Does your organization Measure the "Develop Project Management Plan" process?					Project	Measure
2250	Does your organization Control the "Develop Project Management Plan" process?					Project	Control
2640	Does your organization Improve the "Develop Project Management Plan" process?					Project	Improve
1230	Does your organization Standardize the "Direct and Manage Project Work" process?					Project	Standardize
1920	Does your organization Measure the "Direct and Manage Project Work" process?					Project	Measure
2460	Does your organization Control the "Direct and Manage Project Work" process?					Project	Control
2850	Does your organization Improve the "Direct and Manage Project Work" process?					Project	Improve
1035	Does your organization Standardize the "Monitor and Control Project Work" process?					Project	Standardize
1045	Does your organization Measure the "Monitor and Control Project Work" process?					Project	Measure
1055	Does your organization Control the "Monitor and Control Project Work" process?					Project	Control
1065	Does your organization Improve the "Monitor and Control Project Work" process?					Project	Improve
1310	Does your organization Standardize the "Perform Integrated Change Control" process?					Project	Standardize
2000	Does your organization Measure the "Perform Integrated Change Control" process?					Project	Measure
2540	Does your organization Control the "Perform Integrated Change Control" process?					Project	Control
2930	Does your organization Improve the "Perform Integrated Change Control" process?					Project	Improve
1390	Does your organization Standardize the "Close Project or Phase" process?					Project	Standardize

Best Practice ID	SAM Question	Yes	No	Portfolio Domain	Program Domain	Project Domain	Process Improvement Stage
2080	Does your organization Measure the "Close Project or Phase" process?					Project	Measure
2620	Does your organization Control the "Close Project or Phase" process?					Project	Control
3010	Does your organization Improve the "Close Project or Phase" process?					Project	Improve
7500	Does your organization Standardize the "Plan Scope Management" process?					Project	Standardize
7550	Does your organization Measure the "Plan Scope Management" process?					Project	Measure
7600	Does your organization Control the "Plan Scope Management" process?					Project	Control
7650	Does your organization Improve the "Plan Scope Management" process?					Project	Improve
1030	Does your organization Standardize the "Collect Requirements" process?					Project	Standardize
1720	Does your organization Measure the "Collect Requirements" process?					Project	Measure
2260	Does your organization Control the "Collect Requirements" process?					Project	Control
2650	Does your organization Improve the "Collect Requirements" process?					Project	Improve
1040	Does your organization Standardize the "Define Scope" process?					Project	Standardize
1730	Does your organization Measure the "Define Scope" process?					Project	Measure
2270	Does your organization Control the "Define Scope" process?					Project	Control
2660	Does your organization Improve the "Define Scope" process?					Project	Improve
1075	Does your organization Standardize the "Create WBS" process?					Project	Standardize
1085	Does your organization Measure the "Create WBS" process?					Project	Measure
1095	Does your organization Control the "Create WBS" process?					Project	Control
1105	Does your organization Improve the "Create WBS" process?					Project	Improve
1320	Does your organization Standardize the "Validate Scope" process?					Project	Standardize
2010	Does your organization Measure the "Validate Scope" process?					Project	Measure
2550	Does your organization Control the "Validate Scope" process?					Project	Control

Best Practice ID	SAM Question	Yes	No	Portfolio Domain	Program Domain	Project Domain	Process Improvement Stage
2940	Does your organization Improve the "Validate Scope" process?					Project	Improve
1330	Does your organization Standardize the "Control Scope" process?					Project	Standardize
2020	Does your organization Measure the "Control Scope" process?					Project	Measure
2560	Does your organization Control the "Control Scope" process?					Project	Control
2950	Does your organization Improve the "Control Scope" process?					Project	Improve
7510	Does your organization Standardize the "Plan Schedule Management" process?					Project	Standardize
7560	Does your organization Measure the "Plan Schedule Management" process?					Project	Measure
7610	Does your organization Control the "Plan Schedule Management" process?					Project	Control
7660	Does your organization Improve the "Plan Schedule Management" process?					Project	Improve
1050	Does your organization Standardize the "Define Activities" process?					Project	Standardize
1740	Does your organization Measure the "Define Activities" process?					Project	Measure
2280	Does your organization Control the "Define Activities" process?					Project	Control
2670	Does your organization Improve the "Define Activities" process?					Project	Improve
1060	Does your organization Standardize the "Sequence Activities" process?					Project	Standardize
1750	Does your organization Measure the "Sequence Activities" process?					Project	Measure
2290	Does your organization Control the "Sequence Activities" process?					Project	Control
2680	Does your organization Improve the "Sequence Activities" process?					Project	Improve
1115	Does your organization Standardize the "Estimate Activity Resources" process?					Project	Standardize
1125	Does your organization Measure the "Estimate Activity Resources" process?					Project	Measure
1135	Does your organization Control the "Estimate Activity Resources" process?					Project	Control
1145	Does your organization Improve the "Estimate Activity Resources" process?					Project	Improve
1070	Does your organization Standardize the "Estimate Activity Durations" process?					Project	Standardize

Best Practice ID	SAM Question	Yes	No	Portfolio Domain	Program Domain	Project Domain	Process Improvement Stage
1760	Does your organization Measure the "Estimate Activity Durations" process?					Project	Measure
2300	Does your organization Control the "Estimate Activity Durations" process?					Project	Control
2690	Does your organization Improve the "Estimate Activity Durations" process?					Project	Improve
1080	Does your organization Standardize the "Develop Schedule" process?					Project	Standardize
1770	Does your organization Measure the "Develop Schedule" process?					Project	Measure
2310	Does your organization Control the "Develop Schedule" process?					Project	Control
2700	Does your organization Improve the "Develop Schedule" process?					Project	Improve
1340	Does your organization Standardize the "Control Schedule" process?					Project	Standardize
2030	Does your organization Measure the "Control Schedule" process?					Project	Measure
2570	Does your organization Control the "Control Schedule" process?					Project	Control
2960	Does your organization Improve the "Control Schedule" process?					Project	Improve
7520	Does your organization Standardize the "Plan Cost Management" process?					Project	Standardize
7570	Does your organization Measure the "Plan Cost Management" process?					Project	Measure
7620	Does your organization Control the "Plan Cost Management" process?					Project	Control
7670	Does your organization Improve the "Plan Cost Management" process?					Project	Improve
1100	Does your organization Standardize the "Estimate Costs" process?					Project	Standardize
1790	Does your organization Measure the "Estimate Costs" process?					Project	Measure
2330	Does your organization Control the "Estimate Costs" process?					Project	Control
2720	Does your organization Improve the "Estimate Costs" process?					Project	Improve
1110	Does your organization Standardize the "Determine Budget" process?					Project	Standardize
1800	Does your organization Measure the "Determine Budget" process?					Project	Measure
2340	Does your organization Control the "Determine Budget" process?					Project	Control

Best Practice ID	SAM Question	Yes	No	Portfolio Domain	Program Domain	Project Domain	Process Improvement Stage
2730	Does your organization Improve the "Determine Budget" process?					Project	Improve
1350	Does your organization Standardize the "Control Costs" process?					Project	Standardize
2040	Does your organization Measure the "Control Costs" process?					Project	Measure
2580	Does your organization Control the "Control Costs" process?					Project	Control
2970	Does your organization Improve the "Control Costs" process?					Project	Improve
1130	Does your organization Standardize the "Plan Quality Management" process?					Project	Standardize
1820	Does your organization Measure the "Plan Quality Management" process?					Project	Measure
2360	Does your organization Control the "Plan Quality Management" process?					Project	Control
2750	Does your organization Improve the "Plan Quality Management" process?					Project	Improve
1240	Does your organization Standardize the "Perform Quality Assurance" process?					Project	Standardize
1930	Does your organization Measure the "Perform Quality Assurance" process?					Project	Measure
2470	Does your organization Control the "Perform Quality Assurance" process?					Project	Control
2860	Does your organization Improve the "Perform Quality Assurance" process?					Project	Improve
1360	Does your organization Standardize the "Control Quality" process?					Project	Standardize
2050	Does your organization Measure the "Control Quality" process?					Project	Measure
2590	Does your organization Control the "Control Quality" process?					Project	Control
2980	Does your organization Improve the "Control Quality" process?					Project	Improve
1090	Does your organization Standardize the "Plan Human Resource Management" process?					Project	Standardize
1780	Does your organization Measure the "Plan Human Resource Management" process?					Project	Measure
2320	Does your organization Control the "Plan Human Resource Management" process?					Project	Control
2710	Does your organization Improve the "Plan Human Resource Management" process?					Project	Improve
1150	Does your organization Standardize the "Acquire Project Team" process?					Project	Standardize

Best Practice ID	SAM Question	Yes	No	Portfolio Domain	Program Domain	Project Domain	Process Improvement Stage
1840	Does your organization Measure the "Acquire Project Team" process?					Project	Measure
2380	Does your organization Control the "Acquire Project Team" process?					Project	Control
2770	Does your organization Improve the "Acquire Project Team" process?					Project	Improve
1250	Does your organization Standardize the "Develop Project Team" process?					Project	Standardize
1940	Does your organization Measure the "Develop Project Team" process?					Project	Measure
2480	Does your organization Control the "Develop Project Team" process?					Project	Control
2870	Does your organization Improve the "Develop Project Team" process?					Project	Improve
1155	Does your organization Standardize the "Manage Project Team" process?					Project	Standardize
1165	Does your organization Measure the "Manage Project Team" process?					Project	Measure
1175	Does your organization Control the "Manage Project Team" process?					Project	Control
1185	Does your organization Improve the "Manage Project Team" process?					Project	Improve
1160	Does your organization Standardize the "Plan Communications Management" process?					Project	Standardize
1850	Does your organization Measure the "Plan Communications Management" process?					Project	Measure
2390	Does your organization Control the "Plan Communications Management" process?					Project	Control
2780	Does your organization Improve the "Plan Communications Management" process?					Project	Improve
1260	Does your organization Standardize the "Manage Communications" process?					Project	Standardize
1950	Does your organization Measure the "Manage Communications" process?					Project	Measure
2490	Does your organization Control the "Manage Communications" process?					Project	Control
2880	Does your organization Improve the "Manage Communications" process?					Project	Improve
1300	Does your organization Standardize the "Control Communications" process?					Project	Standardize
1990	Does your organization Measure the "Control Communications" process?					Project	Measure
2530	Does your organization Control the "Control Communications" process?					Project	Control

Best Practice ID	SAM Question	Yes	No	Portfolio Domain	Program Domain	Project Domain	Process Improvement Stage
2920	Does your organization Improve the "Control Communications" process?					Project	Improve
1120	Does your organization Standardize the "Plan Risk Management" process?					Project	Standardize
1810	Does your organization Measure the "Plan Risk Management" process?					Project	Measure
2350	Does your organization Control the "Plan Risk Management" process?					Project	Control
2740	Does your organization Improve the "Plan Risk Management" process?					Project	Improve
1170	Does your organization Standardize the "Identify Risks" process?					Project	Standardize
1860	Does your organization Measure the "Identify Risks" process?					Project	Measure
2400	Does your organization Control the "Identify Risks" process?					Project	Control
2790	Does your organization Improve the "Identify Risks" process?					Project	Improve
1180	Does your organization Standardize the "Perform Qualitative Risk Analysis" process?					Project	Standardize
1870	Does your organization Measure the "Perform Qualitative Risk Analysis" process?					Project	Measure
2410	Does your organization Control the "Perform Qualitative Risk Analysis" process?					Project	Control
2800	Does your organization Improve the "Perform Qualitative Risk Analysis" process?					Project	Improve
1190	Does your organization Standardize the "Perform Quantitative Risk Analysis" process?					Project	Standardize
1880	Does your organization Measure the "Perform Quantitative Risk Analysis" process?					Project	Measure
2420	Does your organization Control the "Perform Quantitative Risk Analysis" process?					Project	Control
2810	Does your organization Improve the "Perform Quantitative Risk Analysis" process?					Project	Improve
1200	Does your organization Standardize the "Plan Risk Responses" process?					Project	Standardize
1890	Does your organization Measure the "Plan Risk Responses" process?					Project	Measure
2430	Does your organization Control the "Plan Risk Responses" process?					Project	Control
2820	Does your organization Improve the "Plan Risk Responses" process?					Project	Improve
1370	Does your organization Standardize the "Control Risks" process?					Project	Standardize

Best Practice ID	SAM Question	Yes	No	Portfolio Domain	Program Domain	Project Domain	Process Improvement Stage
2060	Does your organization Measure the "Control Risks" process?					Project	Measure
2600	Does your organization Control the "Control Risks" process?					Project	Control
2990	Does your organization Improve the "Control Risks" process?					Project	Improve
1210	Does your organization Standardize the "Plan Procurement Management" process?					Project	Standardize
1900	Does your organization Measure the "Plan Procurement Management" process?					Project	Measure
2440	Does your organization Control the "Plan Procurement Management" process?					Project	Control
2830	Does your organization Improve the "Plan Procurement Management" process?					Project	Improve
1270	Does your organization Standardize the "Conduct Procurements" process?					Project	Standardize
1960	Does your organization Measure the "Conduct Procurements" process?					Project	Measure
2500	Does your organization Control the "Conduct Procurements" process?					Project	Control
2890	Does your organization Improve the "Conduct Procurements" process?					Project	Improve
1290	Does your organization Standardize the "Control Procurements" process?					Project	Standardize
1980	Does your organization Measure the "Control Procurements" process?					Project	Measure
2520	Does your organization Control the "Control Procurements" process?					Project	Control
2910	Does your organization Improve the "Control Procurements" process?					Project	Improve
1380	Does your organization Standardize the "Close Procurements" process?					Project	Standardize
2070	Does your organization Measure the "Close Procurements" process?					Project	Measure
2610	Does your organization Control the "Close Procurements" process?					Project	Control
3000	Does your organization Improve the "Close Procurements" process?					Project	Improve
1195	Does your organization Standardize the "Identify Stakeholders" process?					Project	Standardize
2005	Does your organization Measure the "Identify Stakeholders" process?					Project	Measure
2015	Does your organization Control the "Identify Stakeholders" process?					Project	Control

Best Practice ID	SAM Question	Yes	No	Portfolio Domain	Program Domain	Project Domain	Process Improvement Stage
2025	Does your organization Improve the "Identify Stakeholders" process?					Project	Improve
7530	Does your organization Standardize the "Plan Stakeholder Management" process?					Project	Standardize
7580	Does your organization Measure the "Plan Stakeholder Management" process?					Project	Measure
7630	Does your organization Control the "Plan Stakeholder Management" process?					Project	Control
7680	Does your organization Improve the "Plan Stakeholder Management" process?					Project	Improve
2035	Does your organization Standardize the "Manage Stakeholder Engagement" process?					Project	Standardize
2045	Does your organization Measure the "Manage Stakeholder Engagement" process?					Project	Measure
2055	Does your organization Control the "Manage Stakeholder Engagement" process?					Project	Control
2065	Does your organization Improve the "Manage Stakeholder Engagement" process?					Project	Improve
7540	Does your organization Standardize the "Control Stakeholder Engagement" process?					Project	Standardize
7590	Does your organization Measure the "Control Stakeholder Engagement" process?					Project	Measure
7640	Does your organization Control the "Control Stakeholder Engagement" process?					Project	Control
7690	Does your organization Improve the "Control Stakeholder Engagement" process?					Project	Improve
5490	Does your organization "Recognize Value of Project Management"?			Portfolio	Program	Project	
1000	Does your organization "Establish Organizational Project Management Policies"?			Portfolio	Program	Project	
1400	Does your organization "Staff Organizational Project Management With Competent Resources"?			Portfolio	Program	Project	
1450	Does your organization "Establish Strong Sponsorship"?			Portfolio	Program	Project	
1460	Does your organization "Tailor Project Management Processes Flexibly"?			Portfolio	Program	Project	
1590	Does your organization "Record Project Resource Assignments"?			Portfolio	Program	Project	
2190	Does your organization "Benchmark Organizational Project Management Performance Against Industry Standards"?			Portfolio	Program	Project	
3030	Does your organization "Capture and Share Lessons Learned"?			Portfolio	Program	Project	
5180	Does your organization "Educate Executives"?			Portfolio	Program	Project	

Best Practice ID	SAM Question	Yes	No	Portfolio Domain	Program Domain	Project Domain	Process Improvement Stage
5190	Does your organization "Facilitate Project Manager Development"?			Portfolio	Program	Project	
5200	Does your organization "Provide Project Management Training"?			Portfolio	Program	Project	
5210	Does your organization "Provide Continuous Training"?			Portfolio	Program	Project	
5220	Does your organization "Provide Competent Organizational Project Management Resources"?			Portfolio	Program	Project	
5240	Does your organization "Establish Internal Project Management Communities"?			Portfolio	Program	Project	
5250	Does your organization "Interact With External Project Management Communities"?			Portfolio	Program	Project	
5270	Does your organization "Integrate Project Management Methodology with Organizational Processes"?			Portfolio	Program	Project	
5280	Does your organization "Establish Common Project Management Framework"?			Portfolio	Program	Project	
5300	Does your organization "Establish Training and Development Program"?			Portfolio	Program	Project	
5340	Does your organization "Establish Executive Support"?			Portfolio	Program	Project	
5500	Does your organization "Define Project Management Values"?			Portfolio	Program	Project	
5620	Does your organization "Establish Career Path for all Organizational Project Management Roles"?			Portfolio	Program	Project	
7005	Does your organization have an "OPM Leadership Program"?			Portfolio	Program	Project	
7015	Does your organization "Educate Stakeholders in OPM"?			Portfolio	Program	Project	
7025	Does your organization have a "Cultural Diversity Awareness"?			Portfolio	Program	Project	
7045	Does your organization "Establish Organizational Project Management Structure"?			Portfolio	Program	Project	
7055	Does your organization "Adopt Organizational Project Management Structure"?			Portfolio	Program	Project	
7065	Does your organization "Institutionalize Organizational Project Management Structure"?			Portfolio	Program	Project	
7105	Does your organization "Manage the Holistic View of the Project"?			Portfolio	Program	Project	
7115	Does your organization "Manage the Environment"?			Portfolio	Program	Project	
7185	Does your organization "Demonstrate Communicating Competency"?			Portfolio	Program	Project	
7325	Does your organization "Collect OPM Success Metrics"?			Portfolio	Program	Project	

Best Practice ID	SAM Question	Yes	No	Portfolio Domain	Program Domain	Project Domain	Process Improvement Stage
7335	Does your organization "Use OPM Success Metrics"?			Portfolio	Program	Project	
7345	Does your organization "Verify OPM Success Metric Accuracy"?			Portfolio	Program	Project	
7355	Does your organization "Analyze and Improve OPM Success Metrics"?			Portfolio	Program	Project	
7365	Does your organization have a "Project Management Information System"?			Portfolio	Program	Project	
7405	Does your organization "Achieve Strategic Goals and Objectives Through the Use of Organizational Project Management"?			Portfolio	Program	Project	
8900	Does your organization "Accommodate Organization's Approved Frameworks and Governance Structures"?			Portfolio	Program	Project	
8910	Does your organization "Analyze Value Performance"?			Portfolio	Program	Project	
8920	Does your organization "Assess the Realization of Proposed Benefits"?			Portfolio	Program	Project	
8930	Does your organization "Benchmark PMO Practices and Results"?			Portfolio	Program	Project	
8940	Does your organization "Create a Risk-Aware Culture"?			Portfolio	Program	Project	
8960	Does your organization address "Developing Project Management Templates"?			Portfolio	Program	Project	
9000	Does your organization "Establish Enterprise Risk Management Methodology"?			Portfolio	Program	Project	
9010	Does your organization "Establish Executive Summary Dashboards"?			Portfolio	Program	Project	
9020	Does your organization "Establish Governance Policies Across the Organization "?			Portfolio	Program	Project	
9030	Does your organization "Establish Organizational Project Management Reporting Standards"?			Portfolio	Program	Project	
9040	Does your organization "Establish Project Delivery Tips and Techniques Special Interest Group"?			Portfolio	Program	Project	
9060	Does your organization "Establish Resource Allocation and Optimization Processes "?			Portfolio	Program	Project	
9080	Does your organization "Establish Strategic Alignment Framework"?			Portfolio	Program	Project	
9090	Does your organization "Incorporate Performance Benchmarks into Balanced Scorecard System"?			Portfolio	Program	Project	
9130	Does your organization "Report OPM Performance to Strategy"?			Portfolio	Program	Project	
9140	Does your organization "Report Project Program Strategic Performance"?			Portfolio	Program	Project	

Best Practice ID	SAM Question	Yes	No	Portfolio Domain	Program Domain	Project Domain	Process Improvement Stage
9150	Does your organization ensure that "Specialists are Shared Between Projects"?			Portfolio	Program	Project	
9170	Does your organization have a "Consistent Project, Program, and Portfolio Governance Across the Enterprise"?			Portfolio	Program	Project	
9180	Does your organization "Use Mathematically Sound Methods for Prioritization"?			Portfolio	Program	Project	
9200	Does your organization "Use Formal Performance Assessment"?			Portfolio	Program	Project	
7075	Does your organization "Provide Organizational Project Management Support Office"?			Portfolio	Program		
1530	Does your organization "Use Formal Individual Performance Assessment"?			Portfolio			
5170	Does your organization "Use Common Project Language"?			Portfolio			
5320	Does your organization "Certify Quality Management System"?			Portfolio			
6980	Does your organization "Create an Organizational Maturity Development Program"?			Portfolio			
7035	Does your organization have an "Organizational Business Change Management Program"?			Portfolio			
7315	Does your organization "Define OPM Success Metrics"?			Portfolio			
7375	Does your organization have "Intellectual Capital Reuse"?			Portfolio			
9070	Does your organization "Establish Scarce Resource Allocation Criteria"?			Portfolio			
9190	Does your organization "Use an Optimizer to Select the Portfolio"?			Portfolio			
7125	Does "The Organization Manages Self Development"?				Program	Project	
7305	Does your organization have "Estimating Template/ Tools Established for Use Across Organization"?				Program	Project	
9210	Does your organization "Manage Program Resources"?				Program		
9220	Does your organization "Manage Program Issues"?				Program		
9230	Does your organization "Manage Component Interfaces"?				Program		
9240	Does your organization "Plan Program Stakeholder Management"?				Program		
9250	Does your organization "Identify Program Stakeholders"?				Program		
9260	Does your organization "Engage Program Stakeholder"?				Program		

Best Practice ID	SAM Question	Yes	No	Portfolio Domain	Program Domain	Project Domain	Process Improvement Stage
9270	Does your organization "Manage Program Stakeholder Expectations"?				Program		
9280	Does your organization "Plan and Establish Program Governance Structure"?				Program		
9290	Does your organization "Plan for Audits"?				Program		
9300	Does your organization "Provide Governance Oversight"?				Program		
9310	Does your organization have "Strategic Alignment of Programs"?				Program		
1430	Does your organization "Establish Project Manager Competency Processes"?					Project	
1540	Does your organization "Include Strategic Goals Into Project Objectives"?					Project	
1670	Does your organization "Know Inter-Project Plan"?					Project	
2090	Does your organization "Adhere to Project Management Techniques "?					Project	
3070	Does your organization "Encourage Risk Taking"?					Project	
5260	Does your organization "Customize Project Management Methodology"?					Project	
5520	Does your organization "Collaborate on Goals"?					Project	
7135	Does your organization "Demonstrate Competency in Initiating a Project"?					Project	
7145	Does your organization "Demonstrate Competency in Planning a Project"?					Project	
7155	Does your organization "Demonstrate Competency in Executing a Project"?					Project	
7165	Does your organization "Demonstrate Competency in Monitoring and Controlling a Project"?					Project	
7175	Does your organization "Demonstrate Competency in Closing a Project"?					Project	
7195	Does your organization "Demonstrate Leading Competency"?					Project	
7205	Does your organization "Demonstrate Managing Competency"?					Project	
7215	Does your organization "Demonstrate Cognitive Ability Competency"?					Project	
7225	Does your organization "Demonstrate Effectiveness Competency"?					Project	
7235	Does your organization "Demonstrate Professionalism Competency"?					Project	
8950	Does your organization "Define Key Leading Indicators"?					Project	
8970	Does your organization "Document Project Management Case Studies"?					Project	

Best Practice ID	SAM Question	Yes	No	Portfolio Domain	Program Domain	Project Domain	Process Improvement Stage
8980	Does your organization "Encourage Adherence to Project Management Code of Ethics"?					Project	
8990	Does your organization "Establish Competent Project Sponsors"?					Project	
9050	Does your organization "Establish Project Management Template Tailoring Guidelines"?					Project	
9100	Does your organization have "Project Management Case Studies Included in Induction Program"?					Project	
9110	Does your organization ensure that "Project Management Training is Mapped to Career Development Path"?					Project	
9120	Does your organization "Provide Mentoring to Project Managers"?					Project	
9160	Does your organization have a "Consistent Project Orientation Process"?					Project	

APPENDIX X4
OPM3 CASE STUDIES

The following case studies are illustrative of how *OPM3* can be used to increase organizational capabilities and improve business results. These case studies were written by the *OPM3* professionals involved in these specific cases.

X4.1 Advanced Electronics Company (AEC), Kingdom of Saudi Arabia

X4.1.1 Problem Statement

Advanced Electronics Company (AEC) was established in 1989 in Riyadh, Saudi Arabia, as an economics offset company. The charter of AEC is focused around design, production, repair, and support of complex electronic products for military, industrial, and telecommunication end users. AEC has a solid reputation for quality and employment of some of the most skillful engineers in Saudi Arabia. AEC project management practices were originally based on military standards and, over the years, were updated and modified to be more compliant with up-to-date standards. However, as is the case with any growing company that takes on larger and more challenging projects, AEC management realized the need to realign its project, program, and portfolio management (P3M) practices to more up-to-date best practices. Under the sponsor of the CEO, a program management council (PMC) was formed with representation from AEC's main business units for the purposes of looking at the issues and overseeing a self-driven improvement initiative to realign AEC P3M practices to world-class best practices.

The PMC quickly made the decision to benchmark the current organizational behaviors and practices in project management and chose a measurement framework that would encapsulate their plan for improvement. The CEO of AEC chose *OPM3* because the company wanted to be measured not only against organizations in Saudi Arabia or the Middle East, but also against respected international companies. *OPM3* provided AEC with a common scale to start from and the ability to be measured periodically on that scale as the company improved.

X4.1.2 Solution Description

A Certified *OPM3* Assessor® was selected to conduct the assessment and set about a structured method of gathering, analyzing, and interpreting the data over several "waves," producing results which have been the bedrock of an integrated improvement program at AEC.

In the first wave, the assessor interviewed key stakeholders and determined which processes and practices were currently in place and how well they were adhered to. Initial results confirmed that, although there was much good practice within AEC, many project management processes were not formally standardized or actively managed.

The second wave of investigation saw more in-depth interviews with a broader range of stakeholders to determine the full range of *OPM3* Capabilities and Best Practices achieved. This included focused investigations into support functions such as finance, procurement and human resources which were key to establishing a clear understanding of *OPM3*'s organizational enablers.

The assessor used the *OPM3* scoring methodology during interviews and workshops. These results were then fed into the *OPM3 ProductSuite*® software which was used to prepare the final report.

X4.1.3 Results

The results of the assessment confirmed AEC's challenges and the direction they wanted to take. Though their project management performance was generally perceived among the best in Saudi Arabia, this was not due to the standardization, measurement, and control inherent in their project management processes. Moreover, when it came to program and portfolio management, there was a significant opportunity for improvement, though some tacit good practice was evident.

The assessor noted that *OPM3*'s scoring criteria is stringent when assessed for the first time, and the results show that there is much work to be done to ensure that AEC's project management performance is consistent, repeatable, and sustainable; however, there were many good practices in place.

Based on the results of the *OPM3* assessment, AEC obtained a certified *OPM3*® consultant to set up a full P3M capability development program, including the creation of a Corporate Portfolio Office (CPO) and individual P3Os in each business unit using the "hub and spoke" model. The main measure of success will be the improvement demonstrated in a second *OPM3* assessment at the completion of the program when the majority of appropriate processes and frameworks will be in place. This framework will ensure that there is a seamless accountable chain from the development of organizational strategy through to its implementation by means of portfolios of program and projects.

OPM3 ensures that the work AEC has been doing to improve is not happening in a vacuum. In commissioning an *OPM3* assessor, AEC will be able to measure their efforts and successes by benchmarking improvement against a neutral standard, designed to measure the world's best organizations. The Senior Executive Management Board will have a tangible means of monitoring progress. *OPM3* has been instrumental in providing insight, clarity, focus, and momentum for AEC. After 18 months, AEC has a new P3M framework that was developed to help with their goal of portfolio, program, and project excellence.

X4.2 Ambithus, Lisboa, Portugal

X4.2.1 Problem Statement

The Ambithus project is underway in Portugal, representing one hundred organization assessments and improvement plans, based on PMI's maturity model *OPM3*. The project is supported by the European Union and the Portuguese state.

©2013 Project Management Institute. *Organizational Project Management Maturity Model (OPM3®) – Third Edition*

The *OPM3®* Portugal Project is chartered based on the need that the organizing entities want to improve the way the Portuguese industry starts, chooses, manages, controls, and closes projects. This is an opportunity to take advantage of the System of Incentives for Research and Technological Development (R&D) projects to be supported by European Union funding, which is covered under the concept of leading to the creation of new products, processes, or systems or the introduction of significant improvements in products, processes, or systems.

X4.2.2 Solution Description

The *OPM3®* Portugal Project consists of a comprehensive analysis of the state of the Portuguese Industry with regard to the degree of maturity in the adoption of portfolio, program, and project management methodology using PMI's *OPM3* maturity model.

Throughout the research, this study will also produce impacts on the case studies—the companies that are the subject of the project's study, since it will be built and validated with organizational improvement plans that can be adopted by the participating companies.

X4.2.3 Results

Overall, this assessment exercise was intended to create multiple benefits to country stakeholders. For organizations, the intent was to improve the relationship between strategic planning and execution, extending the results of projects, making them more predictable, reliable, and consistent. Other benefits included the identification of Best Practices to support organizational strategy for implementing successful projects and the identification of specific skills that the organization has and which can be "best practices." For policymakers, a country level measure of maturity can assist with the design of future interventions. Sectors with a low level of maturity can receive additional support for executing projects and can be encouraged to form partnerships with more mature sectors. Several other benefits have been identified:

- Development of a specific methodology for intervention in companies with regard to the verification of organizational maturity level.

- Development of an information system to manage administration of *OPM3* interventions at the country level. The data can be used to assess the effectiveness of improvement actions as well as be shared with countries seeking to perform a similar exercise.

- Lessons learned from the project for application in a similar manner to the information system discussed previously.

- Information system that integrates the methods of intervention and could be exploited commercially.

X4.2.4 Additional Description

X4.2.4.1 Planning and Organizing

In this stage, all generic procedures and structured management and control of the project are defined, as well as more detailed planning activities and processes. A cross-functional team consisting of representatives from academia, *OPM3*® consultants, and company representatives was formed to manage project delivery. Particular attention will be paid to documenting lessons learned, identifying areas of good practice, and possible ways to improve future projects.

The team also created specific information systems for this project. A management information system was created for company assessments, and a site was created for registration and online management of all research. This was necessary in order to be able to properly structure and organize research, increasing the efficiency of the more than 20 researchers directly involved. This system was designed by Ambithus researchers who will collaborate in drawing researchers and academics.

X4.2.4.2 Company Assessment

For the company assessments, PMI's *OPM3*® (Organizational Project Management Maturity Model) was selected. The advantage of *OPM3* is its flexibility and comprehensiveness as it contains hundreds of organizational Best Practices, assesses current capabilities of the organization, and maps the steps needed to improve organizational performance. *OPM3* also enables the generation of useful outputs to owners and managers at an early stage of research. As a maturity model, *OPM3* provides a method for organizations to understand their processes and measure their skills as they prepare to improve internal procedures. It also enables organizations to develop a vision of the way forward to improve performance, whether in portfolio, program, or project management. These outputs from *OPM3* can help to maintain the organizational commitment to the project and to support subsequent data collection by researchers.

The study includes 100 organizations that were selected because they engaged in either a large number of projects or had to deliver products and services that were the output of complex projects. Another important condition of the study is that the company's top management is required to fully support the study. The process begins with the signing of a protocol of cooperation which is specified in the objectives and deliverables. This set of rules should specify the name of the internal promoter (project manager) within the company or organization involved, the entity name of organization from the Scientific and Technological System, a participating partner, and the name of the *OPM3* consultant appointed by Ambithus. The objective is to address 100 organizations: 55 that are addressed by the scientific community and 45 that are addressed by Ambithus directly.

The initial process of intervention is:

- Preliminary meeting between the managers and the project sponsor;
- Meeting with top management;
- Meeting with program manager (or person who defines strategy);
- Meeting with the portfolio manager (or person who makes decisions on resources);

- Meeting with the PMO manager (or person who appoints the project managers);
- Meeting with other organizational enablers, like commercial managers, financial managers, marketing managers, and others);
- Meetings with project managers, and
- Meeting with team members.

This intervention process sequence is *OPM3*-complaint, and all the actions are coordinated by senior consultants. Consistent input and elimination of interviewer bias is guaranteed by the established quality control process, which will work preventively by assuring that all collected data is properly recorded in the information system.

Following the fieldwork, a status report for the *OPM3* maturity will be generated and presented to directors and top managers. The presentation of the report will be the working basis for the design of the improvement plan, which will be presented and delivered to the company management. Employees understand that management will participate in this process.

Organizations will be selected from the following sectors:

- **Government.** These organizations provide services to the public and private sector. They are a key part of the enabling infrastructure of the Portuguese business environment.
- **Multinational Firms.** Due to its favorable location, Portugal has attracted a number of multinational firms. These organizations are significant employers and developers of talent in Portugal.
- **Information Services.** This is a fast-growing sector that is an export success story for Portugal. It is formed of new organizations and is seen as a source of future economic growth of the country.
- **Construction.** This sector, formerly dominant in Portugal is now struggling due to changes in the domestic economy and increasing competition.
- **Knowledge Intensive Enterprises.** These organizations create high-margin products with high technology content. They engage in complex R&D projects to develop new products and improve existing ones.
- **Financial Institutions.** These public and private sector organizations directly manage a number of companies that they have acquired in Portugal.
- **Telecommunication Firms.** These are relatively large firms in Portugal that have expanded to operate subsidiaries in multiple countries.

X4.2.4.3 Sector Level Assessment

Upon completion of the company assessment, workshops will be conducted to disseminate and discuss interim results by industry sector. This is done to ensure that both of the companies participating in the study and the overall market will have information on the overall development of the study. It will also serve to confirm research findings and identify additional organizations for study.

Once company level assessments are completed, the findings will be summarized to create industry sector level measures of project management capability. Following the analysis and validation of the results achieved, an industry sector improvement plan will be presented and discussed during seven to nine thematic workshops. The integrated improvement plans will be validated in these events through discussion with sector stakeholders.

X4.2.4.4 Conclusion

The *OPM3* Portugal project is an example of an opportunity to further develop the knowledge of how organizations use methodology, processes, people development, and established standards to improve the manner in which portfolios, programs, and projects are performed. The multisector and multidimensional approach permits new knowledge to be collected and presented and therefore, creates many opportunities to publicly recognize the project results.

X4.3 Mapna Special Projects Construction, Iran

X4.3.1 Problem Statement

Mapna Special Projects Construction & Development Co (MD-3), affiliated to Mapna Group, is a project-based company that mostly operates in the field of oil, petrochemical, gas, utility, cogeneration, and thermal power plant construction industries. A strong matrix structure is being used for the management of different projects, because the project manager is solely responsible for the project integration regarding the client's contract and is also responsible for construction activities. Engineering, procurement, and planning deputies are functional departments providing matrix services for the project. There was a coordination conflict between the project managers and functional deputies, and there was no single methodology for project management because each project manager followed their own style. As a result, approximately 2½ years ago, the Planning Deputy of MD-3 initiated a plan to improve project management processes according to the *PMBOK® Guide.* Four Knowledge Areas were selected for improvement in a 2-day brainstorming workshop with the MD-3 middle and senior management: Project Integration Management, Project Scope Management, Project Risk Management, and Project Procurement Management. The purpose of this project was to improve project management maturity in these Knowledge Areas in two 14-month phases. In addition, a rigorous plan was developed for project management training throughout the organization. MD-3 was able to almost all of the established objectives by the end of first phase. The plan was revised for the second phase to develop a project management methodology which had the most priority for the organization, and the parent company, Mapna Group, simultaneously conducted a project management assessment for some construction subsidiaries including MD-3 in order to evaluate their project management performance.

X4.3.2 Solution Description

X4.3.2.1 Selecting an I Certified Professional

At the beginning, Mapna Group reviewed different approaches for the assessment. Three methods were discussed for this purpose: (1) use an external consultant as the team, (2) use an external consultant to work with the internal team, and (3) use an *OPM3* Certified Professional®. Finally it was decided to conduct an *OPM3* assessment, rigorous type, by an *OPM3* Certified Professional who had access to the *OPM3 ProductSuite*® software. This decision coincided with the certification of one of the MD-3 employees as an *OPM3* Certified Professional®, the first one in Iran. Hence it was agreed to conduct an *OPM3* assessment for MD-3 and other selected subsidiary companies by the internal *OPM3* Certified Professional®.

X4.3.2.2 Plan for Assessment and Assessment

The scope of the MD-3 assessment was determined as Project, Standardize, Measure, Control, and Improve. Selected people were interviewed and some other staff participated in an *OPM3* introductory course delivered by the *OPM3* Certified Professional® in order to transfer basic knowledge of the model to the organization. The assessment took about 1 month and included collecting preliminary data, planning for interviews, opening the meeting, conducting interviews, finalizing data, preparing final report, and closing the meeting. More than 30 people, including project managers, middle managers, and project team members, were interviewed during the assessment. The final reports shows that MD-3 has better performance in Project Quality Management with regard to other Knowledge Areas, in the Executing Process Group as compared to other Process Groups, and project management training when compared to other organizational enabler categories. It also shows that MD-3 requires more attention in the Project Risk Management, Initiating Process Group, and benchmarking. Lastly, the final report elaborates on: (1) some project management strength points, such as developing a construction project success measurement model to calculate the success of completed projects based on defined targets; and (2) areas for improvement, such as not contributing to the performance of the matrix project team members by the project manager.

X4.3.2.3 Plan for Improvement

The new improvement plan for the second phase consisted of three sections. The first section includes improvement of some project management processes, which are the highest priority for the organization, such as Conduct Procurements, Close Procurements, and Plan Scope Management, and revision of the roles and responsibilities of the project managers and some other key individuals on the project. The second section, the most important one, includes development of a single project management methodology for MD-3. This methodology is intended to integrate all project management processes to facilitate project management activities by enhancing the communication and workflow. Finally, the last section includes the application of the methodology in a single pilot project so as to receive feedback and revise accordingly, if necessary.

X4.3.3 Results

While the second phase of the improvement project is still ongoing in the organization, it is briefly discussed here how the second phase plans to use the result of *OPM3* assessment. The most significant contribution of the *OPM3* assessment is to provide good information regarding project management maturity regarding the as-is status of MD-3 and back-up data regarding their strength points and areas for improvement. Initially, the assessment final report showed that MD-3 has a relative maturity in project management in which it endorsed MD-3's initiation to develop a single methodology for its project management. For example, Project Domain and organizational enabler scores (ProductSuite Score) were close, which implies that infrastructure Best Practices in different categories such as sponsorship, strategic alignment, organizational structure, and resource allocation are appropriately supportive for project management processes best practices. On the other hand, the final report shows that most of the project management processes are standardized. This valuable information will be applied as input data to develop a framework for the MD-3 project management methodology, the second section of the second phase. By knowing the project management maturity level, the project management methodology of MD-3 can be tailored to achieve its highest priorities in order to have a holistic view of the project management and clarify all boundaries and interfaces. This single methodology will be presented to MD-3's potential clients in order to assure them that MD-3 is capable for executing their projects within the triple constraints, required quality, and client satisfaction.

GLOSSARY

1. Inclusions and Exclusions

This glossary for the *Organizational Project Management Maturity Model (OPM3®) Knowledge Foundation* includes terms that are:

- Specific to *OPM3* (e.g., Best Practices list)
- Not unique to *OPM3*, but used differently than in general everyday usage (e.g., Capabilities)
- This glossary does not necessarily include:
- Terms whose definitions are readily found in other PMI standards (e.g., *A Guide to the Project Management Body of Knowledge (PMBOK® Guide)* – Fifth Edition, *The Standard for Program Management* – Third Edition, *The Standard for Portfolio Management* – Third Edition, *Project Manager Competency Development Framework*;
- Terms whose definitions are found in the *PMI Lexicon of Project Management Terms*;
- Application or industry-specific terms; and
- Terms whose usage in the *OPM3* context does not differ materially from everyday use.

2. Common Acronyms

BP	Best Practice
GRC	Governance, Risk, and Compliance
OE	Organizational Enabler
OPM	Organizational Project Management (OPM)
OPM3	Organizational Project Management Maturity Model
PPP	Portfolio, program, and project
SMCI	Standardize, measure, control, and continuously improve
SME	Subject matter expert

Area of Expertise. Practical knowledge and skills in a subject that are required to undertake a successful *OPM3* initiative.

Assessment. Evaluation of an organization's successful execution of processes and standards. For *OPM3,* various tools to assess organizational project management maturity exist in the marketplace with variations of granularity.

Best Practice. In general, Best Practices refer to the methods, currently recognized within a given industry or discipline, to achieve a stated goal or objective. In the *OPM3* context, Best Practices are achieved when an organization demonstrates consistent organizational project management processes evidenced by successful outcomes.

Best Practices Directory. The Best Practices directory lists the Best Practices that form the foundation of the *OPM3* content. This directory provides the name and a brief description of each Best Practice. By reviewing the Best Practices directory, the user can become generally familiar with the *OPM3* content. An organization will also use this directory following the self-assessment method to identify Best Practices for any potential improvement effort.

Capability. A Capability is a specific competency that must exist in an organization to execute project management processes and deliver project management services and products. Capabilities are incremental steps leading up to one or more Best Practices.

Categorization. A grouping of components based on criteria.

In *OPM3*, categorizations are groupings that provide a framework for the *OPM3* model to clearly define the relationship between Best Practices and Capabilities. It also allows organizations to focus on alternative approaches to maturity.

The categorizations in the *OPM3* model are the domains of PPP (Portfolio, Program, or Project), SMCI (Standardize, Measure, Control, or continuously Improve), the Process Groups for each of the domains, and Organizational Enablers (OEs). These categorizations can be used to approach *OPM3* from a project management domain, an improvement process, or a Process Group area, respectively. See also *domain, PPP, SMCI, Organizational Enablers,* and *Process Groups.*

Continuous Improvement. Continuous improvement is a total quality management concept based on theories developed by Edward Deming and Walter Shewart. The key principles of continuous improvement relate to four sequential steps in characterizing the performance of a Capability as a Best Practice.

For a Capability to be considered as a Best Practice, it has to demonstrate industry-standard competencies in the process improvement stages (SMCI: standardize, measure, control and continuously improve).

Control. Comparing actual performance with planned performance, analyzing variances, assessing trends to effect process improvements, evaluating possible alternatives, and recommending appropriate corrective action as needed.

In *OPM3,* the progression of Capabilities generally includes determining control limits, looking for root causes for processes that are outside the limits, and identifying improvements to bring the process within the control limits.

When used in evaluating Capability maturities, the collective application of control activities constitutes the third stage of the *OPM3* SMCI quality management model.

Cycle Elements. Groups of processes required to implement *OPM3* iteratively.

Dependency. Dependencies are relationships in which a desired state is contingent upon the achievement of one or more prerequisites.

In *OPM3*, one type of dependency is represented by the series of Capabilities that aggregate to a Best Practice. In general, each Capability builds upon preceding Capabilities.

Another type of dependency occurs when the existence of one Best Practice depends in part on the existence of some other Best Practice. In this case, at least one of the Capabilities within the first Best Practice depends on the existence of one of the Capabilities within the other Best Practice. See also *interdependencies*.

Dependency Relationship. See *dependency*.

Domain. A domain refers to the three distinct disciplines of portfolio management, program management, and project management (also referred to as PPP). Each domain is structured by Process Groups and processes.

Framework. Holistically, the three PMI domain standards (portfolio management, program management, and the *PMBOK® Guide*)—plus the *Project Management Competency Development Framework* and *OPM3*—constitute the total framework of PMI organizational project management practice. Framework may be used to refer to specific components of these key organizational project management proficiencies, such as domains, processes, etc.

Governing Body. The group responsible for guidance and monitoring of portfolio, program, and project management and development work within specific compliance boundaries. These compliance areas include formal corporate ethical, financial, and security considerations, among others, and may be imposed internally or externally.

Improve. Improvement is the process of making something better, developing new qualities and abilities.

The progression of Capabilities generally includes documenting improvements demonstrated to be effective and incorporating them into the standardized process. When the Capability description or title includes phrases like "improve," "increase process value," "process improvements," or "process simplification," it is probably an improvement Capability of the process.

When used in evaluating Capability maturities, the collective application of continuous improvement activities constitutes the fourth stage of the *OPM3* SMCI quality management model. See also *continuous improvement*.

Mapping. A relationship in which one element of a set can be associated with an element of another set. In *OPM3*, each Best Practice or Capability can be associated/mapped to a Category in each of the Project Management Process Groups, Portfolio Management Process Groups, and life cycle phases of a program.

Maturity. Within *OPM3*, maturity comprises not only the state of performance within portfolio, program, and project management, but also the organization's evolution toward that state as illustrated by SMCI.

Measure. The act of identifying what to measure as well as actually collecting the measures that would help an organization understand if the process is operating within acceptable limits.

When the Capability description or title includes some derivative of the word "measure" or "identify," then it is probably a measurement Capability of the process. The progression of Capabilities generally includes determining what to measure, measuring it, and analyzing the results.

When used in evaluating Capability maturities, the collective application of measure activities constitutes the second stage of the *OPM3* SMCI quality management model.

OPM3. See *organizational project management maturity model.*

OPM3 Cycle. An iterative improvement process designed to guide organizations through:

1. Acquiring knowledge about organizational project management,
2. Performing an assessment to evaluate current state,
3. Managing Improvement to gain capabilities identified as needed by the organization, and
4. Measuring the impacts of these changes in the short and long term to optimize business performance.

OPM3 Construct. The process model that describes the dependencies and interrelationships of the *OPM3* components. These components include the three domains of portfolio, program, and project management; the Process Groups or performance domains for each domain; and their four states of process improvement, as well as enablers that support organizational project management. The construct's components are further decomposed into Best Practices, Capabilities, and their respective outcomes to create process model.

Organization. A group of people organized for some purpose or to perform some type of work within an established business. In the *OPM3* context, this can be interpreted as any company, agency, association, society, business unit, functional group, department, or subagency intending to make use of *OPM3*.

Organizational Enablers. Organizational enablers are structural, cultural, technological, and human-resource practices that can be leveraged to support the implementation of Best Practices in portfolios, programs, and projects in support of strategic goals.

Organizational Project Management. Organizational project management (OPM) is a strategy execution framework that utilizes portfolio, program, and project management as well as organizational-enabling practices to consistently and predictably deliver organizational strategy to produce better performance, better results, and a sustainable competitive advantage.

Organizational Project Management Maturity. The level of an organization's ability to deliver the desired strategic outcomes in a predictable, controllable, and reliable manner.

Organizational Project Management Maturity Model (*OPM3*). A framework that defines knowledge, assessment, and improvement processes, based on Best Practices and Capabilities, to help organizations measure and mature their portfolio, program, and project management practices.

Outcome. Outcome is the tangible or intangible result of performing a Capability. In the *OPM3* framework, a Capability may have multiple Outcomes. The degree to which an Outcome is achieved is determined by the existence of deliverables that the process leaves behind when work is completed.

PPP. One of the categorizations in *OPM3* to provide structure for the Best Practices and Capabilities. It is used as a field in the *OPM3* Best Practices list to indicate the three domains of portfolio, program, and project management.

Process Group. A logical grouping of the portfolio and project management inputs, tools and techniques, and outputs. The Project Management Process Groups include Initiating processes, Planning processes, Executing processes, Monitoring and Controlling processes, and Closing processes. Project Management Process Groups are not project phases. The Portfolio Management Process Groups include Defining processes, Aligning processes, Authorizing and Controlling processes.

Process Improvement Stages. The four stages of process maturity, also known as SMCI. The four stages are standardize, measure, control, and continuously improve. A particular process is made capable through the prerequisite attainment of each stage. For instance, as general guidance, to achieve Best Practice in a process in the Control stage, the organization needs to first demonstrate Best Practice in the measure stage. See also *standardize, measure, control,* and *improve.*

Project Management Maturity. Project management processes measured by the ability of an organization to successfully initiate, plan, execute, and monitor and control *individual* projects. Project management maturity is limited to individual project execution and doesn't address key processes, Capabilities, or Best Practices at the organizational, portfolio, or program level. The focus of project management maturity is "doing projects right."

SMCI. See *process improvement stages.*

Standardize. To demonstrate a documented and communicated process whereby the applicable people are following a process within an organization. When the Capability description or title includes phrases such as "have a process for," "document a process," or "standardize a process," it is probably a standardization Capability of the process.

The progression of Capabilities generally includes assigning process ownership, obtaining or developing a process, and then demonstrating that the organization is adhering to the standard for that process.

When used in evaluating Capability maturities, the collective application of standardization activities constitutes the first stage of the *OPM3* SMCI quality management model. See also *process improvement stages.*

Strategic Goals. The definition of an organization's intended achievements in terms of business results may be interpreted from various perspectives—financial, customer, infrastructure, products and services, or by cultural outcomes that are measurable.

Sustainability. A characteristic of a process or state that can be maintained indefinitely. Within the assessment process for measuring a Capability, sustainability must be achieved in order to reach the improve stage.

Value Performance Analysis. Providing business value realization data from value business fulfillment back to the strategy of the organization.

INDEX

A

B

C